THE

HEART

OF

CALIFORNIA

Exploring the San Joaquin Valley

AARON GILBREATH

University of Nebraska Press | Lincoln

Acknowledgments for the use of previously
published material appear on pages 251–52,
which constitute an extension of the copyright page.

Library of Congress
Cataloging-in-Publication Data
Names: Gilbreath, Aaron, author.
Title: The heart of California: exploring
the San Joaquin Valley / Aaron Gilbreath.
Description: Lincoln, NE: University of
Nebraska Press, [2020] | Includes
bibliographical references.
Identifiers: LCCN 2019054554
ISBN 9781496218636 (paperback)
ISBN 9781496223081 (epub)
ISBN 9781496223098 (mobi)
ISBN 9781496223104 (pdf)
Subjects: LCSH: San Joaquin Valley (Calif.)—
Description and travel. | Latta, Frank F.,
1892–1983—Travel. | San Joaquin Valley
(Calif.)—History—Anecdotes.
Classification: LCC F868.S173 G45 2020 |
DDC 979.4/8—dc23
LC record available at
https://lccn.loc.gov/2019054554

Set in Minion Pro by Laura Buis.
Designed by L. Auten.

This book is for Rebekah and Vivian, for giving me the time to write it, and for the deadline to finally sit down and finish. You are the honey, and I am the bee.

This is what California is: a long central valley encircled by mountains.

—Geographer John A. Crow

CONTENTS

List of Illustrations   xi

Acknowledgments   xiii

Introduction   1

1. Down the Kern River   17

2. On Tulare Lake   53

3. Hanford, the Other California Dream   95

4. Uncle Jeff's Cabin   125

5. Through the Swampy Center   145

6. Nocturnal Life   189

7. The End of the Road, San Francisco   209

Further Reading   251

Bibliography   253

ILLUSTRATIONS

Following page 124

1. The boat crew at the Kern River launch site

2. Route of the *Alta II*

3. Frank Latta with Fred Gribble and E. Gay Hoffman

4. Don Latta

5. Ernest Ingalls

6. Richard Harris

7. Jean Latta

8. *Alta* crew arriving in San Francisco Bay

9. Josie Yoi'-mut Alonzo

10. Map of indigenous groups of the southern San Joaquin Valley

11. Yokuts woman collecting native salt grass

ACKNOWLEDGMENTS

The San Joaquin Valley is huge, and so is the list of people who made this book possible. First and foremost, my deepest thanks to Frank and Jeanette Latta for their lifelong dedication to interior California's history and culture. A huge thanks to Bridget Barry at University of Nebraska Press for believing in this book and bringing it to the world, and never-ending thanks to Lucas Church, who took the time to share it with her.

I appreciate all the editors who published some of this material as stand-alone essays or dispatches at *Harper's*, *The Threepenny Review*, *Columbia Journal*, *The Common*, *Hobart*, *Southwest Review*, *High Desert Journal*, and *The Rambler* and who helped improve my text: Greg Brownerville, Aaron Burch, Hannah Gersen, Harrison Hill, Jeremy Keehn, Wendy Lesser, Jensen Whelan, Elizabeth Oliver, Thomas Osborne, and Elizabeth Quinn.

This book wouldn't be possible without William Vollmann's encouragement. When I got stuck and couldn't figure out how to break through the Latta story, I defied all common sense and sent a message to him, a perfect stranger, and his sage advice helped me see my errors and what I needed to do next. As he wrote in his letter, "Have you yet made this trip? If much of it must now be [made by] car, how long would it take? If I were in your shoes, I would make this trip over and over (perhaps in the winter!) and do my best to follow my passion to educate myself for however long it took. If the book requires the rest of your life but will then be entirely yours, why not?" So I bought a plane ticket, rented a car, and scheduled some appointments, and here we are. As my wife, Rebekah, said after we read Bill's letter, "I told you basically the same thing." She had. Apparently, I needed that advice in stereo.

This book is also dedicated to my friend Dean, who taught me a lot about camping in our wild youth and whom I've been lucky to share so many road-tripping firsts with, including first experiencing the Valley.

My warm and personal thanks to Steven Church and Phyllis Brotherton, who offered, respectively, to let me crash at his house and to pick me up when I still planned to boat illegally on various canals. You are good souls. A special thanks to Eric Parker and Phyllis, who read early chapters and offered a lot of insights and spot-on suggestions. Thanks to everyone who took the time out of their busy lives to read the manuscript for a blurb, and especially to Joe Donnelly for his honest editorial input—too rare these days.

Thanks to poet Dana Koester for talking to me, and to her farming in-laws, Allen and Beverly Souza, who spoke with me about farming and fed me their crops. Their perfect persimmons inspired me to plant a Fuyu persimmon in my own backyard. I'm sorry none of our conversations made it into this book.

Thanks to Jim Ruland and to the Circle Jerks' Keith Morris for the Firebaugh info. Thanks to the passionate Beale Reference staff and to the folks at the Cal State Fresno, Fresno County Library's San Joaquin Valley Heritage and Genealogy Center and at the Burlingame Public Library: Jacob Cairns, Nance Espinosa, Chris Her, Gregory Megee, Melissa Scroggins, Elaine Tai, and Gloria Washington. You not only helped me gather Latta's life work; you let me turn the microphone on you to help understand the passion some people thankfully have for this region. The Kern County Fire Department generously answered my weird questions about zip codes and the blurry town limits of Mettler, Lebec, Tejon Ranch, and Arvin. Thanks to Tom Griggs and Diane Mitchell for talking with me about early Valley conservationist Jack Zaninovich back before I knew how to interview people or had ever published an article. Thanks to Larry

Swan and John Parsons for their help understanding the Buena Vista Aquatic Recreational Area.

I owe a great debt to Mark Arax and Rick Wartzman, whose incredible research and expert reporting into Boswell's farming of the Tulare Lake bed gathered details otherwise buried in the proverbial stacks or lost to time. I used certain facts and figures from their book *The King of California* liberally, and I am grateful. My debt to Gerald Haslam is equally great, not only for his passion but for his career honoring the region in literature and for all the details that he unearthed and that I utilized. William Preston did pioneering work in his canonical book *Vanishing Landscape*, piecing together the historical ecology and ethnography of a land that hadn't previously received that appreciative, academic treatment. Even though he told me not to lean too heavily on his research, I did anyway.

Thanks to Calexico for the music that put me in the right dusty frame of mind to write this. A special thanks to Carsten Baumann in Germany, friend in music, who kindly supplied the live recordings that conjured the memories and soaring, solitary feelings necessary to capture this place's magic. Some songs, like live 1998 versions of "Return of the Manta Ray" and "Opening Aunt Dora's Box in 5/8," had to travel around the world to end up back with me, nearly twenty years after I first heard the band perform them.

Big thanks to John Muir, who steered me in the right direction and eventually turned this big, flat valley into my Yosemite. Thanks to the staff at Backyard Social for the beer, burgers, and counter space to write, which I needed at the beginning when I was flailing so hard. Thanks to Carol Lee and her team of master transcriptionists, who revolutionized my process and set me free. Thanks to Elise Makler for her generous funding. And to that asshole Bureau of Land Management staffer who said one thing and did another, I worked around you, just like I work around your fences.

To all the rental car staff who occasionally upgraded my station wagons to larger suvs free of charge, you're the reason I slept better in those cars and awoke with fewer back kinks.

To the people of the Valley, your region is beautiful, fascinating, frustrating, fertile, and culturally rich. It's more ethnically diverse than the so-called progressive city where I live, everyone depends on it for food, and it has as many brilliant poets as New York. Don't let anyone tell you that your land is bland, ugly, or boring. You can decide that for yourself. Thanks for sharing it with me.

Thanks to my dad, who always raised me to appreciate history. When we'd drive to Tucson, he'd point to the peak where Arizona's only Civil War battle was fought. He'd tell me what *palo verde* meant and why Navajo artists included coins on their famous squash blossom necklaces. I only appreciate history because of him. And thanks to my mom, who always supported my artistic pursuits and intellectual interests, nourished my self-confidence, and made me feel capable of tackling intimidating school projects at an early age, even when she wondered why I occasionally tortured myself voluntarily with big school projects.

At the end of his loving tribute to Latta in 1970 in *Pacific Historian*, Troy S. Tuggle wrote how he hoped "that someday, all the widely scattered and little known newspaper articles and other writings of this interesting man may be collected and assembled, perhaps in a single volume, if possible, or a series, for historical posterity to appreciate and utilize." In place of a collected Latta, I hope this book does him some small justice.

And my undying love and gratitude to you, Rebekah, for giving me so much room to stay up late, haunt the library, and work long hours to finish this book during nearly all nine months of your pregnancy. This book was twenty years in the making, and as you said while we drove back from your third ultrasound, "Now you have about twenty weeks to finish it." I didn't realize that a person could sweat so hard in winter weather. And hi, Vivian; this book is for you. One day, you can tell me what you think of it. I'd love it if you helped me write the next ones, or color them. Until then, let's dance to Miles Davis or, better yet, go outside and play.

THE HEART OF CALIFORNIA

Introduction

On June 18, 1938, the *Bakersfield Californian* told the story of local resident Frank Latta's boat launch in an article titled "Kern Boatmen on Way to S.F. via Water."

"Before a large crowd assembled early this morning on the north bank of Kern river at the North Chester bridge," the article said, "the little party embarked in the 'Alta,' a 15-foot skiff, equipped with an outboard motor and homemade paddles for the young crew." The *Alta* was floating from Bakersfield to San Francisco, through what's become one of the most productive agricultural regions in human history. It was an impossible-sounding trip. No one on record had completed it before, and no one has made it since.

A crowd gathered on this warm Saturday as Latta's small four-person crew launched their skiff into the Kern River. "Motion picture cameras purred," the paper reported, "and still cameras clicked making a record of the start of the voyage." The boat's white sides sported the words "Kern Co. Special Bakersfield to Treasure Island," painted with a steady, precise hand. The crew packed navigational charts, food, blankets, gasoline, and a second backup motor. Although Latta's trip wasn't what cowboys would call his first rodeo, it was too arduous for him to complete alone. He needed help protecting supplies from water damage, hauling the boat around dry spots and weirs, and navigating while he took notes. Three kids accompanied him on the entire trip: his twelve-year-old son, Don Latta, and two local boys, sixteen-year-old Ernest Ingalls and seventeen-year-old Richard Harris. Latta taught Ingalls and Harris at the local high school. A fourth teen, Ted Collins, joined them by the fourth day of the trip, but Collins's name simply stops appearing in newspaper articles by their fifth day. The papers never say what happened.

"As the Latta boat swung out from the shore," the paper said, "Don Latta, a youngster, called out to his mother on the bank. 'This is one time, mother, you can't spank me for getting wet,' and he made a paddling motion. The crowd on the levee bank laughed at this sally. In the 'good ship' Alta, were rubber inner tubes sealed ingeniously at each end to contain cameras and other articles to prevent their injury should they become wet. Forward in the bow of the skiff was a small half-deck containing supplies and a set of vest-type life preservers. Some of the river waterways large and powerful with flood currents will make phases of the trip dangerous unless precautions such as this are taken."

Latta, his teenage crew, and their skiff were at the edge of a landscape that was known but, at the same time, still wild. According to the Federal Census Bureau, the American frontier officially ended in 1890, meaning there was no land left to meaningfully explore or settle. However, pockets of rugged, wilder lands remained in the West in the early twentieth century, places where adventure seekers could still experience a more primeval America of unlogged forests and undammed rivers. As widely settled as California was by 1938, the San Joaquin Valley in the state's flat center still offered opportunities for wilder experiences. Cougars prowled its oak woods. Deer nibbled native grasses, and dense cottonwood forest still lined its many rivers, even as cattle roamed the lowlands that once belonged to elk and scrub brush. Latta's boat trip was probably the last of those adventures in this semiwild place, and it marked the beginning of a time when people, not nature, determined the fate of California's water.

Sandwiched between the mountain ranges of the Sierra Nevada and the Coast Range, California's great Central Valley runs 430 miles through the middle of the state. It consists of two long valleys named for their primary rivers: the Sacramento Valley in the north and the San Joaquin Valley in the south. The Sacramento Valley stretches approximately 165 miles from the town of Redding south to the city of Sacramento. The San Joaquin Valley stretches 265 miles north and south and averages 47 miles across, 75 at its widest—wide enough that you can't see its edges on hazy days. You drive through the San Joaquin Valley between LA and San Francisco. You cross it to reach Lake Tahoe and Yosemite. It covers eight million acres; houses over four million people; has some of California's fastest growing cities, four of America's five highest-grossing agricultural counties, and some of the nation's worst air pollution; and is serviced by two large north-south highways. And yet many people who have lived their entire lives in Berkeley and Santa Cruz have never heard this part of their state referred to as the San Joaquin Valley. Some who are aware of it mistakenly call it the Central Valley. Others think of it in terms of vague subregions: the wine country foothills; the gold country; the hot, flat Fresno-Bakersfield section. Most think of the San Joaquin Valley as one long roadside bathroom break, California's flyover country, the West's Midwest, and they try to get through it as quickly as possible. But most things here are gears in the machine that runs one of the most productive agricultural regions in human history. The San Joaquin isn't the wine country. It isn't the gold country. It's its own country, with its own fascinating natural history and settlement history and its own unique climate, produce, and problems.

In November 2014, during the most severe drought in California's five hundred years of recorded history, I retraced Latta's trip through the San Joaquin Valley. Reading about Latta's boat trip in the *Bakersfield Californian*, I decided to follow Latta's route, this time by car, and to try to re-create the story. I'd driven through the Valley many times during the previous two decades. I'd read scores of books about it, spent lots of time exploring its tiny nature preserves, back roads, and overlooked cities, but I still couldn't make sense of the place. The Valley mystified me. Scorching in summer, foggy in winter, and devoid of significant topography, this flat, fecund landscape wasn't beautiful in the obvious sense, and yet it was beautiful. Its history and ecology were more fascinating than it let on. Something about its shapes, colors, and fragrances demanded my attention, just as its underdog status made me want to know it even more.

Frank Forrest Latta was the San Joaquin's most important early historian. Born in 1892 where the Orestimba Creek flows into the San Joaquin Valley near the barely there settlement of Newman, Latta became enthralled by history as a child. Interstate 5 now runs by the creek's mouth, but Orestimba used to cross the Camino Viejo, a road that the Spanish built in the 1700s to connect the Bay Area with Los Angeles. In 1906 Latta's old grammar school teacher Edith V. Hollingsworth suggested that fourteen-year-old Frank interview the people who'd settled their western Merced County school district for a history project. History soon became his life's central focus.

By 1938, the year of his boat launch, Latta was forty-six years old and an experienced outdoorsman. Standing six feet two, with a face that was photographed as quietly contemplative or youthfully happy, he wore a short mustache and kept his dark hair tight on the sides in a military-type crew cut, standing it high on his head. Sometimes he carried a broad-brimmed hat in the field. Sometimes he wore a sport coat and tie. Despite the summer heat, he stood in the boat on this day with his long-sleeved collared shirt tucked into his clean high-waisted trousers and his prescription glasses in his front pocket. He was used to the heat.

His high school project led to a lifetime of work interviewing early Valley residents. He reached those first interviewees on horseback, including James Hitchcock, who came to California on the first wagons to cross the Sierra Nevada when the state was still part of Mexico, before the doomed Donner Party. Ten years later, Latta reached his next subjects in a beat-up, roofless Model T with half a windshield.

In 1916 for two days in August he drove down the Valley's swampy center toward Bakersfield, talking with old-timers about whom to interview and camping outdoors. He bounced down rough roads described in a local paper as "mostly gravel, some oiled"; one was made from a "16-foot concrete pavement with broken edges and cracks every twenty feet." Even though the roads were primitive and the sound of freight trains kept him up at night, Latta described this first journey into Tulare County as the most interesting one he ever made—and he took countless journeys during his long life.

By 1937 his research into early California had him driving dirt roads all over the San Joaquin Valley and Sierra Nevada, interviewing pioneers, trappers, miners, farmers, ranchers, railroad workers, sheriffs, and the people he especially loved, Native Americans in the Yokuts tribes. He searched for these people, to meet them, talk to them, and secure a record of life before modernity erased it. He interviewed people he felt were like himself, with dirt under their nails, not politicians, bankers, or frontier California's upper echelons.

He published a whole book about the Valley in 1937, called *Little Journeys in the San Joaquin*. His best-known books, both about the area, are the massive *Handbook of Yokuts Indians*, viewed as the definitive study of Yokuts culture, and *Tailholt Tales*, the record of one white nineteenth-century settler's life with the Yokuts people. Yet like the Valley he loved, few people outside the region know his name.

Working together as a team, Frank; his wife, Jeanette; and their four kids collected artifacts in tiny towns, from Native rabbit-skin blankets to the hooded tapaderos stirrups the state's most famous bandit, Joaquin Murrieta, used on his last saddle. Somehow, they acquired the 1876 Winchester rifle that Bill Dalton used in California's first train heist. They even owned a huge rusty anchor from a steamship that fished the Valley's massive Tulare Lake, the largest freshwater body west of the Mississippi at the time. They cataloged these items in what the family called the Bear State Library, but Latta specialized in oral history—works primarily composed of the direct words of interview sources, often arranged for effect and supplemented with context and commentary. Latta viewed the subject's words and voice as essential parts of the story, if not more important than the information they gave, then just as vital.

"The man himself is the source," Latta said, using the gendered speech of his time, "the authority." Latta found no distance too great to find a story. He sometimes labored for years to locate key people who'd witnessed or knew participants of particular events. Someone might mention a certain colorful character or old-timer, and Latta would ask locals their whereabouts, following rumors and leads and dead ends until he found the person of interest. He interviewed the sister-in-law of a man whom Joaquin Murrieta supposedly killed in 1852. He interviewed Yoimut, the last member of the Chunut Tribe and last person who spoke their native *Croo'-noot* and *Wo'-wole* dialects. At the end of that two-day Model T trip in 1916, he spoke with Thomas Baker, the founder of Bakersfield. He interviewed so many Native Americans that some nicknamed him *Weé-chet-e*, meaning "little sticks," after the bundles of pencils he brought with him. The approximately eighteen thousand people he interviewed formed the basis of the three thousand articles and fourteen or so books he published. "Often we are in daily contact with remarkable people," Latta once said, "and fail to recognize that fact." He'd talk to anyone who looked interesting.

"After 3:30 that Friday after school was out," Latta recalled in an article, "I hopped in my car and headed clear to this little town in the northern part of the state, and I came up to this fellow while he was feeding his chickens. He leaned against a post and began answering my questions; we talked for eight hours."

As an oral historian, Frank Latta was a scrappier, less monomaniacal version of California's most accomplished ethnographer, Dr. John Peabody Harrington. A voluminous workaholic who studied Native languages and preferred to work eighteen-hour days, Harrington spent the first half of the twentieth century driving all over the West on the Smithsonian's payroll, practically living in the field, taking photographs, pressing plants, collecting baskets, and filling a million pages and hundreds of museum boxes with notes about Native culture. He cut 950 audio discs on a 150-pound portable aluminum disc recording machine that he had to haul in his car on bad roads, and he preserved multiple California languages before they went extinct. Although the two mostly corresponded by mail and rarely met in real life, Latta modeled his efforts after Harrington's.

As Harrington told a young field assistant in a 1941 letter, "If you can grab these dying languages before the old timers completely die off, you will be doing one of the FEW things valuable to the people of the REMOTE future. You know that. The time will come and SOON when there won't be an Indian language left in California. . . . That's why I said to go through the blinding rain, roads or no roads . . . haven't I gone back even two weeks later to find them DEAD and the language FOREVER DEAD?" Unlike Harrington, Latta's interests were wider than language, and he split his time more judiciously between family and work. Harrington worked for the Smithsonian's Bureau of American Ethnology for forty years. Somehow, Latta never signed on with an institution. Maybe he didn't want to. He wasn't formally trained in anthropology, and he was an independent spirit who was able to dictate whom he interviewed and when and to keep all his books in his name.

Harrington and Latta were not lone geniuses but part of a new documentary movement gaining steam in America in the late nineteenth century. In 1879 Congress created the Bureau of American Ethnology. Headed by John Wesley Powell, the ethnographer who mapped the Colorado River and Grand Canyon, the bureau sent out a fleet of scholars during the late 1800s and early 1900s to record Native American languages, tribal knowledge, artifacts, and images and to hold public exhibits. Using portable phonograph machines and notebooks, field-workers created an invaluable lasting document of America's first cultures, while capitalism, racism, and Manifest Destiny were busy eradicating them. As staff workers and affiliated collaborators, the Smithsonian employed Frances Densmore, who spent half a century recording Native Americans' music on wax cylinders, and the famous Franz Boaz, "The Father of American Anthropology."

In the early 1900s, banker J. P. Morgan paid Edward Curtis to spend the early 1900s taking more than forty thousand photographs of over eighty tribes in what stands as the most humanizing and important collection of historic images of Native American cultures, just like *Fortune Magazine* paid James Agee to gather the interviews with poor white farmers that became his influential social document *Let Us Now Praise Famous Men*. During the Great Depression, the Federal Writers' Project sent field-workers to collect the songs, stories, and dialects of working-class rural Americans, the so-called common people. The material collected from former African American slaves proved invaluable; historians still rely on that primary body of work. In the 1930s and 1940s, the Library of Congress commissioned Alan Lomax to drive all over the American South with a heavy disc recorder in the back of his car, hooked to his car battery, where he recorded performances and interviews with musicians like Muddy Waters, Lead Belly, and Woody Guthrie.

Unlike those working for the Federal Writers' Project, Latta rarely had institutional support. He supported his wife Jeanette and four children and funded the family's research by teaching agriculture, drafting, and carpentry at high schools. Instead of recording musicians with audio equipment, he recorded his sources with a camera, pencil, and paper. Latta's subjects never became famous like Muddy Waters, but they were important to the history of the Valley in their own way: the Valley's last stagecoach driver, the last of General Custer's scouts, and the last of the Nutúnutu Tribe. And like Lomax and Agee, Latta gathered their stories because, as he told a newspaper, "I couldn't help it." He believed that history and folklore mattered, and he was happily obsessed.

His technique was primitive; his prose, workmanlike and unadorned. Although easily dismissed as obscure and, perhaps more damning, *regional*, his contributions are unparalleled. Numerous books of California history lean heavily on his research and list it in their bibliographies, yet few modern people, even locals, know Latta's name, just as too few Californians know the name of the valley he loved.

Heavy winter rains in 1937 continued into spring, breaking levees by Sacramento and sending eighty thousand cubic feet of water per second down the Kings River by Fresno; to give some context, thirty thousand cubic feet is rated as a severe volume for the Kings. In March 1938 nearly an inch of rain fell in Fresno in one night. For a semidesert environment, that's a lot. The city gets about eleven inches a year. By April, melting sierra snowpack breached levees near Corcoran and flooded forty thousand acres of farmland, and a thirty-two-year-old named Robert Scutt drowned in a farm ditch after his boat struck debris.

In 1938 the complex system of dams and canals that now manage waterways in the Valley didn't yet exist, so floodwaters undercut roads and disrupted railroads, running hundreds of families from their homes and challenging the wisdom of the settler enterprise. In 1938 those same rivers connected with marshes and lakes into a single hydrological system. Theoretically, a person could float the four hundred wet miles from Bakersfield to the Pacific Ocean, though there was little reason to do so. Latta decided to try. His trip was meant to promote the need for flood control, though it was also an expression of his love for frontier California, even as the dams he promoted would fundamentally alter it.

Latta's planned route would take his team down the Kern River southwest of Bakersfield to Buena Vista Lake near Buttonwillow. From there, they'd float north through Buena Vista Slough to Tulare Lake. Heading north through a confusion of marshes and channels, they would pass over the raised hump of the Kings River alluvial fan into the San Joaquin Valley's namesake river, whose fresh water would, if things went according to plan, shuttle them to Treasure Island in salty San Francisco Bay. These place names hardly add up to a useful mental image, considering how few of these hydrological features still exist. What are important are the water and superlatives.

Back then, like today, the Valley was defined by a continuous cycle of flood and drought. Heavy snowfall would fill the rivers for a few good years. The land would fill with wetlands and ducks. Farmers planted crops as the waters evaporated; then the rivers would dry up for a few harsh years until the floods came again.

Native Americans might have boated from Bakersfield to San Francisco Bay in order to trade, but white people never did. A hunter named Ed Harris took a shorter version in the flood year of 1868, though he only paddled from Bakersfield as far north as Stockton, and he was selling pelts, not engineering. And 146 years later, in 2014, a CNN reporter named John D. Sutter kayaked the 417-mile length of the San Joaquin River, from the high Sierra Nevada to the Golden Gate Bridge. Based on the urban and agricultural demands placed on its inconsistent waters, the American Rivers organization named the San Joaquin "America's most endangered river." Over 95 percent of the river gets diverted for irrigation, and sixty miles of its bed contain no water at all. Sutter wanted, in his words, "to meet the people who depend on it, and to find out whether this dead river could be brought back to life." His route only took him as far south as Fresno, where the San Joaquin River turns north, rather than through the flatlands between Bakersfield and Fresno. Latta went all the way, from the bottom of the Valley to the top.

It isn't clear how Latta came up with his boat-trip idea. One early Bakersfield settler named Mrs. Callie Pettit told Latta that when Sacramento was six feet underwater during the 1862 floods, Tejon Creek, south of Bakersfield, ran so high that you could float from the famous Tejon Ranch in the mountains down to the Valley floor, right up into the floodwaters southwest of Fresno. "If such were the case," Latta wrote in 1937, "the rest of a water trip to San Francisco would have been a simple matter." Maybe this was the origin of the *Alta*'s voyage. He knew the region's flood and drought years. When the snow kept melting and waters kept rising in 1937, he recognized that the water wasn't going away and that this, as an astute student of history could see, was a fleeting opportunity.

What the *Bakersfield Californian* called a "tremendous waste of water" had spread across the Valley in the winter of 1938, and it was time that people "saved [it] for irrigation as needed."

Since Latta's era, the big Sierra Nevada rivers that flow into the San Joaquin Valley have all been dammed. Huge boatable reservoirs now fill those mountains, and nearly every cubic foot of water is spoken for before it even leaves the dams. Instead of recharging the Valley's groundwater supply and filling natural lakes and marshes, canals divert sierra snowmelt to farms and cities through one of the most complex and contentious water-transport systems on earth—the combined Central Valley Project and State Water Project. Thanks to water diversion and an average three hundred days of sunshine a year, the Valley's class 1 soil supports over 250 crops, including almonds, peaches, mandarins, olives, wine grapes, table grapes, raisins, nectarines, kiwis, plums, pistachios, walnuts, onions, carrots, beets, garlic, pomegranates, wheat, lettuce, and 84 percent of the state's dairy products. If you eat any of these, you've probably touched the San Joaquin. The Valley's farmers feed millions of people in America, China, Japan, South Korea, and Europe. California historian Kevin Starr called the San Joaquin "the most productive unnatural environment on Earth." Yet salts from soil and agricultural chemicals are ruining the Valley's soils, and toxins are polluting its water and air. As old farmland gets covered with new suburban tract homes and shopping centers, the words of Valley vaquero Arnold "Jefe" Rojas become more pressing than ever: "Someday we will have to plow up the malls to plant something to eat."

Even if it rained today like it did in 1938, you could never float Latta's route. Buena Vista Lake is no longer a lake; it's a recreation area fed by pumps. Most marshes don't fill unless government agencies let them. This is why I drove. Dams, ditches, and levees make sure that the waterways no longer connect. Even farmers were struggling to connect with the water. In 2014 and 2015 reservoirs ran dry. Some irrigation districts didn't release irrigation at all. Growers relied on established wells to water crops, and thousands drilled new ones. You could do that here. In 2014 California was the last western state to allow landowners to drill wells and extract groundwater on their land with few to no restrictions. The water table kept dropping, and a lot of that well water grew too salty to use. During my trip, few people sensed any light at the end of the tunnel. They felt dread. Some faced ruin. They discussed ways to fix the state's broken system and talked about God and moving away. Longtime farmers knew it would end if they could just endure it. I knew too. I'd read the history. But that's the thing about the Valley: it's feast and famine. Wet and dry years are always on their way.

I don't remember exactly where I first came across Latta's name. It was probably in the works-cited pages of all the books I'd read about the Valley. I know that I kept seeing references to Latta's books *Indian Summer* and *Tailholt Tales*. The latter was expensive and out of print, so I tracked down the first in a Bakersfield bookstore. That's when I first read Latta's words. *Indian Summer* was a slim volume but blew me away, transporting me to another world that looked nothing like the irrigated world that now filled the Valley. *Indian Summer* was just a fraction of his enormous output. When I stumbled on a reference to a boat trip Latta took from Bakersfield to San Francisco, I knew I had to read more. So I started tracking down his books and other sources and focused my attention on this boat trip. Unfortunately, I found nearly nothing more about it: few articles, no books, not even a paragraph in California histories describing the trip. It was bizarre. It was as if it had never happened. So I printed out the original *Bakersfield Californian* articles about it, and I reimagined his trip while I retraced it by car. What did the Valley look like back then? How did its ecology and economy function? As Fresno-born journalist Mark Arax said in the *California Sunday Magazine*, "I pity the outsider trying to make sense of it." I've spent the last twenty years of my life trying to make sense of it.

The story of this region and its indigenous people is the story of a place being almost completely erased in a single century. I believe that this region is important, that Latta's ethnographic work is important, and that helping Americans appreciate the region is important. In narrating Latta's journey, I stuck to the facts, but I have created some scenes from my imagination, constructing particular moments in order to show what the trip might have been like, in order to show readers what the Valley was like before it all got plowed and paved.

For two weeks that November, I visited farms. I visited an almond-processing plant. I ordered ham and eggs for dinner and burritos for breakfast. I hung out in a honky-tonk; gambled at a Yokuts casino; witnessed food scarcity amid all this food; and talked to truckers, travelers, writers, waitresses, a Bureau of Land Management biologist, a truck stop prostitute, water officials, diners, and grocery store shoppers, in an attempt to make sense of the weirdly named towns like Manteca, Turlock, and Ripon and to understand the foul smells and ubiquitous roadside signs telling highway travelers, "Food Grows Where Water Flows," and, "We Buy Pallets." The vintage vw bus parked in the desert behind the gas station. The lone motel on the dark stretch of highway, where only the letters M, E, and L work. The burnt-hair smell in Delano and the smell of sour cheese in Madera. What goes on here? The short answer is interstate and agriculture. The long answer is more interesting.

Along with his boat trip, Latta's oral history inspired me. He talked to anyone, so I did too. He loved the sound of peoples' voices, how they chose their words and phrases, and in huge sections of his books, he gets out of the speakers' way so that readers can hear them talk. His body of work is mostly people talking. Oral history was increasingly popular at the time, though I think that his reliance on others' voices reflects his love of oral tradition as much as his limitations as a narrative writer. John Steinbeck infused his 1945 novel *Cannery Row* with some of this oral history spirit when he decided that "the best way to write this book [was] to open the page and to let the stories crawl in by themselves."

Although I went looking for the Valley, I found a nation incredibly disconnected from the land under its feet and from the people who built the world we inhabit. Different cultures call their predecessors ancestors. In America we call them history. As I read Latta's work, it also became clear that this historian hadn't received the same thorough treatment that he gave his eighteen thousand subjects. This number is likely a slight exaggeration, but this book is still partly for him.

Some residents of the Valley have characterized Latta's boat trip as a legendary local story to me, but although locals know of it, they are few and far between. And despite Latta's contribution to California history, no one outside the Valley had written a long profile of him. The fact is, the story endures among a very narrow group of people, and those people, like Latta's subjects, are aging. There has been no literary survey of him and definitely no narrative account of his boat trip in a magazine. Why? An obsessive personality in the Harrington and Lomax tradition, set against a wilder California— his life seemed so cinematic. Maybe it wasn't cinematic enough. The very word *history* chills the blood of Americans who are forced to memorize dates and battles and regurgitate raw data on tests. But history is fascinating when it's narrated as a story, because people prefer stories over data. We're wired that way.

This book doesn't just narrate history. It's meant to let anyone in California feel the magic of the place where they live, which is what I feel when I read many historical accounts and meet its people, past and present. As Ohlone basket weaver and scholar Linda Yamane said of reading ethnologist John P. Harrington's material on California's Native people, "It's not just words on a piece of paper, but it's saving something from the past that connects with people now." I feel the same about Latta's interviews.

Also, we Americans tend to forget our predecessors. We see the monthly events, not the larger patterns. We think about our children's homework and nightly dinner plans, not millennia. With such bounty in front of us, we forget about the lessons of past deprivations and have the privilege to focus on convenience, business, and low-price products. We live in a golden era. Farmers in the Valley help make that happen.

Life moves so fast, and technology speeds it further each decade, shrinking the lens of perception to a narrow point where the people who sought answers for us in the past now disappear from view. California is a state of emergency—if not a drought, then a flood, an earthquake, a mudslide after a fire—resplendent with fields of poppies. When the next catastrophe strikes, for many people it feels like the first.

Equipped with photocopies of 1938 *Bakersfield Californian* articles, I plotted my course. Latta's exact route was hazy. Did he go through Lost Hills or just near it? Did he sleep in Alpaugh or under the stars? The newspaper record is as specific as dated expository language can be (e.g., "The crew lay over at Lost Hills"). More importantly, parts of the waterways he used now run through the vast holdings of enormous farms—private property—or take the form of irrigation canals, which are dangerous to float and off-limits. Where Latta weaved and curved, I took straight roads and ninety-degree angles. Precision wasn't the point. The point was to see the world that damming had created. He started in Bakersfield, so I did too. I flew from Oregon to Sacramento, drove straight to Bakersfield, and went right to a country bar called Trout's, which was right up the street from the site where Latta put his boat in the Kern River. Then I went to Bakersfield's only natural history museum, followed the Kern out of town, and kept driving north.

1

Down the Kern River

There is no trail but that of wild horses and elk, not a sign
of civilization, not the track of a white man to be seen, and
sometimes the loneliness and solitude seem unending.

—John W. Audubon

Bakersfield's Buena Vista Natural History Museum stands in a downtown whose commercial architecture seems to have been preserved by the desert air. Occupying a bright blue-and-green storefront that could have been a 1950s hardware store, it's down the street from the Spanish colonial art deco Fox Theater, which opened in 1930, and near a Woolworth's that now sells burgers and antiques. But the Buena Vista Natural History Museum celebrates the area's older material.

Founded in 1995 to educate the region about its natural history, the museum preserves and displays local fossils. It offers guided hikes, an annual rock sale, and lectures about topics such as the geography of Grapevine Pass. The museum even has its own lab where visitors use tools to chip at rocks to extract shark teeth. Most of the museum's fossil collection comes from the Sharktooth Hill area in Bakersfield, including one of the world's most intact skeletons of a sea lion–like creature called an *Allodesmus* and a 70 percent complete skeleton of a juvenile baleen whale from the Miocene epoch.

Volunteers run the museum. One volunteer, named Dell, started as a receptionist two and a half years before my visit and now staffed the gift shop. "I didn't study paleontology," Dell told me. "I didn't even know the museum was here. But I've learned a lot. At school

I didn't even like science or anything connected with it, but I love this now."

Dell grew up in Long Beach. After she retired, she moved to Bakersfield to live near her kids. People made fun of her: "Why are you going to Bakersfield? It's a hot place. It's a dirty place. There's nobody up there." "Well," Dell said, "they don't say that anymore. Now they say, 'Ooh, you got oil up there?' 'Ooh, you got money up there?' 'You got movie stars up there?' Yeah, we do. We're like any place else. We got a lot of stuff now, because things have changed." She still loathed the summer heat and air pollution, but after fourteen years the city had grown on her.

The southern part of the Valley is ringed by mountains on three sides. Coastal winds blow Bay Area emissions and industrial waste east through Carquinez Straight and south down the Valley, where it gets trapped in what's called a chemical bowl. Since the bulk of it comes from somewhere else, professionals call this "inherited pollution." Locals often used the Bay Area as a scapegoat for their problems, but not everyone believes the inherited-pollution story. Critics blame the Valley's smog on the topsoil kicked up by tractors, the planes spraying crops with chemicals, and the car exhaust from two major highways. Reading historical records, you see that although the air was once much clearer before tilled soil got into it, visibility was inconsistent. Some days, people on the west side could see individual trees in the Sierra Nevada through binoculars. "The peaks of the Sierra Nevada," wrote Lieutenant George H. Derby, a member of the U.S. Army Corps of Topographical Engineers, "covered with perpetual snow, appeared in close proximity, and rising far above the horizon, seemed as to come down precipitously to the very edge of the water." In June 1864 William Brewer wrote from southwest of Fresno that some days, "the mountains were invisible through the dusty air; the perfectly level plain stretched away on every side to the horizon, and seemed as boundless and as level as the ocean." No matter how inconsistent, conditions have gotten much worse.

On the day before my visit to the museum, the haze came on the heels of a week of dangerously high levels of ozone and fine particle matter called PM-2.5—a hazardous mix of chemicals, microscopic soot, and assorted debris—that sometimes tasted of metal and smoke. According to the EPA, twelve micrograms per cubic meter of PM-2.5 in the air is a "good" rating. Over seventy-five is considered "unhealthy." A few days earlier, PM-2.5 concentrations had spiked at 122 micrograms per cubic meter. Fresno allergist Dr. A. M. Aminian advised *Fresno Bee* readers, especially asthmatics, to protect themselves during periods of bad air by staying indoors or by showering and changing clothes after going outside. "Pollution particles can linger and find their way into your nose," the *Bee* said. "These PM-2.5 specks can pass through your lungs into your body—into the heart, liver, kidneys." That day's pollution read 271 AQI (Air Quality Index) at 10:00 p.m., a level that far surpassed the 100 that's considered moderate. Bakersfield news advised people to stay indoors, meaning no exercise. Some locals compared the air to urban China. They said it was worse than LA. A few months earlier *Time* magazine called Bakersfield "the real capital of air pollution in the U.S." The article said, "School officials in Bakersfield have used colored flags to indicate air quality." They'd added a new color last winter, to signify a worse level than the previous worst. My headache and cough sent me to a natural-foods store where I bought immune-boosting herbal stuff, multivitamins, and zinc, until I realized that it wasn't a cold. The next day, the haze broke, and the blue sky shined through. But no one knew how to fix this pollution.

Dell used to wish that engineers could build giant fans to blow the pollution over the mountains into the Mojave Desert.

She squinted at the front door. "You know, this is a decent day," she said. "When we see blue sky, I mean *real* blue sky, everybody's pretty happy. When you come down the Grapevine, you see it spread out. It just hangs. I always tease my kids. I say, 'Why don't you get out there with one of those things, like a hot-air balloon, and go out there and just suck it all up like a vacuum, up and down and up and down!' My son tells me, 'Mother, do you know how big Kern County is?'"

She leaned against the glass counter. "That's why they want to make the gasoline tax so high: so people won't be driving. They tell you to not drive, to carpool. People bike. I even saw a guy roller-skating!"

People come from all over the world to go on museum digs and to buy meteorites, Dell said. According to the guest book, visitors from as far as Australia and Wales have heard about the museum, from driving by, from Discovery Channel's Shark Week, and from ads in local hotels and the *Bakersfield Californian*. They get a lot of walk-in traffic, too, but a downtown museum is expensive to operate. It is worth the trouble for the way the museum introduces locals to the natural history of a region few think has natural history. It enlarges many laypeople's perception of the Valley, as a living landscape rich with history that predates all the In-N-Out Burgers and smog that they see. For instance, when someone initially told Dell that the Valley was an ocean for sixty million years, she said, "Oh yeah, right. Prove it." "Because I don't think in millions and millions of years," she said.

"I'm pretty knowledgeable," Dell told me, "but I only thought of things in terms of my sons both living here, raising their children and everything. I *lived* at the ocean from the time I was born down south, right on the beach. So when people told me that [about the inland sea], I just looked at them and said, 'Really? Really?' Then they showed me the maps and the different things. I guess the ocean just disappeared, so it's dry land here." Visitors repeatedly told her, "Oh yeah, we've heard that all our lives." They regaled her with stories of digging up dinosaur bones as kids. She shrugged and looked at me with a mischievous grin. "It just didn't seem right to me. . . . But they showed me, and now I am amazed." I could relate.

When I first saw the Valley in the summer of 1995, I told my best friend, Dean, "This place is a dump." Dean and I were driving down Interstate 5, returning home to Arizona from a four-week road trip through coastal California and the Pacific Northwest. We were unshowered, exhausted, and twenty years old. On our second-to-last day, we wound through the mountains of southern Oregon and past the towns of Weed and Mt. Shasta and dropped into a big scorching flatland that didn't feel like California. The place went on forever and was as memorable for its bleakness as it was for the speed at which we drove to escape the greasy July heat. We said it over and over: "This place is a dump." Compared to the verdant coastal forests we'd explored, this landscape insulted our eyes.

We didn't know it at the time, but the nearly five hundred flat miles of I-5 running between the Central Valley's southern end, at the Grapevine Pass, and its northern end, at Redding, are some of the most loathed in America. If travelers stop at all along this highway, it's to visit the gas stations and Denny's that dot the roadside. In the parking lots of these chain stores, drivers lean against their cars to smoke cigarettes, enjoying a moment of sunshine before resuming their trip. Even though the Central Valley feeds them, many Californians refer to the area as the Appalachia of the West, dismissing it as the haunt of rednecks and meth heads, a boring place without beauty or history, a pit, a dump, a hole, "flat as fuck." Despite the ugly commercial architecture, this area can be beautiful. I find it beautiful. But most people experience it the way author A. I. Bezzerides describes it in his 1938 novel *Long Haul*, driving "through the small towns, Fowler and Kingsburg, Goshen and Pixley, Farmosa and Bakersfield, mixing them up, thinking one was the other."

Instead of wasting gas money by using air-conditioning, we drove with the windows open, and the land outside stunk of cow manure and vegetable soup. Hour after hour, the ruler-straight Interstate bombarded us with offensive odors and offered no sign of relief. It had no great curves, no hint of an approaching mountain pass. We didn't understand where we were. The level horizon didn't help. After we watched the mountains disappear near Redding, a solid brown haze stretched in all directions. The land's edges were so dusty that I worried we'd taken a wrong turn and were driving east into Nevada instead of south toward Los Angeles. We weren't. That day, we drove through this flat place for six hours, top to bottom, unaware that we'd driven through the Sacramento and San Joaquin Valleys, until eventually climbing some mountains at its southern end and settling in for the night at Dean's brother's beach house in Marina del Rey. The boardwalk, the cool air, the sound of crashing waves—to us, *that* was California. What we didn't realize was that before large-scale American settlement, the San Joaquin Valley's natural ecosystem was like no other in the American West, which, just like the state itself, was definitively Californian.

In a land of superlatives, paradoxes, and surprises, tarantulas coincided with cranes, marshes met barrens, and summer drought followed spring floods, making it as hard to control as it was to comprehend. Valley grasslands supported Serengeti-sized herds of elk and pronghorn. Kangaroo rats, kit foxes, and rattlesnakes filled the scrub. Cougars and grizzlies prowled the wooded creeks, and in spring the parched soil bloomed.

Traveling with his family in 1850, early Fresno-area settler Thomas Jefferson Mayfield picked so many flowers that the family's horses and packs were soon decorated as brightly as the land. "The two most beautiful remembrances I have," Mayfield told Frank Latta in his first book *Uncle Jeff's Story*, "are of the virgin San Joaquin and of my mother." Driving past the packing sheds and cookie-cutter houses nowadays, you'd never guess this region could make such an impression.

The land that we know as a valley has its roots in the Jurassic. During that famous dinosaur period 195 million years ago, this area lay under the ocean. During the Cretaceous period, a massive chunk of rock, called a batholith, pushed through the shallow seafloor and broke the water's surface, where shifting tectonic plates pushed it upward into the mountain range that became the Sierra Nevada. For ninety million years, those mountains washed their eroding material into the water that lapped their western shore. Layer upon layer of terrestrial residue deposited, all pressed under the weight of new ocean material; these are the shark teeth that hikers find at places like Sharktooth Hill, and the diatomaceous clay that traps salty water under farmers' fields. This shallow sea covered the area until an ongoing series of geological uplifts—the same forces that shape modern California, except with different fault lines and plates—pushed the future Coast Range up from the seafloor. As the sea levels dropped, the Coast Range kept rising and cut the San Joaquin Valley off from its oceanic origins, isolating it, as William Preston put it, "forever from direct association with marine environments and processes." During the Pleistocene the area became the basin we know today, with the Coast Range pushed into its current position, running parallel to the sierra, and separating inland from coastal California.

Just as it had underwater, the terrestrial Valley filled with sierra sediments, creating a flat basin composed of deep layers of alternating soils, including old marine life and salts. Over the last million years, the earth entered a series of ice ages. Glaciers formed atop the Sierra Nevada and carved the valleys that white settlers named Hetch Hetchy and Kings Canyon. As evaporated ocean water turned into glacial snow, the sea levels dropped by three hundred feet, drying the floor of the Valley. The water's retreat left behind a huge freshwater lake called Lake Corcoran seven hundred thousand years ago. At that time, the San Joaquin's rivers didn't flow the way they do now. They drained into Monterrey Bay through the Salinas River. That changed 560,000 years ago after a huge volcanic eruption and more geologic uplift redirected the flow into what became San Francisco Bay. When the last ice age ended 11,700 years ago, the glaciers melted and the Pacific Ocean rose again, between three and fifteen feet per century in places, including San Francisco Bay. But it no longer entered the Valley. This completed the physical separation between interior California and coastal California, which set the stage for the current cultural divisions between the two regions. The water that remained in the Valley was either locked underground between soil layers or pooled on the surface as the lake that Europeans called Tulare. As the earth warmed, the Valley entered its current phase, and Native Americans moved in.

First, the hunter-gatherers appeared eleven thousand years ago, using Clovis points to kill remnant Ice Age bison on the lakeshore.

Then people arrived from the Great Basin, speaking Hokaltekan languages. Then came the Penutians, who learned to harvest acorns five thousand years ago and became the Yokuts.

The area's mixture of forested foothills, wooded waterways, and marshy lowlands allowed members of the Yokuts, Miwok, and Tubatulabal Native American groups to thrive. About 150,000 Native Americans lived in California before Spaniards arrived. Between thirty thousand and eighty thousand of them were Yokuts people living in the San Joaquin Valley. They formed what William Preston called, in his landmark book *Vanishing Landscapes*, "the densest non-agricultural population in North America." Despite the singularity of their lowland terrain and a fairly uniform language, the Yokuts didn't have one leader or capital, so they weren't technically a tribe, though white ethnographers grouped them that way. The Yokuts were composed of about sixty separate, individually named subtribes who had their own leaders, territories, beliefs, and customs. They were the Wowole, Tachi, Chunut, Yokodo, Tulumne, Yowlumne, Wukchumne, Chukchansi, Kaweah, Koyeti, Wechikit, Nutúnutu, and Chaushila, to name a few. These largely peaceful people didn't farm. Instead, they moved seasonally through different habitats, collecting acorns, piñon pine nuts, roots, berries, and seeds and hunting antelope, ground squirrels, deer, ducks, and grebes. In clothing stitched from grass and bark, they fished wetlands in boats made from reeds. They herded rabbits into ingenious nets made from tree branches and plant fibers, gathered shellfish with their toes, and burned grasslands to flush out protein-rich grasshoppers by the thousands. The Yokuts called themselves *Yokoch*, "the people." When asked what that meant, some used the word to mean "they come everywhere," because they were so numerous. Some Yokuts called Tulare Lake *Pah-ah-see*, for the way it swelled and contracted, and the San Joaquin Valley *Chaw-láw-no*.

The first Spanish explorer to lay eyes on the Valley was an early military governor of Alta California, Captain Don Pedro Fages. Born in Catalonia, Fages sailed to Sonora, Mexico, with the Spanish army in 1767. Two years later, he helped lead an expedition to establish the community of San Diego, after which he headed overland with a group to locate Monterey Bay. During his brief time as governor, he made a few forays into the rugged interior. On one of them, in 1772, he entered the Valley while searching for soldiers who'd deserted the Spanish army, and he named the scenic canyon situated at the head of the Valley la Cañada de las Uvas, "the Canyon of the Grapes." *Vitis californica*, California wild grape. Dense mats of wild grapes once grew there. Indigenous people ate its fruit. American settlers turned it into wine. The grapevines grew so thick that Spanish and Mexican soldiers in subsequent eras had to chop their way through—as did travelers on the canyon's wagon road, after Mexico ceded California to the Unites States in 1848. Interstate 5 now runs through Grapevine Canyon, plunging three thousand feet down into the Valley at such a steep, sustained decline that before the road was widened and straightened between the 1940s and 1960s, it was one of the deadliest roads in the West.

Fages named the canyon, but he only referred to the Valley itself as a "great plain." Later Spanish explorers called it *valle de los tulares*, after all the marshes that covered it. *Tulare* is the Spanish word for "reed." Americans anglicized the word to "tules," pronounced "too-lee," rather than "tool." The Mono tribes, who lived in the Sierra Nevada, called the San Joaquin River *typici-h-huu'*, meaning "important river." While scouting potential mission sites in 1805, Spanish lieutenant Gabriel Moraga found a river on March 20, so he named it after Saint Joachim—the father of Jesus's mother, Mary—since that day was the feast of Saint Joachim. It turns out he'd named a small feeder creek, but someone eventually found the main river and transferred the name. In 1826 an unnamed group of Native Americans from the Valley told explorer Jebediah Smith that they called the river *Peticutry*, though his journals don't indicate what that meant. By then, the Spanish had extended the river's name to the whole valley, so when Mexico issued settlers land grants, they listed that name on official paperwork. After Mexico ceded California to the United States in 1848, the state of California named the land around this saint's river San Joaquin County, and like so many things in the whitewashing of America, it was as if no other names had existed.

Before European settlement reconfigured it, the San Joaquin Valley contained habitat types that didn't seem like kinds that could coexist. What army surveyor R. S. Williamson said of the wooded Tule River banks in 1853 holds true for the whole San Joaquin Valley: "The contrast between this beautifully-green spot and the arid plains on each side is very striking." Alkali desert and mixed riparian forest; semidesert grassland and freshwater marsh; swamp and saltbush scrub—those are the scientific names for the habitat types found in the Valley, but I like to think of this as a land both arid and aquatic.

Although this region only receives between zero and twelve inches of rain annually, a lush band of cottonwood, willow, box elder, and sycamore grew where rivers flowed. Huge shaggy oak trees dominated these riparian forests in the Valley, providing a trellis on which thick curtains of wild grapevines and blackberry draped themselves. The valley oak found in the California interior is the largest oak species in America. They grow over one hundred feet tall and more than six hundred years old. Wild roses and clematis grew underneath them; squirrels and woodpeckers moved tree to tree. Ducks and beavers patrolled the river's surface, as tree frogs chirped from shady places. The oaks offered welcoming places to camp, except that cougars and grizzly bears prowled them, too, bedding down while hunting deer and elk.

Moving away from the rivers, the soil dried out, and native perennial bunch grasses grew in tufts. In the space between clumps, wildflowers bloomed or nothing grew at all.

In many grassy areas, small seasonal pools formed. Scientists call them vernal pools in reference to their spring appearance. Locals called them hog wallows for the way livestock cooled off in them. They were delicate ephemeral ecosystems whose tiny plants and minute crustaceans only briefly came to life. Some insects lived nowhere else. Vernal pools formed in places where hard soil kept water from percolating deeper. Flowers bloomed in concentric rings, forming bands of color as the water evaporated, splashing purple on yellow on green, all cinched with a ribbon of white. One tiny flower formed white mats so thick that people named it meadowfoam. Oil extracted from its seeds has a similar chemical composition to oil from sperm whales, which were nearly hunted to extinction because it was an ideal lubricant in watches, sewing machines, car transmissions, and planes. Farmers plant meadowfoam as a cover crop now, and its honey tastes like butterscotch. But that was in wet years. In dry years, the flatlands became a parched hell.

Lieutenant George H. Derby worked for the U.S. Army Corps of Topographical Engineers, and his surveying work brought him through the San Joaquin Valley during a dry year. Entering from the west side in 1850, Derby's party crossed "a perfect desert" with "no forage for the animals but wire grass . . . and no wood at all." Worse than desert, in many places the land was barren, salty, dusty. On the Valley's east side, Derby described the land south of Deer Creek, somewhere near current-day Pixley or Earlimart, as "the most miserable country that I ever beheld. The soil was not only of the most wretched description, dry and powdery and decomposed, but was everywhere burrowed by gophers and a small animal resembling a common house rat. These animals are innumerable, though what they subsist upon I cannot conceive, for there was little or no vegetation." The U.S. Geological Survey sent the young, energetic William Henry Brewer through California in the 1860s to help assess the state's mineral and botanical resources. A good-natured, tireless farmer, Brewer called this a "land of absolute desolation" and described the area around Bakersfield as "patches of alkali grass or saline desert shrubs, in others it was entirely bare, the ground crusted with salt and alkali, like snow." While California was still part of Mexico, explorer Thomas Jefferson Farnham also found the place miserable. "This intense heat, poured down so many months upon the submerged prairies, evaporates the water," he wrote, "and converts the lakes into stagnant pools . . . which send out most pestilential exhalations, converting the immense valley into a field of death."

Death and misery—two common desert features. Despite its seasonal floodwater, the southern San Joaquin Valley was floristically, biologically, and climatologically a desert. It isn't far from the coast. It has the coast's Mediterranean climate of wet winters and dry summers, but Pacific storms that move east dump much of their moisture over the Coast Range, which puts the Valley in a rain shadow. It draws its kangaroo rats, lizards, saltbush, and kit foxes from the Mojave, the same basic genera you find around Barstow and Victorville. But the air holds more moisture than the Mojave, which sits behind the even larger rain shadow cast by the fourteen-thousand-foot Sierra Nevada. Too dry for most coastal plants, too moist for creosote bushes or Joshua trees, the San Joaquin is a climatological halfway point between the inland deserts and the sea, and those conditions, coupled with its physical isolation, gave rise to its own versions of desert species: the Tipton and Fresno kangaroo rats, the blunt-nosed leopard lizard, and the San Joaquin kit fox. In fact, I would argue that you can think of the Valley and its old Pleistocene lake in the same way you think of the Great Salt Lake in Utah, Pyramid Lake in Nevada, and Rogers Dry Lake to the east. Those old Ice Age relics sit in what geologists call the Basin and Range Province, and this land between the Coast Range and Sierra Nevada is its southwesternmost extension. All of this is to say, it's a weird, unique place.

The land goes from desert to swamp in as few natural miles as it did paragraphs in explorers' journals. Marshes weren't all trouble. Life thrived in the muck. Tule elk hid in them. Ducks nested beside them. While his party got mired in the reeds, John Woodhouse Audubon camped on the San Joaquin River in November 1848 and "secured a fine elk and an antelope, three geese and two Sandhill cranes . . . [and] feasted luxuriously."

Thomas Jefferson Mayfield, one of Latta's best-known subjects, provided one of the most memorable descriptions of the early Valley. As Mayfield's family contemplated the wisdom of crossing the swollen San Joaquin River in the spring of 1850, a group of Yokuts, who'd been washing their hair on the opposite shore, swam across to offer assistance. "Finally a young girl about sixteen years of age offered to take me on her back and swim the river with me," Mayfield told Latta. "So Mother took off my clothes. . . . I clasped my hands around [the Yokuts girl's] neck, and she took my feet under her arms and waded into the water . . . until we arrived at the south edge of the stream in shallow water. . . . [The girl] was very proud of me and, holding my hand, kept the rest of the Indians at a distance of several feet. She would talk to me and laugh, but, of course, I understood nothing she said and remembered only the words"; *Chólo-wé-chep*, the girl called him, "little white boy." That image is so tender, so touching, that it attached itself to my brain with the tenacity of a cocklebur when I first read it in college, and it drew me toward this lost world.

The memory of that flat place also stayed with me long after I first drove through it. Back then, the natural world fascinated me. My friends and I hiked a lot and explored Arizona's national forests, and I romanticized so-called "wild" landscapes as a mystical ideal of purity and perfection that made the tamed, gridded, roaded places where we lived seem like failures of civilization. While reading Sierra Club–founder John Muir's canonical 1894 book *The Mountains of California*, a passage piqued my interest.

"The Great Central Plain of California," Muir wrote in the "The Bee-Pastures" chapter, "during the months of March, April, and May, was one smooth, continuous bed of honey-bloom, so marvelously rich that, in walking from one end of it to the other, a distance of more than 400 miles, your foot would press about a hundred flowers at every step." That sounded stunning, but Muir's description confounded me. Honey-bloom? In the place where I suffered six of the most painfully repetitious highway hours of my life?

In the next paragraph, Muir wrote, "And close along the water's edge, there was a fine jungle of tropical luxuriance composed of wild-rose and bramble bushes and a great variety of climbing vines, wreathing and interlacing the branches of willows and alders, and swinging across from summit to summit in heavy festoons." These were the first signs that what I had called a dump contained something interesting. The fact that Muir's descriptions contrasted so profoundly with my own bleak experience only fascinated me more. There had to be some remnants of Muir's garden left in a state park somewhere for me to see, so I decided to find them.

I spent the next twenty years exploring the Valley. I systematically visited every state park, nature preserve, and Nature Conservancy preserve between Bakersfield and Sacramento; drove probably thousands of miles of back roads; visited tiny towns; and read every book I could find about the region, which wasn't many. Something about the Valley captivated me—partly its colors and textures, partly its smells and rural sounds, partly the way it was so unlike iconic coastal California, partly the contrast between its natural history and modernity, the way agriculture so thoroughly erased the past that even locals see it as a land without history. After years of visits, I now see how Mayfield's passage about swimming with the Yokuts girl embodies everything that the original, pre-American San Joaquin Valley was: verdant and pastoral, challenging but promising, filled with welcoming Native people whom Americans mostly eradicated as we reengineered the landscape to produce food and wealth.

After Mayfield's mother died in 1850, his father and brothers went off to make money, and members of the Choinumne Yokuts Tribe offered to take care of the eight-year-old boy. At first, his father hesitated. Leave him with *wild Indians*? Mayfield senior eventually recognized that they could offer his son a safer, more stable life than he could. Mayfield ended up living with the Choinumne for ten years in a village that now lies under the Pine Flat Reservoir. When Mayfield left this second family in 1862, food shortages, caused by white intrusions, and European diseases like measles, smallpox, and tuberculosis had reduced the three-hundred-person tribe to forty people. Sixty-six years later, at age eighty-six, Mayfield told Latta his and the Yokuts' stories. He died a few months later.

In the years since that Yokuts girl carried Thomas Mayfield across the San Joaquin River, American agricultural and urban development have eradicated most of the indigenous people and eliminated 95 percent of the San Joaquin Valley's native habitat. In more detailed accounting of the last two centuries, European settlement has eradicated over 96 percent of the entire Central Valley's original four million wetland acres and 95 percent of its native perennial bunch grassland and has whittled its original 4,000 square kilometers of riparian forest to 416 square kilometers, of which maybe 1 percent remains in a condition healthy enough to be considered intact. Ninety percent of the vernal pools have been destroyed. Sixty million waterfowl used to migrate through the Central Valley; by the year 2000, only three hundred thousand birds remained. Of the eight hundred thousand acres of saltbush scrub that scientists speculate stretched between Fresno and Bakersfield and in the Carrizo Plain, fewer than thirty-six thousand acres, or 4 percent, remain. Those figures are dated. The losses are now probably worse.

Because of the rapid rate of agricultural development here and the value of land, the southern San Joaquin has more endangered birds and other animals than anywhere else in the Lower 48. This isn't the Sierra Nevada, where a series of National Forests, National Parks, and Federal Wilderness areas protect open space. You can't call 4 percent of the original 21,300 square miles a protected landscape any more than you can call a pile of shards a pot. "I supposed," John Muir also wrote, "there will be few left, even among botanists, to lament the vanished primeval flora." But some of us who love the Valley have to tell ourselves that at least it's something, and what these parcels contain offers an enchanting glimpse of the native San Joaquin Valley that the literature thankfully records.

On the first morning of my trip chasing Latta, I climbed over the North Chester bridge's low partition to visit the site of his boat launch. Garbage covered the banks. Bleached cans of pinto beans lay in the sun amid plastic utensils, playing cards, a toilet paper roll, and a pair of gray sweatpants stiffened by dirt. Someone had emptied a whole bag of frozen fish sticks through a short slice along the front. Surprisingly few beer cans laid among the mess. The Beardsley area was known more for crack. An ambulance raced by just before 10:00 a.m., loud and unsettling. Like farmwork, the drug trade started early.

As I descended toward the river channel, an older white woman rode a BMX on the bridge against the direction of traffic, plastic grocery bags swaying from her handlebars, and a Hispanic man hauled two large trash bags of bottles and cans on his shoulder. Overlooking it all was a McDonald's billboard advertising two McRib sandwiches for $4. In the southern part of the Valley, drought and inexpensive food hang over everything like a specter.

When Latta's crew put their boat in the Kern River at Chester Avenue, the Valley's native perennial bunchgrasses had been pushed out by Spanish nonnative annual grasses since at least the 1830s. The condors that used to feast on dead cattle, salmon, and deer were getting shot and losing their food supply. Settlers were cutting down oaks for material and planting cotton and grain in the marshes they'd drained. But because the Kern hadn't been dammed, its banks were still lined with tall trees, and native animals plied the waters. Growing up here, author Gerald Haslam remembered the Kern's riverside forest. He and his friends used to ride bikes across dirt paths to reach its viny shade. They called it "the jungle." He and his girlfriends parked there to make out in the 1950s. He perceived it as wild. Latta's crew also perceived it as wild, since the rushing water threatened their lives. But the Kern they knew was a fragment of the Kern that the river's first European visitor, Father Francisco Garcés, encountered in 1776. Then, it had more species, more water, more animals, and more channels. Biologist Daniel Pauly calls this perceptual experience shifting baseline syndrome.

Every generation sees the landscape they inherit as normal, assuming not only that it always looked this way but that this is how it's supposed to look. To them it seems healthy, natural, biologically diverse. This forms their baseline. As they age, they see species go extinct and land get paved and trampled, and they tell the next generation about its decline, how it's lost, not as great as it used to be—"You should have seen it back then"—when, in fact, the land they knew as grand wasn't as grand as the version before. Our sense of normalcy shifts across time. Psychologist Peter H. Kahn Jr. calls this environmental generational amnesia. In his book *Wild Ones,* Jon Mooallem uses bald eagles as an example. In 1973, when the eagle was listed as endangered, 417 nesting pairs remained in the Lower 48. The population grew to ten thousand pairs by 2007. But when you consider how that enormous, healthy, jump-for-joy number was a fraction of the fifty thousand that lived when the bird became the country's Great Seal in 1782, you get a more accurate sense of the scale of destruction.

The Kern River is one of the most important rivers in the West, and like so many things in the Valley, you can't tell by looking at it. The Valley's hydrology is confusingly complicated, especially since it's been so heavily altered. No significant waterways enter the San Joaquin Valley's west side. The Coast Range is too low and dry to generate consistent surface flow. All the important water comes from the east, originating in snow and springs in the towering Sierra Nevada, which is why the biggest cities developed along the Valley's east side.

The rivers in the north half of what we call the San Joaquin Valley flow north into Pacific Ocean through San Francisco Bay. These rivers are the San Joaquin, the Merced, the Tuolumne, the Stanislaus, the Calaveras, the Mokelumne, and the Consumnes.

In the Valley's lower half, the rivers don't naturally flow north into the Pacific. Historically, they are landlocked. Sediment from the Kings River near Fresno had created a large alluvial fan. That broad but subtle dome, not quite a hill but not level either, rose just enough to keep water from passing over it. Rivers south of the fan flowed south; rivers to the north flowed north. With no outlet, the Kings, Kaweah, Tule, White, and Kern Rivers pooled on the floor of the Valley to form vast freshwater marshes and four separate lakes whose size changed year to year. The Kaweah River enters the Valley around Visalia; the Tule River, by Porterville; and the White, by Delano. Because this southern section of the Valley was a separate hydrological entity, people used to call the land between Bakersfield and Fresno the Tulare Lake Basin, named after the lake that once filled its center. No one uses this name now.

In December 1937 heavy rains began falling in the Valley and continued into spring, smothering the flatlands up north near Colusa. On June 10, 1938, the *Bakersfield Californian's* front page featured a huge photo of a flooded field, under the headline "River Inundates Pastures." On the first day of their trip, Latta's crew floated down the Kern River toward Buena Vista Lake, which would lead them north up Buena Vista Slough to Tulare Lake. Only during the wettest years, like 1938, did Tulare Lake water top the Kings River fan and flow into the San Joaquin River system. There, the southern water mixed with the Merced, Tuolumne, and Stanislaus Rivers, which eventually flowed into the Pacific and would take Latta's crew with it.

Of the Tulare Basin's four lakes, its namesake was the largest. Sprawling across the flatlands between modern day I-5 and Highway 99, Tulare Lake averaged seventy-five miles across, twenty-five miles north to south, with its shores vaguely marked by Kettleman City, Alpaugh, Corcoran, and Stratford. Often covering 200,000 acres, in flood, Tulare Lake swelled to become the largest freshwater body west of the Mississippi River; its highest recorded level was forty-one feet deep and spread across 486,400 acres.

Kern Lake, south of Bakersfield, was the second largest, at eight thousand acres. Buena Vista Lake, west of Bakersfield by I-5, was the third, averaging four thousand acres, and Goose Lake, up I-5 near Lost Hills, was the fourth, though some accounts describe that as more of a pool. Buena Vista Slough connected the lakes. In wet years, the slough ran north and south up the west side, carrying water from Buena Vista and Kern Lakes up to Tulare Lake and turning that whole I-5 corridor into a huge inland sea.

As with everything in this land of extremes, the wetlands' size varied widely year to year. Some winters delivered deep sierra snowpack that melted in spring and swelled the lakes. Some years, the mountains received little snow, and the lakes dried completely. The marshes around them were seasonal in the literal sense: swelling in spring, drying in summer, gone by fall. This was why explorers saw the Valley either as a fertile paradise akin to the Nile, as Kit Carson and Fages did, or as a worthless hell with no future, as Derby suggested. Impressions depended on the season they visited, their precise location (west or east side, between rivers or on the lake), and that year's snowmelt.

The San Joaquin is California's second longest river, but the Kern is the third, at 164 miles, and one of the West's most important. Fed by Sierra Nevada snowmelt, the Kern River's larger North Fork originates at 10,700 feet elevation near towering Mt. Whitney, inside Sequoia National Park. After it connects with the South Fork, the Kern flows through deep, rugged canyons lined with chaparral and oak and used to pass through Bakersfield via three or four distinct distributary channels rather than the one we see today.

Although Spanish exploration signaled the end of the Yokuts' way of life, the Native people were helpful and friendly to early foreign emissaries. They ferried Father Garcés safely across the rushing water in 1776. "They asked me if I knew how to swim, and I answered them 'nay,'" Garcés wrote in his journal. "They convoyed me across between four of them by swimming." Later, in the 1840s, gold-hungry American frontiersman Kit Carson spent time with one Yokuts group to the north whom he called "great friends of the white man" for their generosity and warmth. Despite making his career by killing and scalping Native Americans, even this narrow-minded, xenophobic savage of a man recognized in this village something distinct, people he called "intelligent, hospitable." Yokuts swam Derby's 1851 party across the Kaweah River too. Surely, the Yokuts helped many more white settlers than we'll ever know, ferrying them toward the sites where they'd build the empire that would soon displace the Yokuts completely.

Many Americans later drowned here. The Kern flooded Bakersfield in 1867, 1893, and 1953. People frequently got swept away while taking an innocent swim or got hit by submerged tree trunks and limbs. During the 1950 flood, Oildale author Gerald Haslam watched the raging Kern from atop a levee at age thirteen. "I finally grasped the reality of events," Haslam wrote in his book *The Other California*, "when I saw a large pine tree rushing downstream with a lone, soaked jackrabbit mounted on its barren trunk like a hood ornament. A moment later, the pine seemed to explode as it hit the bridge, then somehow it emerged on the other side, the rabbit still clinging to it." Kids he knew weren't so lucky. The Kern killed his close friend Wally in the late 1940s. Merle Haggard's 1985 song "Kern River" confronts the river's casual brutality by narrating a fictional girlfriend's death. Latta's crew packed life vests for a reason.

When the U.S. Army Corps of Engineers finished construction of Isabella Dam in 1953 under the auspices of flood control, it put all that water in the control of the state government who serviced the local farmers who had advocated for, and often funded, area dams. Now most of the Kern's flow was diverted for irrigation, municipal supplies, and to recharge the aquifers that groundwater pumping depleted. The Kern's water didn't simply build Bakersfield; it transformed the lower San Joaquin Valley into an agricultural empire by irrigating the same alluvial soils it helped deposit. The city grew around it. Although 151 miles of the Kern's upper reaches are now designated as National Wild and Scenic River, its water rarely makes it as far as Chester Avenue. It certainly never flows west to Buena Vista Lake the way it did when Latta floated it.

When I visited the site of Latta's launch, I found the riverbed empty, except for an abandoned shopping cart. What vegetation grew was thin and crisp, an ugly tuft of young cottonwood and willow mixed with lots of invasive weeds. The vegetation on the southeast bank had caught fire, leaving a wide scar of blackened ash below the bridge. The neighborhood hadn't fared much better.

Beardsley Avenue, northwest of the bridge, was one of the city's roughest areas. RVs and trailer parks lined the street, amid small houses and squat apartment buildings where people sat in chairs outside smoking cigarettes. A dusty camouflage Volvo was parked behind a 1970s-era RV with a huge piece missing from its bumper.

It seemed to be someone's residence. On the dirt sidewalk, a white Chihuahua sniffed a black plastic bag and then peed on it. Unconditional signs lined one RV park's fence: No Parking, No Trespassing, and Keep Out.

People biked up and down the street, smoking as they peddled. A California Highway Patrol car drove back and forth too. On his fifth lap in as many minutes, he stopped to talk to a white guy on a neon-green BMX who was talking with a young Hispanic pedestrian. They stood outside the office of an RV park. The Hispanic man leaned over and said, "How you doin', sir?" The cop got out. The kid pulled his pants up by his belt. Soon after, the bicyclist rode off, shaking his head in disapproval and smiling a partially toothless smile, and the cop checked the other man's tattooed forearm. He wore a blue-and-white-striped polo shirt, and his long blue-and-white-plaid shorts reached so far down his calves that they nearly concealed his socks. When the cop placed the man's hands on the wall, he patted him down and cuffed him. Nearby, a tan pug stood patrol, staring down Beardsley.

As the officer placed the man in his car, a young guy walked diagonally across the street, holding a single bike tire, a mug of coffee, and a grocery bag full of donuts, their wet glaze smeared against the opaque plastic. "They arrested him," he told two pedestrians.

One of the other guys called out, "Dude, they spend eight fuckin' hours a day going around so they can arrest people. Dude just got off his shift."

The guy with the bike tire said, "Yup. Fuck 'em." He peered into the Manes RV Park, handed the tire to a tall skinny guy in shorts, and then crossed back across the street, carefully curling his hand around his mug so as not to spill a drop.

While I walked the riverbed, two men worked on cars in front of the Kern River Paint and Body, and two others—one black, one white—sat under a shade tree drinking tallboys from paper bags.

The scene under the bridge was desolate. Discarded clothes and shoes covered the riprap foundation. People slept here, or at least passed the hot days. On the south bank, a bicyclist in a neon vest rode on a bike bath that stretched for miles, peddling in the direction of that lone shopping cart.

After putting in at the Chester Avenue bridge in Bakersfield, Latta's boat drifted west down the Kern River toward Buena Vista Lake.

Like the Kings River to the north, the Kern formed a broad fan that originally affected its flow in a way it no longer does today. Before widespread American settlement, the river emerged from the Sierra Nevada and spilled through any number of distributary channels. Its easternmost route took the river south for twenty miles through what different accounts called the South Fork or Kern River Slough, toward the bleak company farming town of Arvin. Another route, called Old River, ran south along what's now Old River Road. These ultimately led to Kern Lake, which, in wet years, flowed west through the blandly named Connecting Slough to merge with Buena Vista Lake. In 1867 a landslide in an upstream canyon backed the river up. When the water finally ruptured the blockage, it flooded Bakersfield and flipped its course from the southern routes to its current westerly one through downtown. People initially called this channel New River. The city built levees that locked it in place and, in another example of shifting baseline syndrome, made its route along Truxtun Avenue seem like the one and only. None of these old channels determine the Kern's flow today. People do.

South of Truxtun Avenue, Taft Highway crosses the Kern's old channels, which are now irrigation canals watering the lake beds. The land looks flat. From the road, the only evidence that a river ran here is the town of Old River and Herring Road, names that make sense once you understand the system. But the land isn't flat. The valley slopes west toward Buena Vista Lake: Pumpkin Center, elevation 351 feet; Panama, elevation 347 feet; Old River, elevation 344 feet. Latta's crew floated the river's northernmost channel.

On the day the *Alta* left Bakersfield, Latta thought they'd complete the fifty-five-mile stretch to Lost Hills by nightfall. They did but not as expected.

A bridge used to stand where the Taft Highway crossed the Kern River, and as the crew floated west, they hit it. "Saturday, at the outset of the voyage," the *Bakersfield Californian* reported, "Skipper Frank Latta suffered a back injury and a burn when he was struck as the party passed under the Taft highway bridge. In falling from the boat into the swirling water Mr. Latta suffered a burned back from the hot motor in the stern of the little craft. He also wretched his back."

If you study the landscape on Taft Highway just west of Interstate 5, you won't be able to spot the accident's exact location. Maps show the Kern flowing right where it intersects the highway, but those renderings are simplifications. All there is now is a weedy ditch. To the west, a cement-lined canal cuts north to south. That's the California Aqueduct.

As the key connecting element in the massive, complicated California State Water Project, the aqueduct runs 444 miles through the state, carrying water from the wetter, snowier north to cities in the south. This main branch runs along the Valley's west side from the delta to the coast. It doesn't look important, but this water is part of the lifeblood of Los Angeles, San Luis Obispo, Santa Barbara, and desert cities like Palmdale. A vital artery in the state's circulatory system, it's so essential that thousands of lives would shrivel without it, along with their lawns. The old Kern is dead. In this controlled environment, the canal is the Kern's modern incarnation, the shape rivers now take.

According to the newspaper, Latta "was dragged from the boat by a low bridge. The other three boys, Don Latta, Richard Harris and Ernest Ingalls, ducked in time to miss the structure." Drowning was a danger, but hitting a bridge? How does someone not see a distant structure in a land as flat as this? Maybe it happened too quickly to react; rushed under a bridge that barely left room for passage, they couldn't avoid nailing it. The article gives as little away as the landscape does. No coordinates, no details. This is a common problem with tracing Latta's trip.

One of Latta's great oversights was his failure to publish the day-to-day details of what the crew did, saw, and thought in that boat. He was a historian. He knew the value of details. He seemed to publish everything. He published his first book in 1929, a year after collecting the material, and he kept a quick pace with everything he wrote after. Why not write about this trip? Before he died, Latta's home library was filled with maps, newspaper clippings, and obscure documents. If he kept a journal of this trip, he didn't seem like the type to lose it. Apparently, he did publish a brief account of the trip called "Bakersfield to Treasure Island in a Boat." It appeared in 1941 in a small, now-defunct San Joaquin Valley newspaper called the *Westside Progress Review*. Unfortunately, he never included it in any of his books, and neither the research librarians in Fresno nor UC Berkeley's renowned Bancroft Library had copies of the *Westside Progress Review* from that year to share with me. That left the *Bakersfield Californian* articles and my imagination.

The Buena Vista Aquatic Recreation Area appears as an island of pine and lawn grass in a sea of sandy farms. Inside, it looks like any park, with barbecue pits in campsites and big gray plastic trash cans spaced along the road. The Buena Vista Lake it contains isn't the same lake Latta knew. It's an impoundment stocked with fish, and its water is released for irrigation. At least the name survives, and the park does occupy a small portion of the historic lake bottom. The bulk of the original bed lays to the southwest where the Boswell family and corporation farms a large area.

During his lifetime, James Griffin Boswell II was the single-largest farmer in America. He inherited the family land from his uncle, J. G. Boswell Sr., in the mid-1900s, and he grew more safflower and irrigated wheat than anyone else. He may or may not have grown more cotton than anyone else; he didn't like to give too many details away. He owned two hundred thousand acres in the San Joaquin

Valley and thousands in Colorado, Oregon, Arizona, and Australia. Tulare Lake itself often covered two hundred thousand acres, and he owned most of that. In a land ruled by farmers, locals called him the king of kings.

The Boswells built an empire by following the family motto that land was dirt but water, gold. J. G. Boswell II enlarged that fortune by selling water; buying out smaller farmers; growing crops with a small staff, advanced technology, and productive cultivars; and using his mouth, money, and clout to manipulate government water policy in his favor. He was smart, driven, and cutthroat, no matter how aw-shucks he played it. When journalists Mark Arax and Rick Wartzman asked him about the amount of land he owned, he said, "I abhor the word 'empire.' It's a word for nations, for civilizations. Why do you guys have to get into this whole damn 'big' thing anyways?" But the J. G. Boswell Company owned more land than some nations. The bulk of that empire lay to the north, in the drained Tulare Lake bed. Buena Vista Lake was a fraction of the company's holdings. Boswell bought it from a company started by a German immigrant named Henry Miller, who was once one of the largest landowners in America, the Boswell of his time.

Originally Heinrich Alfred Kreiser, Miller's legend has him arriving in San Francisco in 1850 with only $6. He saved money while working in a butcher shop and made his first trip to the San Joaquin Valley in 1854 to buy three hundred cows for $33,000. He brought them back to the bay himself and made a killing selling wholesale beef by the pound. He used his profits to buy more cattle, until he finally turned his attention to the range itself.

In 1858 Miller joined forces with another German, a Bay Area butcher named Charles Lux. Lux was charming and connected. Miller was driven and opportunistic. The Swamp Land Act of 1850 handed over title of federally owned swamplands to states or individuals who could drain and farm it. A widespread legend tells of Miller cheating the Swamp Land Act by having a horse tow him in a boat through dry government land, which he then bought for a dollar an acre. Some of this land wasn't swamp. It was grassland. Some of it featured standing water during flood years but was not year-round swampland in the way the act might have meant it. Miller and Lux created an empire through consolidation, buying sixteen Mexican land grants. They bought out small farmers who were in debt or decimated by floods and drought. By 1874 Miller and Lux owned at least 420,888 acres in San Joaquin Valley, though they owned so much they couldn't assess their holdings exactly. At their peak, they controlled most of the Valley's west side and owned 50 miles along the Kern River and 120 miles along both banks of the San Joaquin River. And as they bought land, they bought cattle, which they used to supply growing San Francisco's hungry residents and to grow them-selves into California's biggest beef producer. They figured out the Valley's secret early: by controlling well-watered land, they usually had enough feed to get their cattle through droughts, because there would always be more droughts.

A local rancher scouted land for Miller and Lux and bought them twenty of the Buena Vista Slough's fifty miles in 1870. All Miller and Lux needed to do was clear the reeds and drain the swamp. It was slow-going work. In 1877 workers building a canal through the slough found two tule elk in the reeds. Native to California, tule elk are North America's smallest elk subspecies, and they fed here in such numbers that in the 1840s, traveler Edward Bosqui said that they "darkened the plains for miles, and looked in the distance like great herds of cattle." There were maybe five hundred thousand when California became a state. By the time the California State Legislature outlawed elk hunting in 1873, they were considered extinct. These two were thought to be the last breeding pair in existence. The elk had so relied on the Valley's tule marshes that they were named for them.

Something about the elk affected Miller. "In the San Joaquin Val-ley," he remembered late in life, "there were wild horses and elk and you could see them running in every direction." He'd first visited as a twenty-something aspirant. Maybe he wanted to preserve part of the land where he'd found his chance for upward mobility. If so, he wrote nothing of it. Miller was no conservationist. He let hunters shoot the geese that shat all over his rangelands in Merced County, because cows wouldn't eat the soiled grass. But with the elk, he acted swiftly.

Miller had state game warden A. C. Tibbett move the elk to a protected area while workers continued draining the slough, and he offered rewards to any employees who discovered people poaching on his property. With a captive-breeding program, the elk population grew from two to twenty-eight by 1895. By 1905 there were 140. The herd was eating thousands of dollars' worth of crops each year, but Miller had enough to spare. To aid the conservation effort, and possibly to protect his assets, he set aside six hundred acres as a temporary elk reserve. When Miller died, his assets were divided, and the elk got moved around. Some people poached them. The population dropped. In 1932 the California State Park Commission bought 953 acres on Buena Vista Slough to use as a fenced sanctuary. Located north of the recreation area, the small Tule Elk State Natural Reserve had the dense reeds and grass and water elk needed. But the dam on the Kern River destroyed the property's riparian habitat, which decimated the elk once again, taking them down to forty-one animals by 1954. The California State Parks Department created artificial wetlands and fed them, so the elk recovered enough that Miller's herd has been moved to sites all over the state. They're one of California's greatest ecological success stories. A similarly miraculous recovery happened with Mexican gray wolves a hundred years later. The species' population got nearly wiped out in New Mexico, Arizona, and northern Mexico. Today, every wild Mexican wolf living in the borderlands descends from seven captive-bred individuals. People have heard of gray wolves, though. Fewer know of tule elk or their original reserve.

Nowadays people fill the Buena Vista Aquatic Recreation Area's campgrounds in summer to water-ski and Jet Ski. People come in winter to fish. The nearby town of Taft stocks Lake Evans with trout every winter. A lot of campers come to compete for prizes in the big fishing derby each November.

A gun club operated nearby, and on my visit the pop-pop of bullets cut through the sound of some camper's copy of Johnny Cash's "Jackson." From the shore, you can see traffic moving down I-5, yet most people don't even know the park is here. The flat, tilled San Joaquin Valley isn't the sort of iconic California landscape that attracts visitors. Few outsiders associate it with natural history, outdoor recreation, or beauty. And yet when he passed through in 1772, Captain Fages also called Grapevine Canyon "Buena Vista Pass" for the "beautiful view" it afforded travelers heading either south or north; the record wasn't clear which. He gave this lake the same name, which makes it the oldest Spanish name in the San Joaquin Valley. At first, it's nice to see that the Spanish name has survived the lake's draining. On closer inspection, the lake has been split into two, and the pieces have been given two Anglo names: the nine-hundred-acre Lake Webb and the smaller Lake Evans. Locals used to call them Lakes A and B, but Taft resident Margaret Schoeser led a campaign to honor the lakes by renaming them for Vance Webb, who created the recreation area despite some public resistance, and Herb Evans, the first director of Kern County's parks and recreation department. As she told the board, the names Lake A and Lake B "are hardly conducive to inviting or luring visitors."

The old muddy lake didn't have a shoreline to sit on. It didn't offer comfort or views. It only swallowed early explorers' horses and generated malaria. But something about its wildness is more affecting than this controlled cleanliness, something that's hard to articulate but that the French photographer Édouard Levé put his finger on when he said, "I prefer a ruin to a monument." That's how the reedy edges of a marsh feel. Its uneven lines register as more powerful than the perfectly edged lawns of suburbia or man-made lakes. Something ingrained in our primate brains recognizes unevenness as ancient and familiar, yet this new lake is beautiful too.

In 1938 Latta believed what many people still believe: that damming rivers is the way to create a stabile society with large-scale agriculture, in line with Jefferson's vision of the yeoman farmer. I doubt he envisioned a greedy capitalistic system where water, like wealth, became concentrated in the hands of the few, serving enormous corporate farms with absentee landowners, and got wasted in this land of high evaporation.

Agriculture in the San Joaquin Valley grosses over $25 billion annually, and California's agriculture industry accounts for about 80 percent of the state's water usage. In 2014 a single almond required 1.1 gallons of water to grow. That was a fraction of the 5,000 gallons required to produce one pound of beef or the approximately 220 gallons for a single avocado. One tomato required 3.3 gallons, but context is key. Over 80 percent of the world's almonds are grown in the Central Valley. The San Joaquin Valley produces the bulk of those almonds.

Before the 2014 drought, one-third of Central Valley farmers' water came from wells; the rest of the water was transported in by the California State Water Project and the federal Central Valley Project. Groundwater provided farms and cities with a sense of security, because during years with little snowmelt, people could rely on wells to water crops and lawns and supply drinking water. Groundwater was the savings account growers tapped in lean times. That was no longer the case.

In the three years before my visit, rain and snowpack had been scarce. Reservoirs dried up. Farmers received little surface water for irrigation. Some irrigation districts didn't release water at all. To protect their crops in the summer of 2014, fruit and nut growers drilled new wells and irrigated with groundwater, often drawing four to five times over what they could put back into aquifers. You could do that here. At the time, California was the last western state to allow landowners to drill wells and extract groundwater on their land with few to no restrictions. Along the Valley's edges, drying wells and shallow aquifers had already led to persistent overpumping, as well as measurable land subsidence. The water table kept dropping, land sunk, and well water grew too salty to use. Some growers cut down almond and fruit trees to cut their losses. Others left fields fallow. As the drought continued into 2015 and farmers got less irrigation, they depended on pumping groundwater even more. In April 2015 California governor Jerry Brown issued an executive order reducing water usage by 25 percent across the state. In response to criticism of the long-term environmental effects of such lax well laws, Brown signed sweeping groundwater-pumping restrictions on September 16. Local agencies have until 2040 to start limiting groundwater extraction and the digging of new wells, which is far too long in many scientists' estimation. "At that pace, it will be nearly 30 years before we even know what is working," wrote Jay Famiglietti, the NASA Jet Propulsion Laboratory's senior water scientist, in a *Los Angeles Times* op-ed. "By then, there may be no groundwater left to sustain." Forecasters feared more dry weather for 2016. That would have been the drought's fifth year. But in the Valley, wet years were always on their way. Farmers knew that, and investors counted on it.

Buena Vista Aquatic Recreation Area used its own wells to fill its lake. When I visited, the manager, John Parsons, was running three and had five off. The summer of 2014, the water table dropped so far that the wells started blowing air, so he lowered each a hundred feet. "They weren't hittin' water," he told me with an unnervingly casual demeanor. "I live in the country and have my own domestic well. Every day I turn the faucet on, I hope the water comes. You never know."

Damming would have happened without Latta's support—he was one voice among many and not influential when it came to public policy—but he echoed the prevailing sentiment of his time. We of the twenty-first century inhabit the world he envisioned, a dry world stable enough to afford the privilege of viewing part of dangerous historic times as bucolic and valuable. Since floods don't wash away our houses and bears don't kill our kids, we can study the benefits of their return, and we can appreciate the elements of a more natural ecosystem. Latta was a man both of and ahead of his time.

To say he wouldn't recognize this lake is to state the obvious. The question is whether he would consider it progress. Damming and flood control make recreation possible. This lake would probably please him, but given the strong love of history that runs through his books, it's clear that he'd also miss the old lake, too, the wild place where Yokuts fished from boats made of reeds. Damming made people's fortunes and produced affordable food, so why mourn a bunch of jackrabbits and mud? America associates advancement with improvement. Cleanliness is next to godliness. So is control. But in that equation, we miss the other intangible elements of our world that we need, something that has to do with what it means to be human.

A thick band of tules lines the modern lake shore. Campers' Doritos bags collect there, and plastic canisters of fishing worms. Someone dumped a large slab of concrete on the bank, which creates a gap in the reeds and a nice view. Waterfowl fly low over the surface. Some bob out there. Others dunk underwater and never seem to come up. Small reed islands stand in the lake, thick enough to support small cottonwoods and imported palms. The lake seems to go on forever. The truth is that a dirt embankment separates it from farmland along the southern shore. A gravel road runs there, forming a clean straight line behind the reeds.

Surrounding the lake are fields—some square, some trapezoidal, all wedged between the irregular routes of roads and canals. Buena Vista Lake's straight back contrasts so starkly with its weaving northeastern shores that you wonder if it means something, some symbol of nature's winding wasteful edges versus humanity's struggle for control, of productivity versus chaos. The Valley was nothing if not a set of conflicting geometries. People cut lines and ninety-degree angles. Nature weaved right across them. It all seemed a metaphor for the Valley's limitations and our illusions of control.

As the sun sets pink behind the Temblor Range, it doesn't matter whether the horizon stops or stretches forever. It doesn't matter whether you're in Ventura or Kern County. You get a chair and a book and a beer under a tree, and you fall a little in love with this place. One day water will be more valuable than gold. For now, we do front flips from boats and splash our friends' faces, and at dusk, sprinklers come on at the lake's west side, watering grass.

I left the park after sunset and found myself a cold drink. The Shell station on Taft Highway was surrounded by miles of desert. Hovering in a solitary dome of light, it looked like the last chance to buy food or turn around, the last station on earth.

It was Friday night. Cars passed on their way home from work. Trailers pulled boats to the lake. People were going camping and fishing, but some of this was also the traffic of a region filling with people, a lake of lights just over the mountains from LA, sparkling in a way it hadn't twenty years ago.

Outside the Shell station, a few cement tables stood in the grass on the edge of the lot. You could feel the moist air cutting through the day's heat. By a sign warning customers of a one-hour parking limit, a man sat inside his sedan smoking a cigarette, and three firemen leaned against their white pickup, sipping tallboys of Budweiser and Clamato.

Inside, teenage girls ate churros in the dining area by the cooler and scrolled through their phones. I bought a bag of Carson's Grandpa Beef Jerky, because the poorly written text on the label made me laugh. "There's something special about an early morning on the lake," it said. "Water. Peaceful silence. Just Grandpa and I fishing together . . . It's these memories that inspired me to create Carson's Grandpa Beef Jerky." It was distributed by a Bakersfield company. The label looked as though someone had created it on their home color printer. It showed two blurry silhouettes pulling a fish from a lake. The dark distant hills, shoreline vegetation, and spreading bands of pink on the water—I raised the bag to study it closely. The scene was too pixelated to be pretty, but it was clear enough that the lake seemed to be Buena Vista.

After passing through the lake, Latta's crew traveled north into Buena Vista Slough. This was the broad marshy channel that connected the lakes in the south to Tulare Lake in the north.

Short sedges lined it. The silver sides of tiny fish flashed in the sunlight, but impenetrable mazes of reeds often stood five to twenty feet tall in some sections. Many wet reed beds stretched for miles, creating what Latta called "an impassable growth." Red-winged blackbirds fluttered inside them. Ducks could hover on drafts, flapping only to hang like kites above the reeds, but people dared not go in there. The gluey mud would trap their feet, steal their boots, encase their horses. Travel slowed to a halt. People got lost. In 1850 Thomas Mayfield's family had to hack through twenty-foot-tall tules after crossing the San Joaquin River. "We were so completely lost in them as we would have been in a forest," he told Latta. Rarely did a tree grow tall enough to let travelers survey their location from its branches. Best to stay out. The beds of reeds growing on dry land could stretch just as far. Besides the elk, Native Americans hid inside them after escaping Spanish coastal missions. Hunters flushed out the elk, but the Native people endured a little longer. Few Spanish officers wanted to chase them in a place like this. The Spanish never built missions in the Valley. It was here in the reeds that Americans later coined the saying "out in the tules." It was a derogatory phrase meaning out in the boonies, the country, the sticks. The tules symbolized nowheresville, a place no one wants to go.

Author and early feminist Mary Hunter Austin briefly lived near Buena Vista Slough. Born and educated in Illinois, a twenty-year-old Mary Austin moved to Bakersfield in 1888 with her widowed mother. The family homesteaded at the southern end of the Valley, near Fort Tejon not far from the slough. After Mary got married in 1891, she and her husband left for the Owens Valley, east of the Sierra Nevada. Austin was a close observer of nature and people, and this rugged landscape gave her lots to look at it. When frontier life allowed the time, she turned those observations into fiction and nonfiction about everything from Native American mythology and Anglo water use to the legend of a woman who wandered the desert west of Buena Vista.

She published her first book, *The Land of Little Rain*, in 1903. It mixed essays and short stories drawn from the Mojave and San Joaquin, and a century later it remains her most beloved, with *San Francisco Chronicle* readers voting it number one in their top one hundred nonfiction books about the western United States. In it she describes the Valley's reedy lands: "The tulares are full of mystery and malaria. That is why we have meant to explore them and have never done so. It must be a happy mystery." She knew malaria well. Her father contracted it in the military and died when she was ten. The connection didn't diminish her fascination. Austin found the area's marshes "ghostly pale in winter, in summer deep, poisonous-looking green, the waters thick and brown, the reed beds breaking into dingy looking pools, clumps of rotting willows, narrow winding water lanes and sinking paths. The reeds grow inconceivably thick in places, standing manhigh above water; cattle, no, not any fish nor fowl can penetrate them. Old stalks succumb slowly; the bed soil is quagmire, settling with the weight as it fills and fills."

Buena Vista Slough crossed the Valley's dry west side.

The west side was different than the east. Drier and hotter than the east side, the west side was less conducive to farming, so people grazed cattle. Some of the dry creek beds have sinister names like Salt Creek, Bitterwater Creek, and Tumey Gulch. Even the names Diablo Range and Temblor Range are cut from the same parched leather. Few had trees, let alone water.

Early visitors hated the San Joaquin Valley's unrelenting west side, which lacked shade, food, or drinkable water. California's most famous bandit Joaquin Murrieta operated here; it was a lawless place where he could rob stagecoaches and pillage settlers and escape to the hills. This is why so many Native Americans abandoned the Spaniards' coastal missions for the Valley. It was huge and poorly mapped. It was the perfect place to disappear.

In the 1850s Derby described the west side as a "miserable barren, sandy desert, with no vegetation but a few straggling artemesias and no inhabitants but attenuated rabbits and gophers." In 1861 Brewer wrote that it "abounds in tarantulas by the thousands. I have seen them where two would cover this page, as they stand, their bodies as large as a half-grown mouse, their hairy legs of proportionate size, their fangs as large as those of a moderate sized rattlesnake. They bite vigorously when provoked, and their bite is generally considered fatal, although I have heard of but one well-authenticated case of death resulting since I have been here; but the bite generally proves a painful and serious affair." It was through this spidery, malarial hell that Latta floated toward the largest freshwater lake in the western United States.

I needed to see this slough myself. One afternoon, I visited a section of it west of Buttonwillow, thirty miles from Bakersfield. The name "slough" had become a misnomer.

I parked on the road's soft shoulder and entered a parched slit in an expanse of rust-colored scrub. Not fifteen feet in, I found ancient glass. Piles of it, blue, green, brown, clear, whole bottles, half bottles, broken tops, and severed bottoms from midcentury Tab, RC, Belfast, Sparklettes, Three B's soda bottles, and numerous streams of twinkling shards that crunched underfoot. Turns out, I'd discovered a de facto dump.

In the arid American West where vacant land was abundant, it was common to dump trash. There was no organized trash collection before the 1950s, so before the era of No Dumping signs, residents of small communities drove into the country and abandoned their undesirables.

While searching the Valley for deserters, Captain Fages visited a village on Buena Vista Lake's southwestern shore. It was the Tulamniu people's main camp. Like the pass he'd named, Fages called the village Buena Vista. He wasn't known for his imagination. When Miller and Lux drained the lake, they unearthed deep mounds of the village's discarded mussel shells—the castaways of subsistence living. Located on the west side of the lake on Tupman Road, south of SR 119, the Smithsonian Institute excavated the Tulamniu village in 1933. What they found was trash. Natural material, sure, which the villagers pulled from the lake, but trash nonetheless, since they dumped it right next to the lake. Trash lasts decades—centuries. This glass would too. "There is no scavenger that eats tin cans," Mary Austin wrote, "and no wild thing leaves a like disfigurement on the forest floor." All people struggle to find room to dump their mess. The desert invites a particular kind of mistreatment, because it seems to offer enough room to accommodate it. My era's trash just seems more egregious somehow—plastic, not bivalve shells; phones, not bird bones—but maybe the bottles weren't so bad. Maybe it was all the same in the end.

The bottles awoke the greedy archaeologist in me, and I gathered all the intact ones I could find. Normally, I would've spent hours on my knees digging for the buried treasure, turning over embarrassing amounts of dirt on this cool California day in order to archive and preserve and beat out other antiquers, going so far as to congratulate myself on removing all that trash. Instead, I resisted that inclination. Digging a deep hole would have made me feel like another destructive force, no better than the trash dumpers. Another part of me wanted to leave something behind for other people to discover, to preserve a little bit of this history and mystery of this desert. So I lugged my bottles and climbed in my car. The rest, I left behind.

2

On Tulare Lake

Everything was water except a very small piece of ground.

—Yaudanchi Yokuts man

On Monday, June 19, the second day of their trip, the winds blew dangerously hard, so Latta's crew waited in the marshlands outside the town of Lost Hills until conditions improved. Latta probably welcomed the delay, as his injuries suffered from hitting the bridge were still bothering him. As the *Alta* weathered Sunday's storm, winds uprooted trees in Bakersfield and left some residents without power. On Buena Vista Lake, which Latta's crew had just passed through, a teenager's sailboat was blown into an offshore willow. To keep the boat from flipping, the owner, Lee Waller, stuck out his foot. But the impact severed his toe, and he and his seventeen-year-old friend William Sabalone spent the night hanging on to tree branches. At three in the morning, Waller's parents realized he hadn't come home. After finding his car on the shore, they woke up the deputy sheriff in Taft, and officers searched the lake in a motorboat at sunrise until finding the boys. "No oil derricks were reported down," the *Bakersfield Californian* wrote, "agricultural damage was slight, and the levees protecting Alpaugh from overflow waters of the Kern river withstood the waves thrown up by the wind." When the winds had died down, Latta and his crew resumed their trip, and on the third day of their journey, they entered Tulare Lake.

The years 1862, 1868, 1906, and 1916 were some of the San Joaquin Valley's flood years, but the land had even more dry years. Until 1937 a lack of sufficient snowmelt had kept Tulare Lake dry for thirteen years. When melting snow finally started filling the lake bed in 1938, the many levees that ringed it could no longer hold back the volume of water rushing from Sierra Nevada rivers, and the water spread across wheat and barley fields, washing away houses and farmers' sheds. Then summer descended.

In the marshes along the lake's edge during flood years, summer heat turned the warm shallow water a vile green. Without depth or strong currents to circulate it, sediment collected. It grew thick with mud and algae. Frogs left clouds of squirming larvae, while fallen bulrushes decayed in the water that collected the bodies of innumerable insects. In October 1861 geological surveyor William Henry Brewer described the lake marshes as "unhealthy and infested with mosquitoes in incredible numbers and unparalleled ferocity." Latta knew Yokuts history, so he knew that by 1833 those same malarial mosquitoes helped wipe out approximately three-quarters of the Yokuts population. Yet the monsoons of tule gnats, flies, and mosquitoes that filled the air as the *Alta* entered the lake astounded Latta. It was impossible not to marvel at the lake's dimensions, not just the water's unbelievable volume, but the grand scale of life and death in it. At sunset millions of bats filled the air to feast on insects. During the day, the sun cooked the murky shallows, and its sulfurous smells traveled far on the breeze, like the thousands of pelicans, ducks, and geese who carried stolen stalks of wheat from nearby fields.

But out on the deep lake, there was no vile green. No muck or feasting mosquitoes. Here the warm breeze blew fresh over the crew's sweaty faces. Visibility was high. The scent of dry grass and moisture filled the air, and the cooler water took on a clean silver sheen. It reached ten, twenty, forty feet deep, and fish cut wide courses through the depths, swimming above sunken grain threshers and fences built by farmers whose respect for the great lake had diminished during its thirteen dry years.

Despite the dangers, this day was probably one of the crew's most wondrous. No one was there to record it but Latta, and whatever journal he kept, I wasn't able to locate. So I could only imagine how the hours passed. I pictured Latta jotting notes and studying his maps as Don, Ernest, and Richard tried to keep the boat on a northeasterly course, swinging their oars in circles and feeling for a bottom that always lay beyond reach. Latta would look up to tell them to hang on to those paddles—those were the only ones they had.

Desert winds whipped up whitecaps, and in places, schools of fish ruffled the water like waves. The larger ones' backs occasionally broke the surface, startling the boys as the boat rocked side to side. They wrapped their fingers around the wooden edges when they kneeled for a closer look. They didn't want to fall in.

"What all lives down there?" Ernest asked.

Latta smiled. "Nothing that will eat you," he said. "Those were only suckers, chubs, and possibly sturgeon, what the Yokuts called *Caw'-cuts*."

The boys nodded, but their hands gripped until their knuckles went white, because when they looked up, they saw water in all directions. No shore. No reeds. Nothing but a single, shimmering, 360-degree horizon and the hazy shape of mountains hovering in the distance. To Ernest and Richard, the view looked like Pismo Beach, though somehow Fresno only lay fifty miles away.

On the fifth day of my trip following Latta, I got off Interstate 5 and stopped at the In-N-Out Burger in Kettleman City. Kettleman is a town of 1,400 people halfway between Los Angeles and San Francisco, and its name reveals frontier ambitions that it hasn't lived up to. When I asked the staff member cleaning the bathroom if he'd heard of the old Tulare Lake bed, his lips pinched and he shook his head. "Never heard of it," he said, wiping the top of the paper towel dispensers.

I said, "The old shoreline is supposed to be right around here somewhere." He said he'd only lived around here for two years and was still getting his bearings. The burger chain built this location twenty years ago, though. "The building," he said, "not the parking lot."

Lake water had left marks on the land here. During average wet years, Tulare Lake often stretched seventy-five miles north and south and twenty-five east and west—about two hundred thousand acres. Its wettest year was 1862, and it covered 486,400 acres, with depths reaching forty-one feet. The thing is, Tulare Lake had no average year. It was a desert puddle in a drying period between ice ages. Some summers, it shrunk to what the *Lemoore Leader* newspaper called "a huge mud hole," leaving millions of rotting fish piled along the receding shore as locals collected the live ones. Other years, it stayed wet. Early gold miner John Barker told Latta that the lake in 1862 was "40 miles wide and 60 miles in length." When Latta mapped the 1862 shoreline from various accounts, his calculations put the towns of Corcoran and Stratford twenty-five feet underwater and the north shore in what he called "the center of Lemoore." The part of Kettleman City that now serves interstate travelers hamburgers and lattes sat safely atop what was called Orton Point in the 1850s. Named for Tulare Lake rancher Julius Orton, the point overlooked the Valley. It's the first real rise of land modern drivers encounter while headed north from the Grapevine grade. Although mosquitoes and the stink of dead fish would have reached it back then, water would not. But over the course of millennia, the minerally lake had left long horizontal stains somewhere around here, and if you looked, supposedly you could see them.

I'd driven a few small roads on both sides of the interstate and hiked up two hills in search of the colored bands, but I hadn't found anything. Had I misread my source? Maybe the stain wasn't on a hill but on a low sandy rise like the one in Latta's photo in *Little Journeys*, which looked like nothing more than the slightly upturned edge of a dry desert creek bed.

When I ordered a burger at the counter, I asked the young cashier if he'd heard of Tulare Lake. He shook his head and smiled. "No," he said, "I'm sorry. I don't know where that is." I explained that it was right here, that we were standing on its western edge, and that it was once the biggest lake west of the Great Lakes. Handing him my money, I described how, during wet years, the water stretched from the town of Corcoran, on the east side, to here. His tan brows raised and hung there, arched. "A lake that big?" he said. "No. That's the first I've heard of it." The information surprised him so much that he seemed to want to know more, but other customers had stepped behind me, so I got out of line and waited for my order.

Granted, fast-food workers might not have been the best people to ask—these were teenagers, not farmers or historians. But the sun was setting, so I didn't have much time. And really, these people deserved to know, since it was the lake that had left unsafe levels of arsenic and boron in the two wells that provided their drinking water.

As the sky darkened further, I pulled into the Starbucks drive-through. "Hi, welcome to Starbucks," said the voice in the speaker. "What can we get started for you?" I asked about Tulare Lake. "Um, yes," she said. "Are you asking me where it's at?" Yes, I was. "Well, you're slightly on the wrong side of the Valley for that. You do need to go a little more towards Tulare, over, like, on the 43. So you're going to travel north on 41 until you see Kansas. If you Google it or on Yahoo, then Kansas will take you to the 43. Tulare's over on that side, so Tulare Lake—I don't even know if it's called that any more—but it's over on that side of the Valley." I was shocked. So far, she knew more about it than anyone. Her name was Gina. She was the manager.

I pushed for more information. Was there still a lake there? "That I don't know," Gina said. "I haven't traveled on that side for a long while." She lived on the west side, in Avenal. Since she knew so much, had she ever heard anybody mention where you could see the lake's old mineral stains here in Kettleman City? "Um, no," she said, in a voice that signaled that either I was an idiot or I wasn't listening, "'cause we're two hours from the coast, so I'm not sure where that shoreline would be." She was losing patience. I explained the lake's size in historic times, how it stretched from Corcoran to Kettleman City. "Oh, that I'm not sure." I thanked her profusely and drove off.

She gave very specific details, but she still had it wrong. That was okay. Unlike the others, she at least made an educated guess that any lake with that name must be near the town of Tulare. It was a smart leap and revealing. There is arguably no landscape in America that agriculture and water diversion have changed more fundamentally than the Tulare Lake Basin. In a 2004 report, the U.S. Geological Survey categorized Tulare Lake as one of California's "discontinued lakes and reservoirs," as if the West's largest lake were an unpopular brand of frozen pizza. As I drove off, I kept trying to imagine what Latta would think of this world where Tulare Lake didn't form the center of the local psyche, a feature that had loomed as large as the Sierra Nevada on early California maps and had dominated the lives of the settlers he'd interviewed in the early 1900s.

As Latta's crew marveled at the wonders, they also got lost. The *Alta* was supposed to dock at the town of Alpaugh on Monday night. When they never showed, people got nervous. Secretary of the Kern County Chamber of Commerce E. Gay Hoffman was one of Latta's main contacts. During the trip, Latta planned to stop in certain towns and call in a report. On Monday, Hoffman told the newspaper that he hadn't heard from Latta. On Tuesday, officials got ready to send a small plane out to search.

The year before Latta's trip, a forty-five-year-old farmer named Kenny Battelle took nine people out on the lake in his new six-person speedboat. He leased the family's four thousand acres to other growers, and with all the standing water, he thought it'd be helpful to check their land by boat. He liked his fun, too, so one sunny Sunday in April, he took his wife, son, two daughters, and the kids' friends out on the flooded lake.

The lake had always unsettled Kenny's wife, Esther. Nearly twenty years earlier, she'd convinced him to relocate the family outside the lake bed. She didn't trust the intermittent flooding. She didn't know how to swim. Kenny moved them to a different house, but this day, he insisted that his boat was trustworthy. Somehow the boat flipped. One of Kenny's daughters, Esther, and two friends drowned. They had packed life jackets, but no one wore them. Latta's crew packed life jackets, too, though no one wore them in any of the photos in the papers.

Surely, stories like this were on Jeanette Latta's mind when she drove thirty miles to Alpaugh Tuesday afternoon. After all, their twelve-year-old son, Don, was on the trip. Jeanette admired Frank's passion, and she supported his interests. In the many towns where his teaching jobs took them, Jeanette helped file Frank's hundreds of papers, maps, and artifacts in their Bear State Library, and she helped run the publishing company they formed to print his later books about Death Valley and the Tejon Ranch. Like Alan Lomax's wife, Elizabeth Harold Goodman, who helped Alan record blues and folk musicians all over the American South, Jeanette and Frank worked as a team. Jeanette and their four kids even went along on many of Frank's research trips. They turned data collection into a fun family outing, crossing whatever rough mountain roads they had to cross to reach Frank's sources. In Sonora, Mexico, in 1936, Frank had to crawl under the car on dirt roads to replace the springs with wooden blocks. He didn't mind fixing cars; as a high school student, he had helped build a barn and school auditorium. The family made the bulk of that Sonora trip with four broken springs and the bumper chained to the axle. But roads were one thing; flooded lakes were another.

Latta's navigational charts of southern Tulare Lake turned out to be flawed. The crew didn't know it yet, but on Monday afternoon they had so overshot Alpaugh that they were approaching the town of Hanford instead, on the Lake's northeastern shore. Despite Latta's years exploring the Valley, the crew were, in the paper's words, "amateur navigators."

If the crew couldn't reach land, they would not have been the first. One Yokuts man whom Latta interviewed described the three nights he and his parents spent on the lake. They were taking a simple trip to see family in a village on an island. Then the wind died and stranded them. The water was too deep to shove off with poles, and after the waves nearly capsized them, they spent the night shivering wet, keeping warm in an embrace. "When it got daylight we could not see the land in any way," the man told Latta. "We could see the Kettleman Hills and the Sierra, but we were away and in the middle of the lake." At the mercy of the wind, they spent the second day fishing, cooking some of their catch, and smoking the rest for later.

Yokuts built small, ingenious firepits on their reed boats, called a *Tri-ahn'-cut*, which they filled with mud to keep the reed surface from burning while they roasted fish and ducks. "We were not hungry," the man said, "and we were not afraid any more, but we did not see how we were ever going to get to land." By sunset, the boat didn't seem to have moved an inch. He found the moonlight beautiful after dark. His mother sang and told stories to entertain them, and they enjoyed their night on the tranquil water. But even patient kids got restless on a twenty-five-by-eight-foot boat. As if to torment them further, the family could see the shore on the third day. They just couldn't reach it. "We stayed out there all day again," he said, "but we got pretty tired of it." When they drifted into a shallower spot after sundown, his parents, ready for the trip to end, spent most of the third night using their poles to approach the shore. In a dark comic twist, a sudden wind blew at dawn and launched the boat one hundred yards from shore within minutes. As trying as that sounded, three nights was nothing. Yokuts routinely fished on the lake for a week straight, listening to coyotes howl on a shore they could not see.

I wondered if Latta thought of that interview while he tried to get his bearings. Did the story make him worry that if their two motors failed, they might spend multiple nights out there? Or did it make him confident that they could survive? I read and reread the newspaper's account of the *Alta*'s mixed-up day, and I imagined the crew at sundown finally recognizing that they'd traveled past Alpaugh and that it was dark enough that they would have to spend the night on the water.

Bobbing on the lake's surface, below the high haze of mosquitoes, was a sheet of cormorants, seagulls, and grebes. The *Alta* passed one of the lake's old sandy islands, and it was covered with white pelicans. Instead of building nests from branches or sticks, pelicans gathered sand with their wings and laid eggs in the divot. If Latta drifted closer to snap some photos, the frightened birds would have lifted into the air and filled it with a thunderous flapping of their ten-foot wings, creating clouds so thick over their heads that the white rain of droppings would send fish nipping at the surface to eat what looked like hail. Early white settlers compared the squadrons of waterfowl to the sound of a freight train and said they darkened the skies. From his years spent among them, Latta knew that Yokuts called ducks *wats-wats*, an onomatopoeia after the way they sounded feeding, and they called squadrons of flying geese *tow-so, tow-so*, which meant "a thousand thousands." All that Latta had read about, all the stories he'd heard, had come to life around him.

But it was time to get serious. Surely, Latta studied the sierra's unmoving topography to triangulate their position, looking for familiar foothills or ridges that would place them somewhere fixed; then he'd turn his head south to guess which part of that long glistening horizon might contain Alpaugh.

Unlike the *Alta*, I reached Alpaugh by midday. It started as a hog pasture on the lake. When wheat and alfalfa fueled the basin's early economy, an LA real estate developer created a planned farming community in 1906, and the Atchison, Topeka, and Santa Fe Railway built a spur line here to ship grain. Now Alpaugh is a thousand-person town with one main intersection.

On one corner stood the old white-sided Alpaugh Grocery Store. On the others stood a school, a Mexican-food restaurant, and a tiny branch of the Tulare County Library. A single sprinkler watered the library's two trees. The branch was closed on Saturday.

During the week, people here worked in agriculture, picking, managing, irrigating, doing office administration. On weekends, men left the grocer holding twelve-packs of Budweiser. People cashed their paychecks and bought prepaid phone cards to call Mexico. A family from Yemen owned the grocery. After the clerk rung me up, he leaned back in his chair to clip his fingernails. The front door stood open, and the air-conditioning was off. Yet he wore a leather jacket, black jeans, and a button-up striped blue shirt, and he stepped into the sunny parking lot between customers, checking his phone and waving at people in the Cesi's Cafe lot.

Down Tule Road, sheep grazed in a pasture across from a lone pomegranate tree, and passing cars steered around a red couch cushion that laid by the canal. In town, water restrictions limited the care of residential lawns, leaving the town the beige color of dirt. In a sense, dirt had always defined the town. It sat on what geologists called Sand Ridge. There were no obvious signs of a ridge. Anyone from mountainous regions would laugh at the name. But the sandy formation that ran eight miles northeast to southwest through here was the largest accumulation of fine sand in the whole San Joaquin Valley, a rare piece of topographical relief on an otherwise level plane, and it peaked beneath Alpaugh.

Deer Creek and White River had deposited the sand over thousands of years in a process that resembled the Kings River building its alluvial fan near Fresno, except on what Latta called "a smaller scale." Technically, the ridge was more of a dune field. The dunes rose fifteen to twenty-five feet high and a few hundred yards wide. In drier years, the dunes connected to the mainland. In wet years, water surrounded them to form three distinct islands. When levees broke ten days before Latta was scheduled to arrive, the men hired to reinforce them raced to higher ground. Thanks to the ridge, Alpaugh itself was fine.

From Alpaugh, Sand Ridge ran southwest to the Bureau of Land Management's eight-thousand-acre Atwell Island Project. Since buying the land from farmers in 1992, a team of scientists had been restoring century-old cotton, oat, and alfalfa fields to native grassland and scrub habitat and encouraging the return of endangered species. The property's full name was the Atwell Island Land Retirement Demonstration Project, but most people called it Atwell. It was the San Joaquin Valley's largest habitat restoration project.

In the Valley, where an estimated 95 percent of native habitat has been lost to agriculture and urbanization, restoration is endangered animals' only hope for survival. To increase endangered populations, you have to create more native-plant communities. Currently, there is no San Joaquin Valley State Park, but Atwell has the potential to act like one. In fact, the way it's positioned near Pixley National Wildlife Refuge, Kern National Wildlife Refuge, and Allensworth State Historic Park—which contains incredibly rare land that's never been tilled—Atwell sits at the geographical center of what could one day be the second-largest piece of natural land in the San Joaquin Valley, after the Great Valley Grasslands State Park farther north. But the project also offers a promising new way to repair the Valley's thousands of salt-damaged farm acres and to decrease pollutants in the water supply. So far, the experiment has shown improvements.

Even though it was Jihadda Govan's day off, the manager of the Atwell Island Project drove thirty minutes from her home in Wasco to show me around the property.

We met outside the Mexican-food restaurant. When she lowered her car window to chat, the sun gleamed on her sunglasses' dark lenses, and a feral dog sniffed around the back of the restaurant. Govan got one of her three dogs from the street here, along with her two cats. "One of the problems in the community that we do have," she said, "are stray dogs." Nearly every time she walked her dogs in Wasco, she saw feral dogs trotting around without collars. "Isn't that horrible? It's like, what the freaking hell?"

We drove two miles down a bumpy road to a huge green field marked with a sign that said Atwell Island Bakersfield Field Office. Atwell headquarters was located in a plain, one-level farmhouse whose low roof ran parallel to the horizon.

A twenty-something in shorts and no shoes sat on the floor, studying a map of the area's old wetlands. She was part of an AmeriCorps winter crew stationed there for six weeks. During the year, the Bureau of Land Management pays for Alpaugh's high school science students to use Atwell as an outdoor classroom. Kids learn about native and invasive species, conservation, and restoration. In return, the program helps stretch Atwell's shrinking budget. It also provides essential community outreach, letting locals know what Atwell does, that they're allies not adversaries, and showing people the subtle beauty of the land they inhabit. This is public land, and Govan hoped the experience gave students pride of ownership and encouraged them to get their families to visit. The previous manager, Steve Laymon, did the early restoration work. Govan inherited responsibility for the next phase: increasing visitation. She envisioned horseback riding, field trips, a visitor's center. "When folks from the community enjoy it regularly," Govan said, "they're going to want to preserve it, protect it."

Even in the T-shirt and gray sweatpants she called her "junky clothes," Govan moved with the lithe confidence of a natural leader, though she admitted she was just as happy outdoors alone. During the week, her commanding uniform included brown cargo pants, a collared shirt, and a round safari hat with a bill that she kept low enough to block the sun and contain her dark curly hair as she ticked off the Latin names of native saltbush species they replanted on the property: *Atriplex spinifera, Atriplex polycarpa, Atriplex lentiformis.*

She offered me bottled water, not tap. Groundwater here contained elevated levels of arsenic, selenium, and boron. "Not super bad, like it's-going-to-kill-you bad," she said, "but just higher than the recommended amount for drinking water." These toxins came not from pesticides or herbicides but from the soil. The old lake bed contained minerals from millions of years of marine and terrestrial deposition. When irrigation percolated through the topsoil, it leached those compounds and concentrated them on top of a thick layer of naturally occurring diatomaceous clay. That Corcoran clay was deposited when this was all ocean floor. The Valley's agriculture sat atop soils that ran ten miles deep in places, yet the clay was 10 to 160 feet thick, so the toxic wastewater never drained that far down. People called it the perched water table. As it accumulated atop the clay, it rose to the surface, taking agricultural pollutants and sea salts with it, and killed the roots of crops. That saline water killed the nearby towns of Allensworth and Traver by destroying their soils. It was the reason land retirement experiments like Atwell existed.

Land retirement means removing land from agricultural service. The Valley's farms have managed various challenges. Lack of surface irrigation and dropping wells are some. Land subsistence caused by groundwater pumping is another. Farming a flat lake bed means wastewater drains poorly. Then there is salinization.

Salinization is the process of land turning too salty to support plant life. In the San Joaquin Valley this wasn't just table salt. These salts included a range of soluble compounds, from sodium bicarbonate to barium chloride, as well as problem elements like selenium, mercury, chromium, and arsenic. In 1992 the Central Valley Improvement Act authorized the Bureau of Reclamation's Land Retirement Program, which allocated money to establish the Atwell Island Project and another plot farther north near Tranquility. That same year, the San Joaquin Valley contained 4.5 million acres of irrigated land, and salinization plagued four hundred thousand of them. Kern County farmers had already removed over ten thousand acres from production. Salinization would ruin at least a million more. The San Joaquin contained four of America's five highest-grossing agricultural counties. Those counties helped fund California's economy, which ranked as the sixth largest economy in the world—stronger than many countries. Salt threatened all of that.

Over the years, farmers and governmental agencies have proposed various solutions for dealing with salt. They've talked about building systems of underground pipes to clear the water. They've talked about treatment facilities and piping wastewater over the mountains to Morro Bay, where, in theory, it would get diluted. So far, no proposal has worked. Before irrigating crops, some farmers with salinized acres preirrigate to flush salts from their crops' root zone. Others try to dilute contaminants and reduce wastewater by recycling irrigation through drip systems or by blending it with other water. As they recycle, they still end up with salty water.

In the end, the most common way of dealing with contaminated water is the most simplistic: pumping it off-site. Removal systems involve canals called drains, which move water to ponds or reservoirs where it gets stored or evaporated or dump it into a river like the San Joaquin for transport. In the early 1980s, farmers tried this at a placed called Kesterson Reservoir near Los Banos.

The federal government built over eighty miles of a concrete canal called the San Luis Drain. The drain poured wastewater into 1,200 acres of open-air ponds within the Kesterson National Wildlife Refuge. The ponds were meant to store the toxic water and let it evaporate until the rest of the two-hundred-mile-long drain could divert fifty tons of salts from the Valley into San Francisco Bay every fifteen minutes. Instead, selenium-laced waste seeped into the ground, and internationally protected waterfowl treated the wastewater like wetlands on their regular migratory flight path. The Valley lays on the Pacific Flyway. Birds not only died by the thousands; the concentrated selenium caused deformed embryos without eyes or beaks. By the time the federal government stopped pumping in 1983, Kesterson was one of the worst ecological disasters in American history. It made national news, but because it happened on farmland in a place few outsiders visit, Kesterson never became a household name like Three Mile Island. The San Luis Drain was decommissioned in stages and plugged, and the feds spent millions sealing Kesterson. That this all happened close to private duck-hunting clubs and routes with names like Wild Duck Road wasn't lost on some observers. The birds' deaths violated the Migratory Bird Treaty Act. Those birds were the canary in the coal mine.

All irrigated cultures have ended because of desertification and related ecological problems, but their decline took many generations. With modern farming technology, desertification is happening with unprecedented speed, and the fate of this seemingly regional California farmland is actually the fate of our national prosperity. The Mesopotamian civilization developed irrigated agriculture in the Tigris-Euphrates river valley around 5,000 BCE. They were the first people to plant cereal grains and brew beer and the first to use a large-scale system of canals and dikes to grow food, and salinization destroyed it. The Sumerian Empire started growing grain in the same region around 3,500 BCE. By 1,700 BCE, salts forced them to abandon their irrigated fields. In the fifth century BCE, Plato wrote about a parallel process, when deforestation near Athens created soils that looked like "the skeleton of a sick man, all the fat and soft earth having wasted away, and only the bare framework of the land being left." This process is called desertification. Modern-day California still has to answer the question of what's to be done with all this salt. What happens in California affects the entire country.

The U.S. Geological Survey estimated that the state would have twenty million tons of salts to deal with by the mid-twenty-first century, but America didn't have the technology to treat the issue on that scale. Certain agricultural interests still advocated for the completion of the San Luis Drain. After Kesterson, many farmers didn't wait. They just built evaporation ponds on their own land. According to both the Geological Survey and the Fish and Wildlife Service, the best option would be for farmers on the Valley's saline west side to take three hundred thousand acres out of production. Interestingly, it was the U.S. Geological Survey that sent William Henry Brewer on the 1863 trip where he found land south of Bakersfield "entirely bare, the ground crusted with salt and alkali, like snow." One hundred fifty years later, the salt keeps coming. Reduced productivity has already pushed many owners to fallow their land, sell it, or convert irrigated crops to nonirrigated uses such as dry-land farming or sheep pasture. At six hundred thousand acres, Westlands Water District, on the dry west side, was the country's largest irrigation district. During my visit, they'd fallowed half their farmland because of the drought, and they were considering turning twenty-four thousand marginal acres into the Westlands Solar Park. The federal land retirement program offered a new choice: sell and they'd restore it to native vegetation.

The Fish and Wildlife Service believed that by selectively eliminating irrigation, they eliminated the cause of the problem. Land retirement also held the potential for other improvements. Fewer irrigated acres meant less wastewater contributing to the perched water table and less water activating soil contaminants. Retirement freed water to irrigate more productive farmlands. Unlike cotton and safflower, native plants like *Atriplex* evolved to live in the Valley's arid, saline conditions, and their low-impact xeriscaping could increase the populations of endangered wildlife, even on land that had been treated with chemicals. It sounded ideal in theory. Atwell functions as a laboratory where researchers could test these hypotheses.

Considering how much food, revenue, and employment farmers produced in the Valley, returning fields to nature was a profound shift in thinking. To many growers, endangered species like the delta smelt represented all the ways environmental interests threatened their livelihood and held the welfare of wildlife over people. But farming was big business, and the federal government paid top dollar for land. Farmers ready to get out of the game sold to real estate developers all the time. Turning land over to nature didn't mean they liked kangaroo rats more than taxpayers. They were simply protecting their interests. Still, many landowners were cautious about liquidating their assets. Some believed that different crops, new technology, and improved irrigation practices offered solutions. In 2001 the Westlands Water District had discussed retiring two hundred thousand acres to the U.S. Bureau of Reclamation but decided against it. "Our goal is to continue farming the land," Westlands Water District spokeswoman Gayle Holman told the *San Francisco Chronicle*. "We have some of the best land in the world." As the *Chronicle* put it, "Many experts said if farmers don't retire the land, nature eventually will do it for them."

Govan opened a door to a back room where huge plastic-wrapped palettes of bottled water stood in the corner beside a fridge. It seemed dystopian, a glimpse of our dry, rationed future where water functions as currency and you can't trust what comes from taps. They'd actually had two break-ins.

On the first break-in, thieves stole lawnmowers, a bed, a mattress, and about twenty-five bottles of water and busted windows and a door. Damages totaled upward of $7,000. Between the pol-luted groundwater and the municipal supply drying up, it costs each Alpaugh household an average of $1,200 to drink bottled water each year. That comes to $400,000 for the whole town. The town govern-ment only spends $300,000 on its municipal supply annually. It's no wonder bottles had become valuable enough for some people to risk a felony for stealing them. Govan didn't live onsite, but after the last break-in, she visited headquarters more frequently and occasionally stayed overnight.

On the side of the house, we climbed into her dusty Bureau of Land Management pickup. Splattered insects covered the grill. When I slid inside, cans clinked on the floorboard. "Those aren't my beers," Govan said. Someone had picked them up from the property. "Also," she added, "I don't drink Bud."

Gravel rattled against the truck's undercarriage as she took off, leaving a tan trail of dust even at low speed. It was a nice clear day, and the November sun felt like spring. The land wasn't much to look at. Scrubby brown shrubs covered the flat expanse, broken by patches of golden grasses. To the untrained eye, these native plants looked indistinguishable from tumbleweeds, if they weren't all tum-bleweeds. I couldn't tell. Govan parked beside a field and explained that some of that brown stuff was a tumbleweed-type plant called *Basia*. It colonized disturbed soil, especially irrigated land and along the edges of restored plots where it didn't compete with native plants. We sat and stared at the scrub. Even to somebody like me who grew up in the Arizona desert and knew desert habitat and plant species well, this seemed more like a vacant lot. "It looks like it's waiting for somebody to do some restoration work on it," I said, "but this is what they've replicated."

She nodded. "This is what they've replicated."

Atwell's Island had several distinct types of habitat. We were look-ing at alkali sink scrub and valley grassland. Sink scrub plants evolved to tolerate salts and alkaline soils. Govan explained that this was how the area used to look. "Historically, if you read the journals of the

Spaniards that were here," she said, "that's how they would describe it, this kind of shrubby place." She'd read tons of early explorers' journals, including those of William Brewer, John James Audubon, John Muir, and the Spanish padres. By June or July the land turned brown, but some explorers described a riot of color here. If it enjoyed a wet spring, native wildflowers like goldfields, alkali daisy, hayfield tarweed, and coastal tidy tips would cover it with yellow, blue, and white, as they had when Mayfield first saw the Valley, and the creamy scent of pollen would fill the air. Govan got excited listing the taxonomic names: *Lasthenia californica*, *Phacelia californica*, *Layia platyglossa*. "*Amsinckia* fiddleheads," she said, "or is it fiddlenecks? I can't remember." She laughed when she couldn't remember all the wildflowers they'd planted either.

She was proud of the work of Atwell's first manager, Steve Laymon, who had re-created the sparseness of the historic habitat, with its spacious distribution of plants. Restoration is a precise process, often requiring seeds to be scattered at specific densities in order to re-create the density that science has determined to be the plant community's presettlement condition. This was one of the first parcels that had been restored. For some restorations, they planted thirty pounds of seed per acre so that the native plants filled in quickly and pushed out the weeds. Since desert natives didn't need much water, Atwell was planted in the fall to utilize California's rainy season. Irrigation only brought more weeds.

After establishing the vegetation, Atwell partnered with the Endangered Species Recovery Program at Cal State, Stanislaus, to monitor the many federally threatened and endangered species that used the area, such as blunt-nosed leopard lizards, as well as with the California Department of Fish and Wildlife, to track the rates of the state's own species of special concern, like the San Joaquin pocket mouse, antelope squirrels, and burrowing owls.

Volunteers helped install burrows to establish populations of the Valley's three species of kangaroo rats and the endangered San Joaquin kit foxes. Monitoring showed that a lot of kangaroo rats used this plot, but not the highly endangered Tipton subspecies. "There's Heermann's kangaroo rats," Govan said, "but then some of these areas, we get a few of the San Joaquin pocket mouse, so that's nice." They had breeding pairs of burrowing owls, resident mountain plovers, and tricolored blackbirds, all federally listed or sensitive species. Kit foxes hadn't taken to the area yet, though staff regularly spotted itinerant foxes trotting on- and off-site. Govan believed they'd get foxes breeding soon.

A native of Pasadena, Govan joined the California Conservation Corps at age eighteen and later left sunny Southern California to study at foggy Humboldt State College in Northern California. Her father had worked as an environmental planner for Caltrans. During her college years, she always worked in natural resources, from forestry to wildlife management to fire application. After college, she landed a position with the U.S. Fish and Wildlife Service at the Sonny Bono Salton Sea Wildlife Refuge near Palm Springs. Another flooded lowland with high salt concentrations, Salton Sea seemed ideal training for her next job as the assistant manager of the Kern Wildlife Refuge down the road from Atwell; the Kern Wildlife Refuge also managed the nearby Pixley National Wildlife Refuge. She worked there for eight years and then moved to a refuge on the Minnesota River near Odessa. The Minnesotans were friendly and the landscape beautiful, and she found comfort in a pub called the Refuge Bar. But she had California in her bones. "I'm a Cali girl," she said. "I'll never leave again." She landed a job at Atwell in fall 2012. The transition to life in the Valley wasn't too hard, because in college her temp position in the California Condor Recovery Program had her driving through here tracking condors' movements from the mountains to the lowlands. "I knew what the area looked like," she said. "So I'm like, 'Oh, Bakersfield's not bad. You know, it's got a Trader Joe's.'"

She still struggled. Sometimes she wondered if she'd only stay a few years. But the more time passed, the more taken she became with the values of the people in the Valley. "It's a mix of different cultures," she said, "because you've got a lot of Hispanics, and you've got that Texas thing. I like it, and it's also the West, where people, for the most part, will accept you on an individual-by-individual basis. They're not necessarily lumpers, for the most part. I think it's just the mix of people, the different places that they came from, and the circumstances, because a lot of people came here during the Dust Bowl where they're very appreciative of the blessings that they have." Local attitudes and peoples' love of hunting and fishing made it easier to talk to them about a place like Atwell. "You got a lot of farm kids here," she said, "and it's an easy sell."

After two years at Atwell, she was getting to know every inch of it with the intimacy of a farmer: *Poso Creek ends south of the turkey farm*; *pocket mice were last spotted right there.* Like a farmer, she worked to make sure her land bloomed, except her plants had been here much longer than cotton, and because they'd evolved for these conditions, they didn't denude it. They replenished.

So far, upward of 4,700 acres had been restored. "We're down to the last one thousand acres," Govan said, "and that's pretty much all in alfalfa, and so when we go to restore that, the best thing is not to disk it, because if you disk it, you stir up trouble." Disking would have involved a tractor attachment covered with circular metal blades breaking up the soil at a designated depth so that farmers could plant seeds in the rows. Unfortunately, disking exposes whatever weed seeds lay in the soil. When restoring native plant communities, Atwell found it best to drill, where little circular implements drilled seeds into the ground after a fire crew had burned the weedy surface. One of the things that impressed staff was how well native shrubs grew in soil that had been treated with chemical fertilizer and pesticides. What they hoped to learn was how much the native plants could help rid the soil of contaminants over time.

She eased the truck onto a patch of gravel and interrupted her explanation. "Why did I stop here? Oh, I stopped here because I wanted to point this out. See that little hole right there?" She pointed to a low bank. Burrowing owls lived inside it. Atwell had many breeding pairs now. Another species that had bounced back notably well were loggerhead shrikes, famous for impaling their prey on barbed wire or thorns. They nested in this plot, along with mockingbirds, western meadowlarks, and horned larks. "I have not seen any thrashers down here," she said, "but the previous manager was a really good birder. I do okay, but he was awesome, and he's seen thrashers. We also have some birds of prey that nest down here, some marsh hawks, and . . . ferruginous." She stopped herself. "Not ferruginous. Harris. Not Harris. I can't remember the name of it now." I rarely remember the names of songbirds, let alone birds of prey.

With the truck windows down, she pointed out the difference between the native saltbush species: one had more leaves; the other was spinier. "So you have some different species of *Atriplex* in here. This is *Isocoma*. This is a golden bush. This is in the sunflower family, and this one I think is somewhat fire tolerant." Any habitat named "scrub" was destined to disappoint people. Visually, it was plain, but its simplicity was deceiving. The sight of a flatland filled with something other than tilled earth or tract homes was what made this landscape so beautiful, as much as the plants that grew on it. The human spirit needed unblemished horizons. It needed emptiness for moments of calm. Here it was, getting rebuilt bit by bit.

We turned south down another bouncy road. Scrub spread in all directions. The Kettleman Hills hung clear and crisp to the west. After hiking the San Joaquin Valley for so long and often having to sneak into off-limits sections of nature preserves to see the good stuff, it thrilled me to get a fully sanctioned tour by a professional.

As the road crossed a small empty channel, I pointed to a coyote who came trotting alongside us, right in the middle of the day. "It's probably a dog," Govan said squinting. "Oh, yeah, that is a coyote. Nice. Cool. Of course I forgot my binoculars."

Govan made a broad sweeping motion with her hand and announced that we'd entered the Ton Tachi wetlands. *Ton* meant "south" in Yokuts dialects. These were once the shallower marshes at the southern end of Tulare, or Tachi, Lake. Sand Ridge divided them from the deeper waters to the north, turning them into what

Spaniards and Yokuts both identified—as if it weren't confusing enough—as a southern Tulare Lake. For Atwell, Ton Tachi was a newer acquisition.

The man who donated this piece of Ton Tachi had farmed a bit of it, but he mostly grazed cattle here. As a wetland, its clay soils held a lot of water. Right now, it was dry. A small canal ran nearby, carrying water to wetlands to the south. Govan was working hard to secure water for this plot. She started to explain the process, how even though she worked for the Bureau of Land Management, Atwell was a multiagency collaboration that got funding from the Bureau of Reclamation. Since the Bureau of Reclamation only paid for upland restoration, Atwell couldn't use those funds to buy water for wetlands, so she pursued other means. She stopped herself, possibly to spare me the details, possibly to spare herself the irritation on a Saturday. "It's kind of convoluted," she said.

For a place that used to be covered with water, it now cost between $10,000 and $15,000 to fill two small ponds. She had three wells that could potentially fill Ton Tachi; one was broken. She'd submitted a formal request for special funding to fix the well, which took a year and a half to get. She had an estimate for repairs and a contract. Now she needed to secure the money to pay the electrical costs of pumping clean well water, and that required waiting for other paperwork to pass like selenium through many dense layers of bureaucratic strata. Reimbursement was always a challenge with federal projects, especially ones like Atwell, which was by definition an experiment to see if land retirement had larger social and economic benefits. Expensive or not, she preferred to keep two ponds full here. As the water table continued to drop during the drought, the pumps had to work harder to pull water from the deep aquifer beneath the salty perched water table, and that increased the cost. One pond required forty acre-feet to fill it. An acre-foot of water cost $60 to $65 in a wet year and $140 to $150 in this drought. Plant restoration alone cost an average of $1,500 an acre. The bureaucratic stuff sucked, she said, but seeing this covered with ducks and buzzing with songbirds made it worth the effort. AmeriCorps built an observation deck nearby, which the Alpaugh students loved. People were giving Govan a hard time, saying, "Jihadda, you should have water in there," so she felt stuck between the proverbial rock and a hard place.

She stared out into the distance. "So it's just kind of tough." Wrapping your head around Tulare Lake was tough too.

In addition to dividing Tulare into south and north lakes, Sand Ridge used to form three separate islands in Tulare Lake. Spanish explorers called the westernmost one Calaveras, or Skull, Island.

According to Latta, "Skull Island has been the basis of several very remarkable tales concerning a great Indian battle which is supposed to have taken place there in prehistoric times. Dr. Cartmill, Tulare pioneer, visited the place in the early 1860's and reported the place to be almost covered with human skulls and other bones. In the 1870's the bones were still reported to be as thick as ever. Visitors found skulls and fragments of skeletons over the entire higher portion of the island. Digging revealed several buried skeletons together with fine obsidian spear points and other objects of Indian manufacture." In the 1870s a ranch hand named Jose Messa traveled regularly through the area to tend cattle. During one trip to Skull Island during high water, Messa found beads and skeletons on the shore, and he figured out once and for all that this wasn't a battle ground. It was a Yokuts burial ground where high winds and waves were eroding the graves.

Farther east the ridge formed Pelican Island at the mouth of the Kings River. According to Latta, in 1833 this island was ten to sixty feet wide, a mile long, and never over eighteen inches above water. "If we are to accept the statements of pioneers," he wrote, "pelicans nested on this island as thick as they could sit."

Skull Island. Pelican Island. The names read like something out of a C. S. Lewis novel. The Bureau of Land Management's project drew its name from a more conservative sounding middle island between the others. White settlers called it Atwell's Island, after its first American owner, but it started as a seven-hundred-person village named Bubal.

Since the lake held an abundance of food, the Wowol, Chunut, and Tachi Yokuts tribes lived there in both seasonal and permanent habitations. The Tachi were the lake's largest group, with four thousand people. The Wowol had about 1,300 members. The village of Bubal was the Wowol's largest settlement.

Bubal used to be located on Tulare Lake's western shore, but the Wowol seem to have moved it to Sand Ridge because of all the Spanish territorial activity to the west near the Camino Viejo. There, between the northern and southern wetlands, the people could keep dry, access lake and grassland food supplies, and conduct trade in a vast network that spread as far as the Mojave Desert on the other side of the Sierra Nevada. In wet years, you needed a boat to reach Bubal. In low water, the island stretched nine miles long and two across. The lake was low enough that when Spanish priest Father Juan Martín searched the area for mission sites in 1804, he walked over Sand Ridge to Bubal. Granted, he came to take Yokuts children away to work at the coastal missions and learn about salvation, his "harvest of heaven," as he put it. He'd gathered two hundred kids when he arrived at Bubal. Fortunately, the village chief put a stop to that, and Martín left empty-handed. But like many Spanish padres, this religious imperialist left an important record of the region and Native Americans before American settlement.

It took a while for most Americans to notice the island through the eighteen-foot-tall reeds. The wealthy attorney "Judge" A. J. Atwell and a business partner Ike Goldstein knew it was there but didn't realize how big it was. Grazing their sheep in the sierra foothills one night, high above the Valley, the moon lit Tulare Lake, and the island's true size revealed itself. Atwell told his partner, "Say, that would be a fine place to raise hogs." A few weeks later, they scouted the island on foot and hired a Yokuts man to ferry the first hogs over on a reed boat. This was in 1859 or 1860. Surrounded by water, Atwell didn't need fences to contain his animals, and they loved the natural grasses and green tule shoots. Locals started calling it Hog-Root Island, then Root Island, and then Atwell's.

Buyers liked the taste of Atwell's pigs. But when other people started keeping pigs there, the animals started eating the lake's freshwater mussels, and customers grumbled about the meat's fishy flavor. Farmers set the pigs free and started grazing cattle in the 1870s. "The place was infested with coyotes," Latta wrote, "continuously watching for an opportunity to fall upon hogs, antelopes, calves or cattle unfortunate enough to mire down in the boggy margins of the lake. Captain Conley and Lewis Atwell once came upon the carcasses of 40 cattle on the north edge of Atwell's Island. They had been driven into the mire by coyotes and had bogged down, to finally be eaten alive. Three or four were still living but were so torn and mutilated by the coyotes that they had to be shot."

The U.S. Army forcibly moved the Wowol to reservations in 1854, but some families returned to build secret houses in the reeds, trying to get back to their old lives. It didn't last. Cattlemen kicked them off.

Judge Atwell used to take his son Arthur duck hunting on the island. "When my father first obtained possession of Atwell Island," Arthur told Latta, "there were still many of the [dome-shaped] Indian houses standing there. These houses were made by weaving and tying the standing tules into a thatch which shed water as well as a good shingle roof." Built ten feet high and twelve feet in diameter around a firepit, their doors faced south to keep the water out when the north wind blew. While duck hunting, the Atwells would hide in the houses during rainstorms. Arthur once spent the night in one. The next morning, he woke up a few feet from a dead Wowol. The records don't say, but the dead Wowol was probably abandoned by any family because settlers ran them off their own island. Or perhaps the Wowol person died from starvation or maybe got murdered, while hiding from white ranchers.

During those early cattle years, Americans started planting wheat on the shore as Tulare Lake receded. Farmers thrived between floods. They built levees to solidify the lake's edges, but planting on a lake was a calculated risk that often left farms wet.

During wet years, moving cattle and equipment by boat could save people a sixty-mile detour. In the 1870s and 1880s, Tulare Lake had at least five boat docks. There was Atwell's Landing on the northeast shore. There was Rhoades Landing near Lemoore, Buzzard's Roost near Corcoran, and one at the old Thomas Creighton ranch southwest of Tulare, where there's now a Nature Conservancy preserve. In 1870 there were no settlements on the lake's west side, so two cattlemen named Cox and Clark built an adobe and boat landing three miles south of Kettleman City, near the In-N-Out Burger where I ate. The adobe became an important trading post for Yokuts and white travelers, until commerce shifted and it crumbled away. Three miles south, on the same northwestern shore, was Gordon's Point.

Jack Gordon was an infamous hog farmer who was shot and killed in an 1865 duel in the Sierra Nevada. His landing stood on a low sandy spit that extended a half mile out into the water, and it created a cove that boats used for shelter in storms. Fisherman called it Terrapin Bay for the staggering number of turtles that lived there. Turtles coated the sandy shoreline and drifting mats of reeds. "When disturbed," Latta wrote, "they popped into the water in a solid mass making a roar like the surf on a beach."

Coastal restaurants made turtles into soup, so fisherman hauled them in with huge nets called seines. Each seine was one hundred feet long, with a sixty-foot rope attached to each end. Two men would walk through the shallow water, spaced two hundred feet apart, and scoop up everything in their path. When the seine got too heavy, they cinched the ropes and pulled the net to shore. Turtles sold for $4 a dozen. Fishermen stuffed live ones into barley sacks two dozen at a time and shipped them to San Francisco, where they were distributed up and down the coast. Eighty to a hundred turtles was a nice catch. Kern County exported between 180 dozen and 300 dozen turtles in good years. When fisherman exhausted a section of shoreline, they moved to another.

Fishing quickly became a lucrative industry. Between the 1860s and 1880s, enterprising people built and imported boats to harvest the lake. "The abundance of fish of all kinds," the *San Francisco Picayune* raved in 1851, "is absolutely astonishing." Fishermen bragged about harvesting eight tons of fish using a single draw of a seine. Duck eggs were a delicacy. So were the ducks themselves. Fisherman caught catfish and trout, carp and chub, salmon and sturgeon, mussels and frogs, but perch sold the best. They threw back whatever wouldn't sell.

A longtime fisherman named William J. Browning ran the largest lake operation, and he told Latta, "We threw back some fish so often we came to know them by sight and gave them names." Browning's biggest single haul weighed 2,200 pounds, and that was after returning twice that to the lake.

Weeks of work turned fishing camps into foul places circled by hungry seagulls and coyotes and stained the dirt with the grease of dead sucker fish. Suckers were good money. Some brothers in Lemoore laid the little fish on metal racks to render their oil in the sun, and their outdoor camps got filthy, covered with fish bones and barrels of leaky oil, which Browning dryly told Latta was "a lovely place to be away from." Even though coastal diners might not have known exactly where their food came from or that a giant lake lay to the east of the mountains, fish stew was popular. This transaction of inner California's natural riches to urban consumers was one of the first of a now-entrenched commercial exchange—moving produce from the Valley to the coast—and it was the first example of coastal Californians depending on the interior without even knowing its name or their debt to the place. The American frontier was filled with dreamers, laborers, lunatics, and every stripe of opportunist and schemer, and the lake was its own frontier. With money to be made, the boats came one by one.

In the 1870s the U.S. Navy built a thirty-two-foot-long schooner called the *Alcatraz* to move people between the island prison and San Francisco. In 1878 a cranky shoeless eccentric used ropes, paddles, and horses to haul the retired boat down into Tulare Lake. Renaming it the *Water Witch*, he planned to make a killing fishing and gathering bird eggs. He was a bad businessman, and he ended up a subsistence hunter, eating most of his catch, which earned him the nickname Eating Smith. After a few failed excursions, he sold the boat to these guys with the fish oil camp, who sold three hundred dozen Tulare turtles in one year, until a storm wrecked the boat and they sold it to someone else.

In 1875 Judge Atwell and his old sheepherding partner got in on the action and built a steamer called the *Mose Andross*. Named after a friend who worked for the U.S. Land Office in Visalia, where the Atwells lived, the boat started as a sailboat, but because the lake winds were too unpredictable, they converted it to a steamer. The boat hauled cattle and passengers and could tow barges. When the lake started drying up in 1879, the owners ditched it on the receding shore near Lemoore, where some people salvaged the engine to use in a sawmill, and others turned the hull into a small ferry that worked the shrinking lake. Then there was the *Alta*.

Alta means "upper." It was the term the Spanish used to distinguish the upper half of their Californian territory from the Baja half. In 1862 Tulare Lake was spilling its banks, so an investor named Thomas Flaxman, with his eyes on the fishery, paid a crew of experienced sailors to take a steam-powered stern-wheeler named the *Alta* down into the lake. These men knew the waters. They'd spent time running freight up and down the San Joaquin River from Stockton to where the river bends near Fresno. Since boats could only reach the lake in high water, boats had to get in and out quickly, before their passage evaporated. Maps only helped so much. Captains relied on skill and the stupidity that passed for valor.

The *Alta* got down the river alright. At some point near the bend, they brought some vaqueros onboard. The captain assumed that since the cowboys knew the area, they'd know which channel would lead to the lake. "The passage was made without difficulty through the hardest part of the route," Latta wrote in *Little Journeys in the San Joaquin*, "and then the vaqueros lost their way. Everything was covered with tules and water and no channels could be seen. Soon after dark the first night after they left the San Joaquin river, they began to have trouble. They were aground most of the time. The water was only three feet deep. The sailors carried the anchor ahead and put it in the tules. Then the captain had the engineer draw in on the anchor chain. This pulled the boat up to the anchor." They did this over and over, inching their way south until the crew was exhausted and quit at midnight.

"In the morning when it came daylight there was no water in sight and there never has been since," Latta wrote. The crew left the boat where it stood, two miles southeast of the old Elkhorn stagecoach station near modern-day Burrel. The vaqueros trudged back to the ranch through the mud. The sailors walked forty muddy miles to Firebaugh, where a boat took them and their bad news to Stockton. The *Alta*'s hull stayed on the baking cattle range for years. Set a half mile off the stagecoach route, passengers stared as they passed it, while locals picked its valuables and burned the hull for firewood. Somehow a Kingsburg butcher shop got hold of the pilot's wheel and used it to hoist sides of meat. The boat never even made it into the lake.

Although the newspapers initially called Latta's boat the *Alta*, it was actually the *Alta II*. He named it after the original. Latta knew his history, and part of knowing history is knowing where you fit into it. With that association, the name *Alta II* seemed cursed. You're supposed to christen your ship with a bottle of champagne, not the name of an abandoned ship. But even if his small boat didn't sink and his crew didn't drown, Latta probably knew that this voyage, like the first *Alta*'s and the Wowols' final trip to Atwell's Island, would be the last.

The Yokuts said, "Once there was a time when there was nothing in the world but water. About the place where Tulare Lake is now, there was a pole standing far up out of the water, and on this pole perched a hawk and a crow. First one of them would sit on the pole a while, then the other would knock him off and sit on it himself. Thus they sat on top of the pole above the waters for many ages. At length they wearied of the lonesomeness, and they created the birds which prey on fish such as the kingfisher, eagle, pelican, and others. Among them was a very small duck, which dived down to the bottom of the water, picked its beak full of mud, came up, died, and lay floating on the water. The hawk and the crow then fell to work and gathered from the duck's beak the earth which it had brought up, and commenced making the mountains. They began at the place now known as Ta-hi-cha-Pa Pass, and the hawk made the east range, while the crow made the west one. Little by little, as they dropped in the earth, these great mountains grew athwart the face of the waters, pushing north. It was a work of many years, but finally they met together at Mount Shasta, and their labors were ended. But, behold, when they compared their mountains, it was found that the crow's was a great deal the larger. Then the hawk said to the crow, 'How did this happen, you rascal? I warrant you have been stealing some of the earth from my bill, and that is why your mountains are the biggest.' It was a fact, and the crow laughed in his claws. Then the hawk went and got some Indian tobacco and chewed it, and it made him exceedingly wise. So he took hold of the mountains and turned them around in a circle, putting his range in place of the crow's; and that is why the Sierra Nevada is larger than the Coast Range."

Govan stopped her truck beside a field they'd planted with native golden bush and *Atriplex spinifera*. She pointed out the places where birds flipped things over with their beaks in search of insects. "On the refuge in spring," she said, "they come off the refuge when the sun comes up in the tens of thousands. It's insane. It's all you can hear." After all those thousands of years covered in water, those ducks and a few upturned bits of vegetation were most of what remained of the old lake—no more Terrapin Bay, no more island of pelicans. Just canals and cotton.

When Govan told visiting children that this used to be a lake, they said, "What happened to it? Let's go check it out!" The old maps floored them. If these kids pursued careers that impacted landscapes, Govan wanted them to remember their Atwell visit. She wanted them to remember when, back in the day, some lady explained to them how altered this flat brown landscape was. Hopefully their experience would shape them enough to make policy decisions that preserved the pieces of their turf that weren't yet altered, so future generations would know that farms and cities and slick fashion magazines weren't all that the world contained.

"We're mimicking what was already here," Govan said, "or what Mother Nature, however you want to say it, put here, and it benefits a lot of species. And it's beneficial to us, too, to know kind of what it looked like, because you lose touch. You forget that." She believed that it was important for everyone to keep in touch with the natural world, because it let us see how we fit into the great web of life. This was especially important in the Valley, where human beings laid the strands of the web, because it showed people that our idea of beauty wasn't the only idea of beauty.

"Yeah," she said, "people kind of pooh-pooh on it. They're just like, 'Oh, what's so great about this?' It's like, well, these birds sure think it's awesome. That's what's so great about it. If you build it, they'll come." She carried a reverential, almost spiritual, respect for the land. "I grew up Muslim," she said. "That's where I get my first name." Jihadda didn't enjoy that religious experience. She found it constrictive, and when she moved to Wasco, she vowed that if someone invited her to church, she would go. She'd been attending a church for two years. "But as I learned more and more about the Bible," she said, "Adam and Eve and whatnot, I just think, 'Here are these other places in the world, on this globe, where these people had paradise. How do you know where this was?'" Meaning, maybe Eden was in multiple locations. Maybe it was right here on this patch of San Joaquin dirt. The Yokuts led a great life. Wasn't this their Eden? Not that she preached gospel to visitors. This was just one way to think about a landscape whose most dramatic feature was a twenty-foot rise of sand.

"It doesn't have to look like the mountains," Govan said. "Not everything can be Montana and piney and fir trees and this and that.

You know, there's beauty here too." Govan steered the truck down the dirt road.

Talking about Yokuts' history, she mentioned how she was reading as much about them as she could, trying to understand not just the ecosystem from a scientific perspective but how first nations used it. "There's this one book," she said. She bought it recently. It was out of print but worth the money, about a guy named Thomas Jefferson Mayfield. He lived with the Yokuts as a kid from 1852 to 1862, and he told a historian the whole story months before he died. "Anyway, it's called *Tailholt Tales*."

I nearly jumped out of my seat. She knew Latta's most famous book too! To keep my composure, I kept my voice down, but I was bubbling with joy. "Yeah," said, "I've got it." Or at least, I had the new condensed version called *Indian Summer*.

Jihadda smiled. "Isn't that the greatest book?"

"I love it," I said. That book was the reason I even knew about Frank Latta. Mayfield and Latta were the reason I was sitting in that truck at that moment.

She said, "I was in tears at the end of that book. I was like, oh my God. I read about the ethnography of the area and all these others, but that one was just like, wow." Mayfield's story deepened her appreciation of the work that the staff did at Atwell, but the part of Latta's book that affected her the most was that part that most affected me too. It was one sentence. When Mayfield's family rode through the Valley in 1850 for the first time, they picked so many flowers that their horses and packs were soon decorated as brightly as the land. "The two most beautiful remembrances I have," Mayfield told Latta, "are of the virgin San Joaquin and of my mother." The original book runs eighty-eight pages, but Mayfield's heart is in that one sentence. "Living with them and being able to illustrate both worlds and just how beautiful the San Joaquin Valley was when he saw it," Govan said, "that got me."

The Yokuts who raised Mayfield used to boat down to the lake to fish and trade. "And I guarantee he came here to spend time when he was a child," Govan said, "because it was a dry spot."

It thrilled me to finally meet another person who appreciated that book and this area as much as I did, because kindred spirits were few and far between. Govan was trying to show other people what Mayfield saw, to give them their own ah-ha moment. That required playing strong defense.

Being this large and in the middle of nowhere encouraged a sense of recklessness instead of respect. Looking like a weedy lot didn't help. Atwell partnered with people who did de facto security and monitoring. A huge site like this needed many sets of eyes. But along with break-ins, people snuck around trying to steal things, dump trash, and throw parties. Govan used to stack brush by a pond, and a trained fire crew would burn it. "Some dorks came up here Fourth of July weekend and burned those piles," she said. One of the three piles stood six feet high and twenty-five feet in diameter. Fortunately, the wetland had water in it, which kept the fire from spreading before the fire department arrived.

When asked why he littered the highway, desert writer Ed Abbey said, "After all, it's not the beer cans that are ugly; it's the highway that is ugly." Govan minded the cans. And the dumped car parts, appliances, and asphalt shingles, along with the feral cats, who hunted endangered wildlife.

The beer cans still lay on the floorboard when Govan paused to investigate cigarette butts on the shoulder. She found a box filled with white canisters on the property once. Law enforcement said they contained ingredients used to make meth. Recently, some off-road driver tore through the Tipton kangaroo rat habitat along Homeland Canal. She shook her head, "I need to talk to people about what they can and can't do here." She frequently found emaciated dogs along that canal. They never came when she called them. Someone recently dumped two Chihuahuas at Atwell headquarters. She kept dog food there for that reason. Worse yet, a guy murdered his girlfriend and dumped her body on a small canal that feeds the Homeland. A man supposedly found her while collecting trash. She was wrapped in plastic and folded like cardboard.

Govan parked the truck near three hundred acres of what staff called the pasture. It had never been farmed, only grazed.

We got out and walked across the dry grass. In a neighboring field, rusty harvesters sat where the owner had abandoned them decades earlier. To the north, silhouetted trees hovered in the distance.

She said, "You see the ridge?"

I looked around. The horizon stretched forever. I pictured the Spanish fathers walking their horses across it, their brown robes caked in mud. I pictured Yokuts weaving reed boats on a shore that left no trace by the Kettleman Starbucks.

She waved her hand to mimic the land's subtle slope.

Yes, I said, I did.

A breeze rattled the grass.

To me, Sand Ridge was the ultimate embodiment of Americans' relationship with the Valley: we stood right on top of it, it supported us, and we didn't even know it was there.

New federal conservation areas often start with dedicated funding. Atwell never had a dedicated source. The project cost $650,000 to run per year. It used to get $400,000 to operate annually. At the end of 2014 the Bureau of Reclamation was going to cut Atwell's funding, forcing it to operate on $500,000 for five years. Govan was trying to secure other funds.

Besides the research into land retirement's ability to reduce the perched water table and salinization, Atwell offered American taxpayers many other services. Atwell is one of very few large pieces of public land in the Valley where residents could enjoy open space, broad vistas, and native habitat that connects us to the past. The people holding Atwell's purse strings might not be able to quantify those benefits the way they could count the number of feet the toxic water table dropped, but those functions are a core part of the function of public land. And they are qualitatively essential to our hominid brains and sense of identity. If part of the Atwell experiment was, in the Bureau of Land Management's words, to "assess the effects of land retirement on drain water and ground water levels," then it was proving successful.

A 2010 report conducted at Atwell showed that land retirement had locally reduced the size of the toxic perched water table, forcing it further from the root zone. This could benefit the farms surrounding Atwell. Researchers would need more funding to find out.

Back at headquarters, Govan and I studied maps with the AmeriCorps crew. They had a map from 1886 that everyone thought was cool. "Speaking of Latta," she said and disappeared into a back room to find a signed copy of Latta's book *Handbook of Yokuts Indians*. She came out empty handed. "I know it's around here," she said with a shrug. She found it days later and sent me a photo. "To Yoimut," the typed dedication said, "who provided the imagination and information that made this volume possible." Beneath that, in large looping blue script, he signed, "FF Latta, January 1949"

Following the *Alta*, I traveled across the lake bed, too, first heading northwest across its center from Alpaugh to Kettleman City, then north on Highway 43 to Stratford along the lake bed's west side.

Leaving Alpaugh felt like leaving the shore for the open ocean. No towns lay west of it, no visible farmhouses. For twenty-five miles lay nothing but cotton, space as vacant as the days when water pooled here. Instead of water, this was now the kingdom of the Boswell Corporation, where tiny roads with little activity dissected the fields. I saw no people, no cars, just soil, horizon, and sky.

The Valley's emptiest stretches are my favorite stretches—I get tired of people, and I love the spacious view. But in Latta's day, such vacant quarters would have been the riskiest. Nowadays, no people means fewer irritations. Back then, no people meant no help.

In a place this vast and rural, you can still feel stranded. The empty places between Alpaugh and Stratford, Kettleman City and Corcoran, can make you anxious. You better get food *now*, you think. You regret not stopping at the last minimarket to buy two cans of iced coffee— one for now, one for later. The roads here feel so far from the world. Wedged between rows of cotton, irrigation ditches stretch forever into the dusty horizon, the same horizon against which you saw the last Starbucks miles away. The sight of all these fields ignites a desperate, hoarding impulse. You start feeling greedy, clutching at all you consider essential, as if the tiny road wouldn't eventually lead to another suburban-looking strip of fast food on I-5 or Highway 99. You know it will. You just don't know when. You stare at the 360-degree horizon of this empty quarter and feel lost. Goodbye civilization! Hello nothing!

When I reached the old section of Kettleman City on the lake's western shore, a Hispanic woman was walking three kids down Standard Oil Avenue in the afternoon. Dogs barked. An old pool table sat in a yard beside a vintage green pickup truck, and a glass stood on the table's edge. Then the town turned itself over to fields. Tulare Lake's dry northwest shore outside Kettleman City was the opposite of city, a land defined by people's absence.

On Highway 43 north, a pickup passed me hauling a crashed biplane on a flatbed trailer, its bruised, chipped body set on top of its detached wings, the corpse of a bird that failed to take flight. Semis pulled in front of me and slowed me down. There was no other traffic to slow. Latta's crew floated along the shore to reach Stratford—this time, playing it safe by keeping the land in sight. The road to Stratford took me along the old lake bed's northwestern shore. According to old maps, the lake shore stretched as far north as Stratford. According to Haslam's book *The Other California*, the lake often stretched farther north to neighboring Lemoore and south to the Allensworth state historical monument. According to Latta, talking about Tulare Lake involved playing the "Where was the old shoreline?" game. "Let us now see," he wrote in *Little Journeys*, "where their level would place the shore line of Tulare Lake." Allensworth? Yes. Corcoran? Yes. But in one year, the southern shore stretched south to the town of Alpaugh; in another year, it would reach farther east to Allensworth. Trying to understand the lake's complicated shifting boundaries could get so confusing that it made you want to quit trying. Of the challenge, Latta wrote, "One might as well ask, 'How big is a cloud of smoke?' Tulare Lake was never stationary long enough for us to learn how big it was."

From the road, the area just looks flat, but the Tulare Lake bed actually slopes up in a bowl between Corcoran and Kettleman, Alpaugh and Lemoore, on up to its reed-choked outlet near Halls Corner. Besides the lake's fluctuating size, the wind blew strong enough to push the shore atop the flat bed, like an egg on a hot greased skillet. "The wind had considerable effect on the shoreline of Tulare Lake," Latta wrote. "When the north wind blew for several hours the lake would begin moving south. If the wind continued for several days the south level would rise as much as a foot. The north shore would move southward as much as three or four miles, uncovering extensive mudflats and swamp bottom. When the wind stopped, the water went back to its former shore lines. So the lake really wandered about over an area of many square miles slightly above the actual stable lake level." The Chunut man who told Latta about sleeping in his family's boat for three nights also described how, when the north wind blew, the Yokuts on Atwell's Island sometimes woke up with water in their beds.

Once Americans forced out all the Yokuts and seized the lake bed, they fished and made their living farming. First, people planted wheat. Harvesting flat fenceless lots was easy. Wheat didn't need irrigation, and it liked the sun. Of the Tulare Basin's crop, 90 percent was wheat in 1884. After its dry-farming period, the region moved to cotton, partly because the Boswell family bought the region and planted cotton. This was the center of J. G. Boswell's empire, a land so vast that even the nation's largest farmer could do nearly whatever he wanted without people noticing.

People call the San Bernardino area the Inland Empire, but the name fits the Tulare Basin too. Two nation-states existed here, neither of which many outsiders have heard of: the Yokuts nation, the largest nonagricultural population in presettlement North America, and J. G. Boswell's nation. There are scores of reasons to loathe Boswell's business practices and environmental record. In a region that grows over 250 different crops, cotton is one of the top five that require the most water and chemicals. But I had to admit that Boswell puts every part of that cotton plant to use, not to be generous, not to be environmental, but to make money.

Nothing valuable gets wasted. The cotton seed gets pressed for oil that ends up in everything from cookies to mayonnaise, as well as cosmetics and gunpowder. Ranchers feed cows cottonseed. The fine hairs that cover the seeds get used in dollar bills, toothpaste, and lunch meat casings. Monetize all pieces of the plant to maximize profits. Many growers can't do that with their crops. Grape skins and seeds can be used after the fruit gets juiced, but lettuce and kiwis are one-use wonders. Cotton, as much as I loathe its production, is incredibly versatile. This was one reason J. G. Boswell liked it so much. Thanks to the way trends turn today's clothing into tomorrow's trash, part of my frugal, environmental mind couldn't get past the fact that fashion trends move so quickly, that clothing gets retired quickly, and that obsolescence means that most of the five hundred pounds of fiber that came from a bale of cotton got wasted. By extension, that means that so much of this land gets wasted. That frustrated me. The part that impressed me was how far that bale of cotton beyond the fiber actually got stretched.

Productive as the land was, there wasn't much to see from the road, definitely no evidence of lakeshores or concentrated wealth. In fact, in full daylight, the lake bed felt sinister, scorched brown and tenuous, held together by a frayed network of drying canals, like a fish drawing breaths in a net. It was unpopulated enough as to seem forsaken, though it was actually one of the most managed lands on earth. I never found the mineral-stained shore I looked for outside Kettleman. The only evidence of the lake I spotted was also the subtlest: the words "Westlake Farms" painted on the side of a long silver propane container near a low metal building.

Not far away, a huge orchard had recently knocked over its nut trees because of the drought. Their stiff, crooked bodies lay among their shattered branches. Growers had a lot at stake.

Twelve miles outside Stratford, amid lush living orchards that suddenly came to life on both sides of the road, a billboard for Tachi Palace casino said, "Come for the Fun."

Stratford was tiny: 1,200 people. Instead of surrounding a town square, the small town center was built around an elongated circle lined with one-story commercial buildings. Most were unoccupied. One had fallen down completely, exposing a large gravel foundation behind the standing front wall.

La Fuente Market and Hardin's Grocery were the circle's hub of activity. Two filtered-water machines and a vacant liquor store separated them, near a pay phone that no longer worked. Off the circle, Sadler Honey Company occupied a shed near Crisp Warehouse. Crisp had a scale-and-grade house for commodities and offered both "Ag Commodity Storage" and "Seed Processing Grain Sales." Two young girls in hairnets walked to a house across the street, on their break. Next to Crisp, six men in hairnets hung out in the A&M Market's lot. It was 5:15 on Monday. They spent their break leaning against the brick fence. When one guy looked at his phone, he started trotting back to the warehouse, as the two girls strolled out of the house toward Crisp, carrying a white Styrofoam take-out container and sharing a drink. A loud noise boomed from inside the facility, under the beeping of a backing forklift. I studied the door, waiting for smoke or people to rush out. Was that an accident? None of the men in the market turned their heads.

Overhead, a loud jet roared as it dropped low in the distance, headed for the Lemoore Naval Air Station to the north. Down the street, a man in jeans, brown boots, and a blue ball cap carried a twelve-pack of Bud Light through the town circle, and a washing machine stood in a house's front yard, with a wooden sign on top listing For Sale. The yard had no grass, so there was nothing for the machine to kill. In an arid land, it was refreshing to see so little lawn grass. In fact, after driving the lake bed, it was nice to be back in town.

After camping outside Stratford on the northern shore of Tulare Lake Wednesday night, the *Alta* broke camp Thursday morning and aimed for the land on the other side of the Kings River. They were two days behind schedule.

The Kings spilled more snowmelt into Tulare Lake than any other river. By the time it reached the lake's north shore, the river split into a web of sloughs and channels so large they got their own names: Clark Fork, North Fork, Faull Slough, Boggs Slough. All the sediment they deposited over thousands of years formed a vast alluvial fan that kept Tulare Lake and its other rivers from flowing north into the San Joaquin River and the ocean. Farmers eventually turned that web of sloughs into a web of canals with names like Settlers Ditch, often keeping the course of the original waterways, and their efforts turned one of the San Joaquin's most verdant, fertile areas into one of the world's great raisin grape regions. To outsiders, it looks like any other part of the Valley, unless you're really looking. Latta's crew were looking. They needed two of those sloughs to reach San Francisco.

Historically, Tulare Lake released its excess through a series of channels on the north shore, the largest of which was Fish Slough. Fish Slough flowed into Fresno Slough, which carried water forty miles north into the San Joaquin River. Latta wrote, "In its natural state this outlet was overgrown with swamp-grass, tules, swamp-willow and other native plants, which probably raised the free level to as much as 215 feet. Pioneers describe the vicinity of Summit Lake as having been covered with an impassable growth of tules and swamp willow 20 or more feet in height. Only by climbing an oak tree were early travelers able to get their bearings." Latta said that 1878 was the last year the lake spilled into Fresno Slough naturally. "According to historical records," he wrote in *Little Journeys*, "Tulare Lake was above the 207 foot level and discharging into [the] San Joaquin river in 1844; from 1850 to 1851; from 1852 to 1855; from 1862 to 1865; and from 1868 to 1877." By the time the *Alta* reached these sloughs, farmers had been channelizing some of them since the late 1800s, and dry spots and impoundments forced Latta's crew to walk their boat around them. But first, they had to find Fish Slough.

Considering the trouble they had finding Alpaugh, they probably didn't feel wildly confident. The boys might have doubted Latta's navigational skills. Latta might have doubted himself. He got them lost on a lake. This area was a maze. How would they get through? No Lake Exit sign marked their channel. Few if any obvious ripples would have shown the current's direction. They would have had to float north, triangulate their vague position on maps, and enter a mess of bulrushes, algae, and clouds upon clouds of mosquitoes darkening the bright gaps above the reed beds and humming like the electric lines that would one day run through here. Once they did that, they would hope that they'd entered the right channel. If they hadn't, the shallow water would peter out, and they'd have to hack through tall reeds and carry their boat across dry land to find another channel, their pants caked with mud in ninety-degree heat. If they chose correctly, they would float through shallow water, with all their doubts, aching joints, and bated breath, waiting for it to peter out too. Good synthetic sunscreen didn't hit the American market until the 1950s, so the crew would have been pretty red at this point, including the fingers they crossed about their chosen direction.

The *Alta* left the lake five miles west of a tiny place called Halls Corner. Halls is still there. It stands where two long roads intersect. It has a traffic light now, as well as stores that sell seed, hay, and gravel. I know nothing about Hall, and there isn't much to his corner. Instead of following Latta's route north through the Valley's center right now, I headed east toward Highway 99, to take a brief detour away from the ghost water. I wanted to photocopy some of Latta's old books at the Fresno public library and hear some of these stories in his own words. First, I needed a place to spend the night.

3

Hanford, the Other California Dream

Neither the Crusades nor Alexander's expedition to India
can equal this emigration to California.

—C. N. Ormsby

From Stratford I drove past the Yokuts' palatial Tachi Palace casino
to Hanford. Until this week, I'd never heard of Hanford.

When I exited the freeway in the dark, I entered another quaint
time capsule downtown, this one built around a large grassy court-
house square, with the old-school Superior Dairy ice cream parlor
on one corner, the historic Fox Theatre on another, and an imposing
brick building between them that looked like a castle. I'd traveled over
170 miles from my starting point in Bakersfield, and even though
Latta hadn't boated here, I wanted to explore this charming old-
fashioned place. But it was getting late, so I found a parking lot on
the train tracks next to the Comfort Inn.

I'd already arranged my bedding in the back of my rental car. That's
how you make car camping work—secrecy. Many days had passed
since my motel room in Lost Hills, and three more would pass before
I got another. In 1862 William Brewer met a shepherd in the Diablo
Range of Stanislaus County who hadn't seen anyone in three weeks.
Once in a while I liked it that way. Camping suited me more than
motel sterility, and in this land of highways, the cramped backs of
cars passed for tents, and that saved me money I didn't have to spend
in the first place.

When I lifted my head from the pillow at sunrise, the world outside was white. Fog swirled around power lines. It absorbed the tops of water towers and a rusted packing shed. The sky had no dimensions. It seemed both distant and within reach. Sleeping semis parked in the dirt across the tracks. To the east, the sun pushed a single concentrated point of light against the flat sky, and the sky pushed back. It didn't take long to find a place to eat.

The Star Restaurant, Hanford's oldest dining establishment, stood on the next block along the southern edge of downtown. At 9:00 a.m. that Tuesday, two tables and eight of the restaurant's ten booths were filled. "Rudolph the Red-Nosed Reindeer" played overhead. A paunchy man told the cashier, "Time to climb in the truck," after he paid his bill, and a solitary senior citizen with dark, puffy eyes ate in a sunny corner. Christy Cordoba, the waitress, kept swinging by his booth asking, "How you doing George?" "You need some more coffee, George?" He didn't speak. His glasses had a sun visor that flipped up as he read the paper. When George went to pay, he shuffled toward the register in a blue windbreaker and blue sneakers, leaning on a cane. "Bye, George," the cashier said. "See you tomorrow."

Open since 1901, the Star and its neighboring buildings formed a row that looked like a Wild West movie set, with thin wooden beams running up to worn wooden balconies and eaves. To the left stood the grand Artesia Hotel, where an artesian well fed the lobby fountain in 1891 and where small businesses now operate. To the right, two vacant storefronts awaited tenants. In the Star, historic town photos hung above each booth, mixed with multiple copies of the Norman Rockwell poster where Rockwell paints himself beside the caption "Every Job Is a Self-Portrait of the Person Who Did It." That also seemed true of restaurants' relationships to towns. Like Hanford, the Star was antique but not retro. It survived because it slung good food and conversation and everyone went there, and it just happened to be in an attractive vintage building. Cordoba worked the room.

One of her regulars asked her, "Hey, where's my water?"

Cordoba's booming voice cut through Bing Crosby's "White Christmas." "You didn't ask for no water. We're on a drought!"

By 9:20 the fog had cleared, and a cloud of pigeons lifted from the water tower to make aimless figure eights before landing back on top.

Cordoba's father served on the chamber of commerce. He used to be the president, and she grew up in a house on the town's nice north side, but she always partied south of the tracks.

"I'd run away," she said. "They didn't know where to find me. I was w-i-i-i-ld." She was thirty-seven now, with a teenage son and a young daughter she feared might turn wild too. She'd worked at the Star for ten years and loved it and her boss. At night she went to school, studying criminology to go into corrections.

Allen, heavyset with soft arms and a round face, sat on the counter's last swiveling oak stool, hunched over his coffee. He lived in the opera house on the other side of the block. Built in 1893 to seat seven hundred, it was once the only opera house between San Francisco and Los Angeles. After a fire destroyed the fourth-floor stage in 1929, it became a series of hotels before its conversion into apartments in 1986. Rent was surprisingly low for such a beautiful building. Some claimed it was because of bedbugs and bad management. Allen said that it was because this was Hanford. He'd rented a one-bedroom there for fourteen years and had known Cordoba for ten. "She's an excellent waitress," he said, "best in Kings County."

Cordoba did a fake curtsy. "I had to go to school for that."

She had a solid-colored band tattooed across her bicep, hoop earrings, and thick mascara. Her dark ponytail draped against her white T-shirt as she refilled waters and took food orders, but she took marching orders from no one. Attending to fifteen tables and nine stools alone from 6:00 a.m. to 2:30 p.m. required intelligence, grace, and speed, and she couldn't afford to wait for people to figure out toast or biscuit. "Oh, yeah, no," she said, sorting tickets. "I don't have time."

Hanford's small size charmed many people but felt smothering to others. "I could walk outside and see someone I know," Cordoba said. "That's not always good." No matter how much Hanford grew, it couldn't loosen the ties that bound a lifelong resident to the people they'd spent their life around. Why exactly had I come to Hanford, she asked. People frequently asked me that in the Valley: What was I doing *here*? Just looking around, I said.

The Southern Pacific Railroad established Hanford in 1877, the way it had established Tulare, Earlimart, Goshen, Lemoore, and Tipton when it laid tracks in the 1870s and 1880s. The Kings River flows north of Hanford. The Kings' high water table and ample surface water supported a vast, spacious woodland of large oak trees by what became Kingsburg and Laton. Farther west, the woods opened into a moist, mushy grassland whose channels required ferries to cross.

After riding on the sweltering plain for six days in 1864, William Henry Brewer welcomed the shade and good water here. "And what a relief!" he told a friend in a letter. "We are again in good spirits." This wasn't like the land around Bakersfield or Corcoran, where the scrubby saline desert needed help to bloom. This was prime, naturally irrigated farmland. As the Spanish father Pedro Muñoz wrote while searching for a mission site in 1806, "All the meadows are well covered with oaks, alders, cottonwood, and willow. The river abounds with beaver and fish." He was another self-appointed savior trying to collect Yokuts to "save" their souls and make them work as slaves in the coastal missions, but the Americans lucky enough to settle the Kings delta found the same lush, easy land that Muñoz described. The Kings provided so much water that before it was dammed in 1954, not all farmers needed small ditches to irrigate their fields. Some actually dug wells just to lower the water table.

Hanford's location supplied ample water for crops and productive gardens. Like many towns near the old lake, people grew cotton, alfalfa, and wheat, and those feed crops helped turn this into a dairy town. Hanford is the seat of Kings County, but for a medium-sized town, its architectural beauty and strong economy had always set it apart. Even when its roads were dirt, it had metropolitan sophistication and the reputation as an oasis in the desert. It's the kind of place that should house an exhibit about a local visionary like Latta.

In 1908 a Southern Pacific Railroad employee named Andrew J. Wells wrote a small book designed to publicize the Valley and expand the railroad business. "The streets of Hanford," he wrote, "are well shaded and the whole place attractive for reason of vines and palms and a variety of ornamental trees. An opera-house, a free library, good hotels, schools and churches, a creamery, packinghouses, condensed-milk cannery, fruit cannery and winery, and solid business blocks attest [to] the prosperity of this young town." The town still wows people today.

California TV personality Huell Howser filmed a Hanford episode of his PBS show *Road Trip with Huell Howser* in 2008. Howser produced another popular show called *California's Gold*, which explored historic and scenic locations, from military forts to overlooked places like Weedpatch. In both, he did the classic mic-in-hand street interview with everyone from surfers to chefs. This Hanford episode still sent out-of-towners from far afield to eat at Star and Superior Dairy. The Star predated Superior by twenty-nine years. When the Star opened, this was Front Street. Three thousand people lived in Hanford, and they parked their horse-drawn wagons on the dirt. It was dizzying to imagine all the cultural developments the restaurant had lived through: horses to cars; three thousand to fifty thousand residents; TVs to laptops. Latta was nine when it opened.

Eddy Funahashi owned the building and Ed's Tick Tock Jewelers next door. When his grandparents and great-aunt and great-uncle opened the restaurant, many California businesses followed the rampant institutional racism of the era and served only white customers. But the Star welcomed everybody, including the large populations of black cowboys, Chinese railroad workers and shepherds, and Mexican and Portuguese farmworkers, and it provided a safe space for people of color to congregate. As Funahashi told a local magazine, "They would turn no one away." Despite their hospitality, racist, fearmongering Caucasians sent the Funahashi family, along with 120,000 other Japanese Americans, to internment camps during World War II, where they were treated as threats to national security.

The Star closed, and someone stole the contents of its basement, including Eddy's grandfather's violin, which he talked about until his dying day. Friends maintained the property, and when the war ended, a fellow Japanese family became the first in a series of owners the Funahashis leased to. Now Rotha Roger Nop runs it. Nop grew up in Cambodia, escaped the Khmer Rouge, and owned a Los Angeles doughnut shop before stumbling onto the Star when it was between owners. At first, he just managed and kept the books. When his cook quit one morning, he started cooking too.

Sunset and other magazines have published articles about Hanford. Despite the publicity, Cordoba said that a slew of longtime downtown businesses had closed, and others had to compete with the nearby Super Walmart. Many locals liked the megastore. They had mixed feelings about the proposed Costco.

"I think it's good," Allen said.

Cordoba raised one brow. "I'm assuming it's a good thing."

Allen estimated that between 60 percent and 80 percent of residents had some connection to agriculture, including him. In the early 1900s his great-grandparents had a dairy not far from downtown, which the high school bought and turned into a baseball diamond. His parents grew up in Hanford and raised him outside Fresno. For work, he drove eighteen-wheelers and dairy tankers between San Diego and the Bay Area, until some sort of back injury sidelined him. After he started having seizures, the state revoked his class A commercial license. He hasn't driven semis since. "Not a big thing," he said, "or I guess I'm where I'm supposed to be."

Back in the 1950s and 1960s, people in Fresno used to get to know their neighbors. But Fresno is now California's sixth-largest city by area, so Allen returned to Hanford when the fabric of Fresno's community felt frayed. Hanford had no ocean views. Many days, smog obscured its scenic mountain backdrop, but it had preserved the civil pace he liked in Fresno as a kid. "Fresno is just traffic," he said. "I don't like traffic." When he grew up, it seemed to take forever to reach downtown; Fresno's rural space had filled with one long nightmare that he hoped wouldn't swallow Hanford.

Even though Fresno was twenty-eight miles away and was still separated by farmland, its congested spirit hung over surrounding towns the way mortality hung over people—far enough that you didn't have to see it but close enough to know that it would get you eventually. Many Hanford locals disliked Fresno. They took advantage of its Trader Joe's and medical facilities but complained about its drivers and crime. A symbol of the good life's ruination, it functioned as a barometer to measure a certain quality of life and as a case study of the way places go wrong.

Right now, Hanford doesn't have Fresno's suburban sprawl or density. Being set off from Highway 99 has spared it the usual chain store clutter of local highway towns, and isolation has so far spared it the bedroom-community fate of nearby towns like Clovis and Fowler. Travelers don't even know Hanford exists. But it's downtown zoning ordinances and organizations like Main Street Hanford that help preserve its small-town feel by dictating what kind of stores can open where and how they can look. The idea is to preserve a somewhat unified, turn-of-the-century appearance; protect older buildings; control density; and keep out skyscrapers. When a historic building burns down, as the Vendome Hotel did in 2012, its replacement looks more like Hanford than a suburban mall. The restrictions reminded me of Santa Barbara, where codes required every new downtown building to look Spanish colonial to match its historic architecture. Still, Allen saw changes from the inside.

"I don't know if you can tell," he said. "It's slowly filling up." I couldn't. This was my first day here. It seemed the right size to me. But Allen feared that Fresno would tarnish what he called Hanford's hidden jewel.

Working-class Californians kept leaving the coast for the interior, because they could find an affordable house with a yard here, a good school, small-town values, and a slower pace of life. As one Modesto real estate agent told author Gerald Haslam years ago, "We have a rule of thumb that for every extra mile you drive to the Bay Area, you save $1,000 in the price of a house." Maybe they couldn't find the same tech, entertainment, or finance jobs they could on the coast, but they could get steady agriculture and manufacturing jobs, jobs in schools or government, admin or retail, work in factories for Frito-Lay and Del Monte, or they could test their devotion to the area the way many Modesto residents did by commuting two hours each way to jobs in the Bay Area. It was nuts. Between the economy, food system, and water supply, the ancient physical divisions between coastal and interior California were rapidly dissolving. Geographically, it's clear where the Valley ends and the coastal slope begins. Economically, parts of the two had become one region, sending the Valley farther from its agricultural base and blending it culturally with the industrial urban Bay Area. "Whether we like it or not," Modesto's mayor Carol Whiteside once said, "our region is now far more closely linked with the Bay Area than it is to the rest of the Central Valley." Long commutes between both regions created a new reality that Californians had to deal with. A high-speed rail line between LA and San Francisco offered one way to fuse them more smoothly.

People had been discussing the pros and cons of high-speed rail since the first surveys were conducted in 1993. California senator Quentin L. Kopp and Representative Jim Costa's Senate Bill 1420 established the High-Speed Rail Authority and sought funds for construction. In 2008, 52.7 percent of voters approved $9.95 billion in state funds to build the train. Then things got complicated.

People filed lawsuits. Land surveys dragged on, and voters started wondering whether this would become a Boston Big Dig situation. Officials asked for patience. Like the bullet trains of Japan and the Trans-European Transport Network, California's high-speed trains would travel over two hundred miles per hour and shrink hours-long travel times to minutes. By getting commuters off the road, the system aimed to reduce statewide congestion, fatalities, and emissions. The system would create 300,000 temporary jobs and 450,000 permanent jobs, connect 80 percent of the state, and save drivers money. No one could deny the fact that California's traffic was terrible or that its population was growing. Accepting congestion as a baseline only ensured that it got worse, said Representative Costa. High-speed trains were a long-term solution. Unfortunately, the bulk of the tracks would run through the Valley, and to a region that already felt like too many governmental and environmental outsiders like me dictated the terms of its business and life, that aroused suspicion.

Sure, trains would ease the commute, but ease of access would encourage more urbanites to move to the Valley and ruin the quality of life they sought here. Instead of small towns, critics said, the train ultimately serviced people in LA and San Francisco, people who could zip in and out of their affordable inland homes without having to know their neighbors or get too involved locally, creating more fair-weather residents who treated small towns as investments instead of communities, people without roots. Allen didn't trust it.

"It's just going to take up a lot of valuable farmland," he said. "It's a big mistake, pumping so much money in and out, when they could be pumping money into water restoration, which they should've started years ago." He understood the state's need to examine every detail before building tracks and stations, but he still found the pace and expense ridiculous. They changed the routes so often that Kings County might not even get a station, he said, and if Hanford did, how many jobs would it create? I sympathized with his skepticism. But following Latta, I saw this railway as the next stage in an ongoing process where each generation created an improved system of transportation that came with its own set of future problems to solve. In the 1800s, horseback rides took days. Steamboats got stuck in rivers. Old trains got derailed and delayed. Model Ts broke down. New cars get trapped in traffic so dense they might as well have broken down. Highways weren't efficient with this many cars on them. Building more freeways wouldn't alleviate congestion the way fewer cars and better trains would. If rivers and bumpy roads were the highways of Latta's day, then high-speed railways were the highways of tomorrow. The original railroad built Hanford. When Amtrak established local service, it didn't destroy the Valley. It created a convenient $5 Amtrak ride to Fresno that locals constantly talked about, yet many still resisted high-speed rail.

A sense of territoriality permeated the debate. Outsiders had designed much of the rail system, outsiders who freely ate the Valley's food and drank Sierra Nevada water but didn't set foot here if they didn't have to. If you want to live here, many locals argued, then work here like everyone else. For people only commuting through the Valley, for urbanites who take all those hi-res pictures of their pretty dinners and vibrant farmers' market produce, take a look around. This place feeds you. It's time to respect it.

I like high-speed trains. The entire United States would benefit from a national rail system as reliable and efficient as Japan's, with collapsed travel times and an end to our addiction to fossil fuel and cars. I also like the Valley's residents' determination to maintain their identity, agricultural productivity, and autonomy. Not with water, because they wasted the hell out of it and didn't always understand how it worked. But with the trains, commuters, and coastal migration, they had reasons for caution, and they did need to protect their farmland. The country needs its food, and the Valley deserves its jobs. And really, too few coastal folks respected this region before the rail project, so why would they expect locals to welcome them with open arms because they decided to move or commute through here?

Two months after my breakfast at the Star, an event in Fresno commemorated the official groundbreaking, although the train would eventually get hung up on where engineers and politicians would build the train stations, leaving resisters to ride the small Kings Area Rural Transit bus system town to town and to decide if they were ready to get on the right side of history.

Another issue that riled Allen was water. Even though he didn't fully trust the government, he believed that the government should use state money to fix the Valley's water problems instead of building the train. "Drought wouldn't be so bad," he said, "if they had dams built or aquifers that would've provided or held back water for instances like this." That wasn't true, I said.

First off, you don't build aquifers. Nature does, and people were draining them.

Second, there already were dams on every major Sierra Nevada river that flowed into the Valley, from the Stanislaus by Modesto to the Kern in Bakersfield, and the land was still dry. The problem is consumption and snowpack, not damming. You can't fill a dam if no snow falls in the sierras. Unlike Latta's generation, Allen didn't want dams. He wanted *more* dams, because he believed that by building additional impoundments, you could trap more water to release to the main impoundments for agriculture. They already did that on some waterways. There still wasn't enough water to fill the reservoirs, and dry rivers can't recharge drying aquifers. The state's Department of Water Resources monitors 154 large reservoirs in California. During my visit, most suffered historic lows, from the enormous Lake Shasta up north to Lake McClure near here, exposing shorelines people had never seen before. Would more dams raise those levels?

It disappointed me that even an engaged, lifelong resident with a history in agriculture didn't understand how his water system worked. Maybe he just repeated what he heard on the news and from other agricultural workers. We all parroted watered-down third-generation information to some degree, including me; you can't read every primary source. But his was a grossly inaccurate portrait of hydrology. I only partially challenged him. No native wanted to hear this from some outsider, and in order to talk accurately about solutions, I needed to understand public perception. For that I needed to listen. So as he spoke, my inner voice yelled *Come on, Allen!* internally.

He went on about the train money and dams: "I know there's Folsom Lake at the Sacramento, that there's a dam there. I don't know of any other dams up there, just the Folsom." Up there are the enormous Shasta, Oroville, and Comanché Lakes. Folsom is small compared to the other reservoirs near here, like New Melones and Don Pedro.

"I don't necessarily agree with what the politicians are doing," he said, "but really nothing you can do about it. Well, some of them want to restore, you know, build more dams, which I know Devin Nunes has been trying to push that for years, and now they're finally realizing, since we're in a drought, yeah, we should, but it's just getting it started when you've got environmentalists, if they find a rat or something on a piece of ground, or, oh, this is this natural habitat, and so they'd put a stop to anything. A lot of the water just goes out to the ocean. From the Sacramento Delta, that water goes out to the ocean. We have the San Joaquin River, which the water eventually ends up in the ocean. That river runs year-round."

No, it doesn't. It did one hundred years ago. Once it leaves the sierra, sixty miles of it are completely dry year-round.

"Yeah," he said, when corrected, "at least it was. I don't know about now." He also didn't know about the "rat or something."

Only about 5 percent of the Valley's native habitat remains for kangaroo rats and other native species. Farms and cities use the rest of the land. Furthermore, the rats at Atwell were part of a grand experiment scientists were using to improve the groundwater that people like us drink. That project isn't just for rats or environmentalists. It's for farmers and kids and citizens affected by salinization. On top of that, Bureau of Land Management properties like Atwell are by definition multiuse! His mix of confidence and misinformation frustrated me, the way it had people acting like they knew exactly what they were talking about, while characterizing the so-called opposition as the misinformed ones. That delta water that "just goes out to the ocean" isn't just going to waste like some broken toilet. The ocean is the natural outlet for all San Joaquin Valley water, and there wasn't as much water flowing from it as there used to be, especially that wasn't salty. Where else was it supposed to go, over Donner Pass into Nevada? *Read better sources!* I yelled to myself. *Do more homework!* Sure, he knew more about local feed crops and farming than I ever would, but since he didn't even know that a huge stretch of the San Joaquin River was dry and that every nearby sierra river was dammed, then he didn't know Valley Hydrology 101, so he didn't get to make declarative statements about supposedly simple solutions to "solve" the drought like he did.

In order to get his argument straight, I repeated back his ideas about trapping more water and asked why the state wasn't doing that right now. "You'd have to ask the politicians that," he said.

"Whenever they have a drought," Allen said, "they always call it the seven-year drought. So, that's mother nature." And people in the Valley just had to ride it out. That's how life had always been here. Savvy, wealthy businesspeople like Miller and Lux and Boswell bought enough water and acres to survive cyclical floods and droughts; now modern megafarmers used their size, portfolio, and power to do the same. The drought cycle was the same, so I expected floods and heavy rains by 2016 or 2017. But those wouldn't ultimately quench California's growing thirst. Most of what had changed were the water table conditions.

With little to no surface irrigation in canals during the current drought, farmers pumped well water to irrigate crops. As the table dropped, people dug more and deeper wells, and the overpumping caused the land's surface to drop and made the aquifer saltier. People around here talked about the challenges of groundwater pumping and salts, because they worried about staying in business, but like many concerned citizens and farmers, Allen believed that pumping restrictions were the true enemy, not overpumping. Dams and more wells were his answer. Obviously, I thought he was wrong.

"Especially with Madera County drying up," he said. "I heard that Madera County, on the west side, a lot of land's drying up over there. There's a lot of restrictions on pumping. They're going to start metering how much a farmer uses." That's a good thing. People have overlooked overuse for too long. The reality is, digging deeper wells only lessens farmers' ability to use the aquifer to survive future droughts, and there would be future droughts. They can pump now, but how long will those wells stay wet when they've already dropped hundreds of feet and aren't getting replenished? If Americans want farming to endure in this dry land, farmers need to grow crops that use less surface water, not dig deeper wells. So far, that isn't happening enough.

California, not Wisconsin, is the nation's leading dairy producer. In 2015 the state had about 1,500 dairies with 1.77 million dairy cows that produced 20 percent of America's milk. Despite its aridity, two-thirds of the state's dairy comes from the San Joaquin Valley.

People raise beef cattle on the west side by 1-5 and dairy cattle on the east. Rather than pasture, most milk cows here eat what's called feed crops, such as hay, corn, milo, and different silage, even local almond hulls and cottonseed depending on the stock and price. In the early 1900s, alfalfa from nearby towns like Alpaugh supported Hanford's dairy industry. As local yields drop, some dairies import out-of-state hay, but most feed is still locally grown. On average it takes 67 gallons of water to produce an 8.4-ounce glass of milk, which means it takes 144 gallons of water to produce 1 gallon of milk. Ninety-five percent of that water goes to grow feed. Feed producers often use dairy farmers' cow manure as fertilizer. It's more ecologically sound to monetize manure recycling than for farmers to use chemical fertilizer, but the amount of water required to grow feed still makes producing dairy in a drought-prone region with saline soil an expensive, unsustainable proposition.

Unlike bucolic wooded rural Illinois and Vermont, where dairies are often small, the Valley has what are called megadairies. Some milk a couple of thousand head a day. Farmer A. J. Bos milks ten thousand a day on family land by Bakersfield. It's hard to picture that scale. It's also hard to imagine how neighboring Tulare County can justify being the state's largest milk producer—27 percent in 2013—when its wells kept going dry and residents without reliable taps were applying for the State Water Resources Control Board's free bottled water delivery program. Many dairy farmers cut costs by irrigating crops with water recycled from their barns, called barn water. Some growers received government subsidies to conserve water by leaving their land fallow. Others fallowed acres to focus their limited resources on growing better feed on fewer acres. All Americans need these farmers to stay in business, just as the farmers surely want to stay in business. To do that, the Valley needs new, drought-adapted crops and efficient production methods that change, not perpetuate, the status quo.

Many local ranchers and farmers had no intention of quitting farming because of a seven-year drought, Allen said. They'd survived past droughts and would survive this if they played it smart and had the finances. Fortunately, economics were moving some farmers to switch from feed and dairy to walnuts and almonds. During the drought, so many progressives wrote articles like *Mother Jones*'s popular "Your Almond Habit Is Sucking California Dry" and complained about how thirsty California almonds were, but compared to dairy cattle, nuts looked efficient. Many fellow progressives I knew in Oregon worried about the wisdom of Californians producing almond milk while they freely ate ice cream and California cheese. I pointed out the contradiction and explained that when nut growers use drip irrigation systems and soil-moisture gauges that time water's release, they stretch their resources and reduce waste, and it takes much less water to turn a profit and create protein. It's something Allen thinks farmers should've done years ago. But drip systems cost money to install and maintain, and it's time-consuming to learn a new crop, so that discourages small dairies. At the same time, wetter states like Iowa, South Dakota, Oregon, and Nebraska were actively courting California dairies with more water; fewer regulations; and cheap, ample feed crops. Understandably, some farmers were moving their herds cross-country. Others stayed and suffered.

"What I've seen with kids stepping in," Allen said, "the kids don't know how to manage it like the parents or grandparents did, so they end up losing it, because they borrow against it or borrow against the land." Although it made sense to grow less thirsty crops here, farmers needed economic incentives to do so, not regulatory ones, and I believe one of the ones they deserve is higher profit margins. Meaning, they deserve to make way more money than they currently do. The reason is simple—they feed the nation. "Without that," he said, "everybody in the world will feel it."

Allen and innumerable residents of the Valley used that phrase to defend their right to water, improve public perception, and establish their importance: "This valley feeds the nation." That could not be truer. Residents of the Valley were proud of their important contribution, and you could sense a bit of injured irritation in the phrasing. They were tired of people not giving them credit, and they demanded a little recognition, if not respect. The drought, salinization, and agricultural longevity are business problems for farmers in the Valley to solve, but because millions of people rely on these farmers for food, these are also national issues. All Americans should be concerned and informed about what happens here; instead of causing more divisions between voters, farmers, and consumers, we should work together to create solutions and economic incentives to solve these problems in a way that ensures that farmers can keep farming and make a living. Because it would be better for everyone if the Valley were to feed the nation things it actually needs more than ice cream, milk, and cheese. My main concern was not a rat but sustained productivity. Besides paying more for groceries, I didn't know how to make that happen.

The thing I can never reconcile about farming in a capitalist system is why farmers so often live in debt or on the cusp of bankruptcy season to season when it was their food that kept our civilization alive. What kind of life is that for the people who provide essential services? People all over the world love actors and basketball players and TV personalities, but we don't need them. Yet they, not growers, are the big American breadwinners. I know many Americans can't afford this luxury. I know that many Americans barely scrape by, eating the inexpensive food that we have, but I feel willing now to pay more money for my groceries if I know that the added profits will help keep farmers in business. We all want inexpensive food, but Americans have paid so little for so long that we expect that deli meat, wheat bread, and onions are supposed to be this cheap. Are they? The reason consumers pay so little for food is because of a complex system built on chemical-dependent max yields, bioengineered crops by companies like Monsanto, government subsidies, cheap water, and cheap migrant labor. Those products get passed through capitalism's supply-and-demand grinder and nature's fickle seasons, which puts them in a precarious state both inside and outside the free market in a way that I don't fully understand. But what I know is, through it all, we consumers have gotten used to inexpensive and available food. That's our baseline. It's a dangerously naive position, since small, true family farmers make too little money for the role they play in society. Smaller farmers deserve more stability, because America wouldn't exist without them, so why not pay them more? I think many Americans share my concerns, even though they share my confusion about how agricultural economics work. And I still think that one way to improve the farm industry is for people like me to pay more for small farmers' products. They're certainly worth more.

When I told this to Allen, his brow scrunched. "You want to pay five dollars for a gallon of milk?"

"I don't drink milk," I said, which I admit is an irrelevant answer, "but I feel like if that's what keeps the food coming, that's sort of the social contract."

Allen tried to help me understand economics. "They've got their overhead," he explained. "The price of milk that the dairymen get, if it's too low, they're not going to be able to run their dairies, because the cost of feed has gone up so much, and that, in turn, affects everybody." That overhead was exactly why I was willing to pay more, especially for ice cream and milk, which are luxury items, not essential foods like vegetables and clean water. With tax laws and complex economics, I was out of my league. I could only think out loud as a consumer and a person here to try to understand. He didn't fully understand it all either, and the idea that our economic, social, and ecological ties could bind all Americans' fates in a way that would create a "social contract" escaped him.

"So if feed crops in the Valley require a lot of water," I said, "and the Valley feeds the nation, what's the solution?"

Allen shook his head, "There really is none."

It was complicated, maybe too complicated. Someone like me certainly wasn't going to figure it all out, but it mattered too much to not try.

When I wondered how long this area could remain one of the most productive areas on Earth, he said, "As long as the government will let it." Yet he blamed greed as much as increased water costs for the skyrocketing price of feed.

The prices of different feed changed independently of each other, but during the drought, local hay had gone from $135 a ton to $265 a ton. And it takes many tons to feed animals. Unfortunately, the price producers got for their milk hadn't gone up with costs. So depending on their level of debt, some smaller dairies feared they'd have to sell to bigger dairies or let the bank take over, ending their family's long tradition of farming and taking not only their jobs but their most valuable possession with it—their land. "There's plenty of feed," he said. "It's greed. I attribute it to greed." Producers knew someone would pay those prices, even if it was someone they'd known for years or seen at a place like the Star. "Money's what makes the world go around." Milk too. This place was swimming in it.

Despite our disagreements, I appreciated our ability to have a respectful exchange without getting called a communist or tree hugger, and it impressed me how engaged small-town residents were in the Valley with local issues and how much they appreciated their town's history, like how Jimmy Stewart lived in the opera house for a while and Amelia Earhart once visited Hanford. Many big-city people I knew, including myself, mostly paid attention to national politics and took more interest in the new artisan burger joint down the street than in the origin of the street itself. It was also refreshing not to have to listen to people talk about their food allergies or their dog's special diet over breakfast. The city could get grating.

Allen clutched his ninety-five-cent coffee. Besides friendliness and old buildings, Allen thought everyone should come to Hanford to eat at the Star and get sassed by Cordoba. "Yeah," he said with a smile. "It's good to get harassed."

Bruce Bowen agreed. Dressed in a blue "Bimbo Bakeries USA" sweater, the silver-haired fifty-eight-year-old sat in a booth and sawed into a pancake that filled an entire plate. Bowen grew up in Fresno and moved to Hanford twenty-five years ago to drive delivery trucks for Rainbo and Orowheat. He'd retired and was living off some rental properties and landscaping work when his old boss asked him to deliver Bimbo merchandise three days a week. He worked out of Visalia and could have bought a house there, but he stayed for the same reason as Allen: Hanford now is how Fresno was when he was a kid.

When Bowen moved here, he didn't know anybody. After a few visits, the grocery store staff started calling him by name. The farming community was salt of the earth, he said, and the church organizations were filled with really nice people. His daughter moved away, but she missed the tight-knit community and moved back. "It's like everybody kind of watches out for one another," he said. "It's just that way."

Like most people I met, he raved about local attractions like the car shows, the Renaissance fair, and the annual chili cook-off. Through mouthfuls of food, he suggested that I visit the China Alley Historic District, the Romanesque Hanford Carnegie Museum, and the old haunted jail, called the Bastille, and then talk with Dan Humason, who owned the Hanford Fox Theatre and used to run the projector as a kid. Everyone called him Danny.

Bowen's phone buzzed. "That's my boss." He wedged the phone between his shoulder and cheek and ate while discussing how well their baked goods sold from a certain market's display. After he hung up, he insisted that I visit Superior Dairy.

To most people, Superior was as old as Hanford, and nothing better personified the city's winning combination of dairy, community, and antiquity. Since 1929, Superior has made all its own ice cream. Superior's original owners distributed throughout the Valley from the Hanford location. It was one of the oldest ice-cream parlors in the state. Countless locals grew up eating there, dropping in with their families after church or passing Friday nights in its booths as teenagers. Nowadays, people drive from as far away as Modesto to eat giant sundaes. A lot of high school and college kids work there, because customers are nice and the owners let employees study on the clock, especially when business slows during winter. For kids, Superior is a rite of passage. Bowen's daughter, Hannah, got her first paying job there and used the money to buy her first car. "She went out and got her own apartment," Bowen said, "moved out, and I was like, 'Hold on,' you know? But now she's doing great." Now she was twenty and worked as a waitress at the Yokuts' Tachi Palace casino and at In-N-Out; she was saving for nursing school.

As much as I appreciated Superior's doo-wop charm and its place in the local routine, as an outsider, I saw its cost. The question wasn't whether people deserved a nice ice-cream cone and a summer job. It was whether there are better ways to use the Valley's water and soil than to produce luxury goods, when there are wetter places to do that. To most people, agricultural discussions aren't about matching crops to landscape. They're about jobs.

The thing about Hanford, Bowen said, is that if you want to work, you just have to go out and ask for it. "I'll tell you what," he said, "if a kid shows any fortitude or interest in work ethics, people around here will hire them."

He no longer knew if that was true in Fresno. He avoided Fresno and stayed in Hanford, where he could bike around town and park in front of whatever building he wanted. He loved Hanford's simplicity, just as he loved pulling his 1965 Aristocrat trailer to the state park in Pismo and hanging out by the ocean. One of his favorite things was Hanford's farmers' market, where food venders took over downtown and blues and rock bands played on the street. What I heard was hometown pride from someone who'd found his sunny niche where he could make steady money; still afford real estate; have good times in good weather with family; and enjoy a relaxed, active lifestyle. It was literally the California dream, and people were living it far from the iconic coast. The dream, though, has some problems.

Hanford's tap has a bad reputation for smelling like rotten eggs. It wasn't from agriculture, people said; it was natural hydrogen sulfide in the soil. The Valley's water has always had problems, some areas worse than others. During the 1864 drought, William Henry Brewer camped at a "stinking, alkaline" slough between Firebaugh and Fresno that "had the color of weak coffee." Brewer continued, "It smelt bad and tasted worse, and our poor animals drank it protesting. We drank well water which looked better and tasted better, but I think it smelt worse. But in this dry, hot, and dusty air we must drink, and drink much more often." Hanford residents insisted that the sulfur wouldn't hurt you, just repel you, and there was no harm in that. Bowen's boss wouldn't drink fountain soda in Hanford, because she could taste the funk through the syrup. Bowen lived here too long to notice. He held up a glass and stared through the ice. "This water's, I think, filtered."

When he asked Cordoba, she laughed. "Filtered? Smell it. Does it smell filtered?"

I sniffed Bowen's glass. It didn't smell sulfurous.

Months before my visit, the city started chlorinating the supply. Instead of sulfur, people joked that it would now taste like pool. Hanford folks said, no worries—they'd get used to that too. I was worried. Thirteen wells supplied the city, and the city recently retired a few affected by arsenic and dug new ones. What was everyone ingesting?

So many times during conversations on this trip, I wanted to interrupt people to ask, "You know you're being poisoned, right?" These were good people who made me laugh and gripped my hand saying hello, people who fed the ducks with their grandkids and passed the hot sauce without asking, and they were living in the middle of the world's largest sprayed field. America's fruit basket was a chemical bowl, and along with the millions of bellies it filled with food, it filled itself with poison. How could they not expect to get sick? Farmers applied 2.7 million pounds of chemical herbicides, fungicides, pesticides, fertilizers, and defoliants every year to the Valley's fields. The region had what are known as cancer clusters—locations where particular cancer rates were unusually high for the local average. Shafter had bad wells. Fresno has bad wells. Fowler, McFarland, and Earlimart had cancer clusters in the 1980s. It required group delusion to act like the same forces didn't affect life here. Was it a miracle that cancers were widespread, or was it not as dangerous as I assumed?

According to one 2004 study by the Cancer Registry of Central California, the whole Central Valley had California's lowest cancer rates. "However," the report said, "this is due to the larger percentage of Hispanics who reside in the Central Valley. Hispanics experience lower rates of cancer than non-Hispanic Whites and African Americans." The incidences of many cancers were declining in the Valley, though the region's growing population, not agricultural chemicals, had increased the number of cancers being recorded. Kern County had the San Joaquin Valley's highest rates of cancer, and a number of scientists were studying links between farm chemicals and cancer there. I still didn't trust the chemicals.

Here houses stand down the street from orchards that planes spray on low-wind days. If suburbanites look at a farmhouse set between fruit trees that get sprayed by crop dusters, they might think those exposed residents were nuts. But look at many suburbanites' kitchens, their bedrooms, their kids' playground. They're all downwind. That farmhouse is theirs. Nineteenth-century coal miners entered the dank tunnels knowing they'd come out coughing blood. Why did we think we could live amid all this poison spray and groundwater flushed with selenium and not suffer the same fate? Miners had the canaries in the coal mine to let them know what was and wasn't safe. We have ours, but we pay them little attention. People treat the Valley's size like they treat the ocean, thinking that all that space will dilute the dangerous agents we dump in it, but with this many people dumping into this crowded a place, dilution is a delusion.

For all the times people talked to me about tap water and drought, for all the times they used the phrase "armpit of California," not one person mentioned that they lived inside a chemical soup. Not one person mentioned these invisible agents. Americans get upset about scores of invisible agents, including electrons, allergens, microbes, free radicals, encroaching governmental controls, lawsuits, perfume, threats of violence, downsizing, and debt. People develop phobias about standing near microwaves and living near cell towers. And lately, germophobia has struck America with the fervor of Beatlemania, causing seemingly stable people to compulsively wipe down shopping cart handles and open bathroom doors with their feet. So why weren't people here more openly unsettled by agricultural chemicals? With toxic molecules on the leaves and dirt and air, you'd think a germophobic nation would be living in paper surgical masks, compulsively brushing invisible particles from their sleeves with a special lint roller. Was there a diagnosable San Joaquin Valley chemophobia condition? Were they just not discussing it with me? The flipside of the California dream is delusion. People know it. They just didn't talk about it to me. "Our children are at risk as never before," farm-labor activist Cesar Chavez said years ago. A man told author Gerald Haslam, "The farmers are the ones who move everything in California. They are bigger than the government. And they want the chemicals." Even the fog's toxic. UC Davis environmental toxicologist James N. Seibert found sixteen pesticides in tule fog back in the 1980s. Lord knows how many are in there now. Because of the way it lingers in the lungs, toxic fog was more damaging than polluted air.

Part of people's delusion had to do with their sources of information: people didn't believe all that so-called liberal, environmentalist crap. They believed their friends and family. Maybe I didn't hear about it because if locals got scared about agricultural agents, it would destabilize their whole world. They'd have to move. They'd have to feel guilty about their jobs. They'd have to view their nice neighbors and sweet Uncle Bob as more sinister characters than they'd like to admit, people who had the best intentions and really loved those feral cats but who made the difficult trade-offs that working adults supposedly had to make to survive. That would not only completely mess with their head; it would require them to start a whole new life. And they liked their life. Hanford was beautiful. They were lucky to have been born here or to have found it after too many miserable years in LA, and hell if they were leaving now. I felt lucky. A random passerby saw me photographing the Woolworth in downtown Bakersfield and said, "If you like old buildings, you should check out Hanford." The moment the fog lifted this morning, I wanted to buy a house here. It was one of the most beautiful towns I'd ever visited, the sort that my dad always described as the pinnacle of midcentury American life. Now I was sitting in a booth across from Bowen, trying to resist discussing poison.

I slipped out the Star's back door and passed the opera house. The building was incredible, and it was the tip of the iceberg.

Hanford was part of the Main Street American Network. The tourism center led guided walks that took participants "back in time." I cut aimless figure eights through downtown, passing the Lacey Milling Company, the Bastille, and small nameless storefronts in between. The more I walked, the more Hanford worked its magic on me. I found myself strutting through a midcentury fantasy of a simpler life with fewer cars and crowds, because when this town put its head on your shoulder, you squeezed it oh so tight, tasting milkshake on your lover's lips in the back of your father's Plymouth, and you felt lucky to have landed here rather than Sacramento or San Bernardino or crazy San Francisco.

Studying the mom-and-pop storefronts, I could imagine headlines to magazine articles about Hanford:

California's Hidden Mayberry
The Big Little Town That Will Steal Your Heart
Bucolic California Offers Amenities as Wholesome as Its Beloved
    Ice Cream

People held the door for each other. They put their trash in garbage cans, and when they missed, a pedestrian stopped to pick it up. People did that elsewhere, but in this setting, these acts appeared old-fashioned. So did businesses' names. Inside Reba's Hair Designers Plus, a woman with a thick silver dome pruned another woman's silver hair. A jowly man in jeans, cowboy hat, and turquoise Navajo belt buckle slipped into the Sequoia Club at 1:44 p.m., while a police officer stopped at a nearby light and waved to a pedestrian.

A group of men in hard hats touched up the windows on the new Vendome Hotel. The original burned down two years earlier. It had operated in this location since 1899, though part of the building dated back to 1891. The brick and mortar weren't reinforced, and after the blaze, crews knocked down the remaining walls. It hadn't been a hotel for years. The upper floors were boarded up, but six small businesses used the ground floor. The fire destroyed them all. Crews were building a replacement that matched the original, except this time with an elevator. The reborn Vendome would have street-side storefronts and apartments upstairs. Many people expected it to be one of downtown's most gorgeous buildings.

Between 1849 and 1851, San Francisco's business district burned down six times, but as historian Martha Bentley told the local paper, fire also shaped Hanford. An 1887 blaze decimated the early, wooden Hanford business district, so residents gathered to discuss incorporating into a city to get infrastructure like fire protection, water, and paved streets. They didn't want additional taxes, so they hesitated. When another fire torched downtown four years later, they incorporated.

After the 2012 Vendome Hotel fire, Tom Miller, who owned Miller's Jewelry on the opera house's ground floor, talked to the paper about how many historic buildings weren't up to code. "I think about it all the time," he said. "I have fire insurance, but what can you do? This building burned once." In a vintage city, he had reason to fear.

When I finally reached the Fox Theatre, it was closed. Part of the ceiling collapsed eight months earlier. It was built in 1929, and the old joints gave way. The Fox shows movies and hosts concerts by big names like Willie Nelson, Lyle Lovett, and Jackson Brown. That would have been one hell of an uproar if the ceiling had killed Willie. Fortunately, no one was in there when the roof caved. Restoration would take two years and $4 million. As bad luck would have it, part of the renovated ceiling would collapse above the stage three months after the theater reopened in September 2016, five minutes before a concert.

I walked down Seventh Street past Grandma Lou's Thrift Store, which opened the previous June. Though the owner lived forty minutes away in Fresno, she opened her store up in Hanford because it only had one thrift store and Fresno had too many. "Being on Main Street has been good," she said. "It's a really cute town." She sold me two dollars' worth of sew-on zippers in their original 1960s packages.

An empty store named Kirby's stood next door. Gigi's Boutique was having a storewide 20 percent–off moving sale, though it wasn't clear where they were moving. Next door, Country Hutch Fine Furniture and Accessories sat vacant, a red Available sign in its dusty windows. Charming, attractive, and walkable downtown Hanford didn't seem to offer enough to ensure a draw. Some analysts said that web sales were killing brick and mortar as a business model. Next to Country Hutch, Cosmic Corral Books and Gifts for the Soul had a handwritten sign urging pedestrians to Support Small Business and to Shop Small. Surrounded by vacancies, the words felt more desperate than empowering, part of an ongoing conversation about what people wanted Hanford to be versus what it had become.

As I walked the streets, this whole town resembled the zippers I'd bought—still in their original packaging, waiting to be discovered. I kept wondering how a functional time capsule town preserves its charm in one of the fastest-growing regions in America's most populous state. Things frozen in time defrost. One side effect of being off the beaten path is that isolation can make it harder to keep businesses open, and the more that enchanted visitors like me sing a town's praises, the more people might ruin what made it attractive. People say growth is inevitable, but history is littered with towns that turned into ghosts rather than into Fresnos.

Of course, historical research had brought Frank Latta here before me. In the early 1930s Latta drove from Shafter to Hanford to interview Yoimut, the last member of her Chunut Tribe and the last one who spoke their native *Croo'-noot* and *Wo'-wole* dialects. Latta spelled her name Yoi'-mut and her tribe Choo'-noot. He was exacting that way. I wondered why she moved here rather than other lakeshore towns and what downtown looked like then. Did Yoimut live in town or on the edge? If she lived today, would she be an opera house renter or live in the country amid the green fields? Cotton killed her tribe. She probably wouldn't want to look at it every day.

Wandering through the town square, I met Richard Phelps, who had been maintaining city facilities for the last six years. Wearing khakis and a blue collared shirt, he stood in front of the Hanford Civic Auditorium, facing the Fox Theatre and park benches, and described Hanford life.

Had Latta visited Hanford in the twenty-first century, he would have interviewed people like Phelps. Phelps's family had lived in the country before moving into town when he was nine. "I mean, it was a different world back then," he said, "a lot of fun." When it had fourteen thousand people, it felt like the city ended at Twelfth Avenue. Now houses stretched deep into old farmland. Like many small-town kids, he'd gotten restless and moved away. He landed in Utah, where he built cabinets and custom furniture for fifteen years. The older his parents got, the harder it became emotionally to live so far. When his grandmother died, he moved back. This happens a lot. Hanford was the kind of place where distance gives enough perspective to show people what a special town they have. Phelps discovered that a lot of old friends had never left.

When he left town in the 1980s, the historic auditorium was solid green. With no distinction between the face and moldings, it looked like someone had dumped paint from a helicopter. When he returned, they'd repainted it more carefully, using the original powder blue, with each of its eight front columns painted white and details done in cream and gold. Phelps ranked the auditorium as Hanford's nicest building. A grammar school stood there until they built this in 1924. When the school came down, the city attached its clock high above the auditorium entrance. Phelps wound it twice a week. "Right now, it's not working," he said. "We're waiting for the guy to come and look at it, but we have to go up there and wind it twice a week. It's not electric. Has weights and everything."

Phelps found it amusing to now maintain buildings his family had known for two generations. He used to hang out in this park as a kid. Now the city paid him to take care of it. Phelps grew animated describing all the buildings. You could tell he was glad to be back, except for the summer heat. "I mean, it just gets gross and crazy," he said. "By the end of the summer, you're just tired of it, you know?"

I did. People felt that way about winter back home in Oregon. By February we all get sick of the rain and cold. Sometimes Hanford stayed hot until November. Fortunately, not this November.

Of course, Phelps eventually mentioned the sulfurous water. Only Phelps mentioned how Tulare Lake affected it. His dad used to hunt ducks on the lake, until Boswell drained it. "It's quite a ways from here," he said. "If you look on a map, usually they have it drawn out on a dotted line where it was originally, you know?" I sure did.

At sunset I aimed for the famed ice-cream parlor. New Yorkers mention Central Park less frequently than Hanford residents mentioned Superior Dairy. It stood on a corner across from the square, and in the dim shade of dusk, the storefront glowed like a beacon, its long, bright window lighting the street.

A crisp white building with dark trim and red tile roof, Superior's striped awning only added to the Mayberry effect. I love diners. I love midcentury coffee shops and drive-in movies, so when I stepped inside, I immediately thought, *Oh my God, I love this place.* Pink booths lined the walls. Pink stools ran along a long counter, and curling metal lamps hung from stamped white ceiling tiles. The past had come to life.

Six teenagers in bubblegum-pink shirts worked that night. One handed me a paper menu and fed me four samples. Another, named Andrea, leaned against the counter, reading a huge algebra textbook for an upcoming test.

Andrea scooped my small strawberry ice cream into what looked like a pint and then set a small waxed cup on top as a lid. When I tipped over the lid, it was full too. This place was insane. "It's the second-oldest restaurant in Hanford after the Star," she said before resuming her studies.

I sat at the counter and ate from the lid. I let spoonful after spoonful melt on my tongue, savoring the velvety texture and fresh summer flavor. As Andrea leaned over her textbook, I slid into *Happy Days* bliss, with the counter and oldies music and young customers on dates. This place was *Happy Days, Fast Food Nation,* and the Food Network rolled into one. All around me, people immersed themselves in the same decadent ritual. Savoring spoonfuls. Licking cones. Closing their eyes and moaning. You didn't taste fresh ice cream like this very often, and you rarely saw historic restaurants being casually used into a state of slight disrepair because historic was normal.

I told Andrea this ice cream was my dinner. She said she had that same dinner a lot.

I washed my cream down with water that didn't taste like sulfur. Superior's was filtered.

The street went dark by 9:00 p.m. The aquifers were dropping, and the land was turning to salt, but tonight we licked our cream, savoring the fruits of farmers' labor while ignoring the effects.

With all my questions and concerns, I admit I'm a buzzkill. But inside Superior, I wasn't thinking about water or drought or anything but that moment, and that was the problem. When we die, the cost of our material existence and gluttony all become someone else's problem. Eating all this bacon and heavy cream, some of us will die long before our world does.

I walked across the street with my water in hand and gave my pint to a homeless couple on a park bench by the Bastille. They were the first homeless folks I'd seen here in Mayberry, and it was pure chance that I found them. They started shoveling it with the plastic spoon I brought. "This is good," they said as I walked off, "very good. Thank you!"

Walking back to my car, I checked out the Artesia Hotel's lobby. Some people thought it looked like an old western brothel. I paced the lobby, studying the architecture and small businesses: the Marriage and Family Therapist, the bankruptcy attorney, the salon. A woman stepped into the lobby and screamed, "Ah! You startled me!" She pressed her palm to her heart. "You don't expect to see anyone in here now. I'm such a weenie."

"No weenie," I said, apologizing. I explained that I was checking out the historic photos and this famous fountain.

Her name was Sandy. She and her husband ran their own photography business, called Weiii Photography, in here. "Don't ask about the name," she said. "It was Eddie's idea." They were finishing moving their office from a unit upstairs to a ground floor unit that had just opened. Sandy showed me around the building and where the horses used to park on the dirt under the front eaves.

Outside, she stared up at what stars you could see through the moisture. "It's a special place," she said.

The color of the moon. The sound of a train. Friendly conversation. I was sad to have to go.

As I drove out of town, moisture clung to the fields and loosened the edges of tall shaggy trees, and it reminded me of Californian William Everson's poem "Fog":

There has been fog for a month and nothing has moved;
The eyes and the brain drink it, but nothing has moved for a
    number of days;
And the heart will not quicken.

1. The boat crew at the Kern River launch site.
Courtesy of the *Bakersfield Californian*.

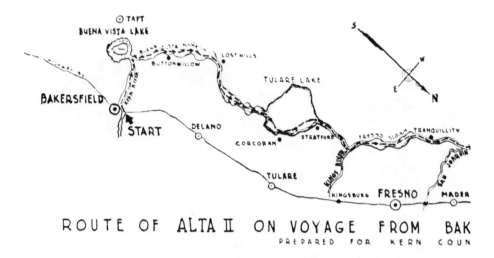

ROUTE OF ALTA II ON VOYAGE FROM BAK

PREPARED FOR KERN COUN

2. Route of the *Alta II*. Courtesy of the *Bakersfield Californian*.

3. Frank Latta (*center*) with Fred Gribble (*left*) and Chamber of Commerce secretary E. Gay Hoffman. Courtesy of the *Bakersfield Californian*.

ERSFIELD TO TREASURE ISLAND, SAN FRANCISCO.
TY CHAMBER OF COMMERCE

4. *Alta II* crew member Don Latta. Courtesy of the *Bakersfield Californian*.

5. *Alta II* crew member Ernest Ingalls. Courtesy of the *Bakersfield Californian*.

6. *Alta II* crew member Richard Harris. Courtesy of Kern County Museum. Used by permission.

7. Jean Latta, January 8, 1943. Courtesy of Kern County Museum. Used by permission.

8. *Alta* crew arriving in San Francisco Bay, July 1, 1938. Courtesy of the *Bakersfield Californian*.

9. Josie Yoi'-mut Alonzo, December 4, 1934. Photo by Frank Latta. Yosemite National Park Archives, Latta Collection.

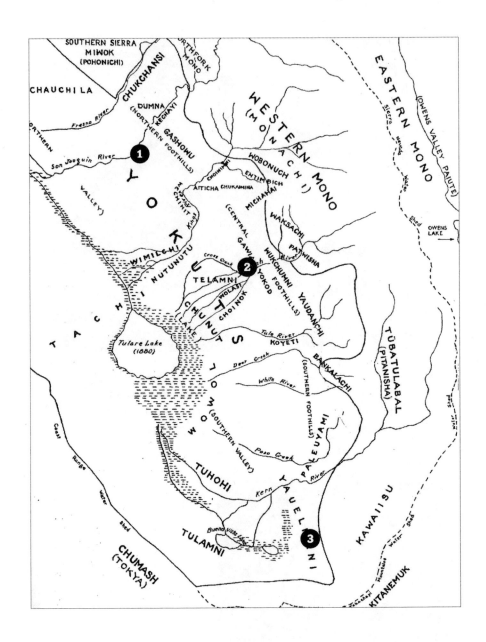

10. Map of indigenous groups of the southern San Joaquin Valley by anthropologist Anna Gayton, 1948, based on research by Alfred Kroeber. Image appears in *Indian Summer*. Used by permission of Julie Savasky.

11. Yokuts woman collecting native salt grass. Photo by L. Radanovich. Yosemite National Park Archives, Latta Collection.

4

Uncle Jeff's Cabin

The question of history cannot easily be avoided
in this Valley, for the past visibly abuts on the
present here—change is difficult to deny—
and the long horizon hides little.

—Gerald Haslam

Fresno, California's fifth-largest city by population, stands fifty miles
northeast of the old Tulare Lake. Even though Latta didn't boat close
to Fresno in 1938, he'd traveled through the area countless times,
collecting stories. Nearby, in 1928, he met Uncle Jeff Mayfield, the
man who told him his most important story.

Latta toiled in relative obscurity, recording the people who made
their living off California's demanding soil. Because few people wrote
about Latta, I had few secondary sources to work with to bring him
to life, which meant I had to treat him as his own main source. To
do that, I needed to hear more of his stories. Who was this person
I was following? Why did he spend his time searching for stories?
And why did he find local life so compelling?

Downtown Fresno's Central Library was humming on Wednesday
night. People watched videos on computers; kids dropped books into
return slots. When I stepped into the San Joaquin Valley Heritage
and Genealogy Center upstairs, the small reference room was empty,
except for one librarian reading a book at the desk. "Welcome!" he
said. His name was Chris Her. Born in nearby Sanger, Her was thirty-
two and had worked at the Fresno library for over fourteen years.

"Looking for something in particular?" he asked. I told him I'd come from Oregon to photocopy some works by Frank Latta, and he leapt from his chair. "Latta is an interesting character." Like Latta, Her appreciated historical obscurities that the rest of our era ignored.

He led me to a dim aisle where, shuffling left to right, we scanned the spines for particular call numbers. Some of Latta's books were scattered around by subject. The rest stood here—his well-known *Handbook of Yokuts Indians, Joaquin Murrieta and His Horse Gangs,* and *Dalton Gang Days,* as well as lesser-known works like *Black Gold in the Joaquin* and *Saga of Rancho El Tejón.* For years, I'd only seen some of these titles in other books' bibliographies; they were long out of print or too expensive to buy used. A small publishing company in Exeter, California, republished a few under the name of Latta's Bear State Press. But limited demand and a limited budget meant they printed limited runs, and that created prices only collectors could afford. The worst part was that limited editions put some excellent material out of the hands of the general public, which was the opposite of Latta's intention.

I removed one thin volume called *Pioneers of the San Joaquin.* I'd never heard of it. As it turns out, it wasn't one Latta published. An archivist long past had glued physical copies of his early 1930s newspaper columns to hard cardstock and bound them.

"Latta did that a lot," Her said. "He'd write columns for local papers, then gather them as a book." He didn't gather them all. That was why the library had such a hard time securing copies of all three thousand of his articles. So many of the regional outlets he published in had ceased operation, and hard copies hadn't always survived, like "Bakersfield to Treasure Island in a Boat," the account Latta published in the *Westside Progress Review* newspaper about his boat trip. "Yeah," Her said, typing furiously at his computer, "looks like no one has it. Sorry."

Unlike modern magazines' narrative profiles, Latta set up each one of the page-long oral histories in *Pioneers of the San Joaquin* with introductory remarks: "Can you imagine how it would be to know two languages which no one else in the world knows how to speak, or to be the last survivor of your race?" went one of his intros. "Within the southern end of the San Joaquin Valley," began another, "there is living probably the last remaining man who scouted under General George A. Custer." And "The wish of an historian, searching among pioneers of the San Joaquin for data, would be for archives left by an earlier historian who had accumulated a great fund of information dating back into the unlettered past."

A great fund of information was exactly what Latta had left, but how many people were reading it? This room's ascetic stillness heightened the sense that these stories were relegated to the furthest margins of collective memory.

After these introductions came blocks of direct quotations from the interviewee, mixed with dates, settlers' names, summaries of the pioneer achievements that made them unique, and occasionally overwrought exposition. This was Latta's style.

Flipping through *Pioneers*' pages, stern faces stared back at me from black-and-white photos. These people wore overalls and sun hats, tan suits, and tight-necked dresses. Their features were faded from reproduction and time, but most were grim. Only a few smiled. Pioneer life was demanding; maybe they also felt like specimens under the lens.

These were the people Latta spent his life searching for, the people he had rescued from complete obscurity, cataloged on a dim library shelf beside the people I had yet to meet—Yoimut and William J. Stockton, Wah-nom'-kot and Uncle Bud Akers—photographed by Latta on porches and in fields, telling their stories for generations to hear.

I set the *Pioneers* book facedown on the copy machine glass, and before spending the next few hours capturing these voices, I opened *Tailholt Tales* to read how Latta found Thomas Jefferson Mayfield. Mayfield was the source who established Latta's name as an important oral historian; the source whose interviews became Latta's first book, the book that he would always be known for; and the voice I liked hearing best.

In May 1928, at age thirty-six, Latta spent four hours interviewing a Yokuts tribes member in the mountains outside Visalia. Because of the language barrier, one misunderstood word at the beginning of their four-hour conversation somehow changed the course of their exchange, and when Latta wrapped up, he realized not only that most of the material was useless but that he needed a new system. Ideally, he needed a native English speaker who understood the Yokuts language as well as the Yokuts did.

Latta had started creating lists of translated words from different Yokuts dialects when he was twenty-four, and he patiently assembled the lists into dictionaries complete with pronunciations: "sister," *aw-gáwish*; "squirrel," *skée-til*. Seven years later, while teaching high school, he started systematically interviewing Yokuts in his free time, trying to record elders before they passed away. He understood how susceptible the historic record was to accidents and neglect, how the Spanish adobe structures he photographed one year got toppled in heavy rain the next, and he regretted the stories no one recorded—like the story of Chappo, the Potwisha's last chief, whose account of his first contact with white settlers in the Sequoia National Park area died with him in 1890.

Using his collected words, Latta drove the Valley, meticulously gathering ethnographic information and direct quotations that, as he put it, preserve "a dream among the ruins of an extinct civilization" recorded "from the lips of the departed." He interviewed Sínel, a Tachi doctor known for having "supernatural curative powers." In Hanford he interviewed Yoimut, last of the Chunut Tribe, who'd taken the name Josie Alonzo and pointed out that Yokuts' practice of burning good clothes after a person's death was no different than white people burying people in good clothes in expensive coffins, so why the fuss? And Latta drove four hundred miles through the Sierra Nevada with Las'-yeh, an eighty-year-old Porterville woman who used her friend Toi-eh'-yets as an interpreter so Latta could catalog her Koyeti Tribe's place names and traditional stories about the sierra's origins, why roadrunners' heads are striped red, and how rainbows end up in the sky. Las'-yeh had spent years gathering this information from elders as she watched her tribe disappear; Latta provided the way to permanently document and relay it to the rest of America. For many interviews, Latta had no interpreter, and his limited language skills meant that nuance got lost, details stayed hazy. It was detail that Latta wanted: how Yokuts learned to use bird wings to dust their houses; how they threw huge Tulare Lake clam bakes; how they made chewing gum from milkweed; why women didn't smoke tobacco.

At some point, Latta met a Wukchumne woman named Wah-nom'-kot near Visalia. The wife of the tribe's last chief, she also went by the name Aida Icho. Latta helped Wah-nom'-kot's family build a tourist exhibit to display their tribe's baskets on Highway 99 near Tulare. In return, Wah-nom'-kot helped Latta interview other Yokuts, performing essential communication functions, gaining people's trust, and helping him find more sources. Wah-nom'-kot wasn't with him on that day in May when he interviewed the Yokuts tribes member.

Frustrated by the wasted interview, Latta drove out of the foothills and met his friend Mrs. John Cutler in Visalia. She was an early settler and frequently helped him with research, clarifying details about pioneer life. He told her about the day's frustration because of the one word, and he told her how much he wished he could find a white person "who had been raised by, or who had lived with the Indians," and who could interpret the languages' connotations and denotations. Cutler encouraged him, saying that if he would look "for such a person and not give up, sooner or later he would find what he was looking for."

He drove to the town of Tulare to run an errand, and when he parked in front of the Tripletts' family store, his friend Mr. M. C. Zumwalt walked up. Zumwalt was an early Tulare pioneer, and he knew that Latta was always searching for a story. "I was just now going to the store to telephone you," Zumwalt said. "Mike Mitchell of Ducor knows an old man at White River who was raised by the Indians on Kings River. He has been over this part of the valley with them, and on Tulare Lake, and he knows more Indian than all the Indians in the country."

Surely, Latta's brow raised. He'd heard of other white men being raised by Native Americans. He might have even located a few, but their stories never panned out. Latta trusted Zumwalt, but as he later wrote, "Surely this was too good to be true." That was my sentiment exactly. Reading this version of events in the introduction to *Indian Summer*, I couldn't help wondering if this sequence happened as quickly as he described or if Latta invented it. Even those devoted to history are prone to mythmaking and self-aggrandizing. Whatever the time line, things worked out well.

The next day, Latta drove to Ducor, a tiny town of four hundred acres set against the Sierra Nevada's foothills, where Mike Mitchell confirmed Zumwalt's claim. They piled into Mitchell's Model T and drove up a winding dirt road between the spacious oaks, over rocks and ruts where dry creek beds cut across the gravel, to White River. This mining town used to be called Tailholt, named when a stagecoach passenger grabbed "holt" of her dog's tail to keep it from chasing a cat, but White River sounded more civilized. Mitchell grew up in Tailholt, where his family ran a store and hotel. He knew everyone, and the Mitchells were as close with Mayfield as the old-timer would let anyone get.

On the front porch of the town's one store, a thin bearded man with white hair sat in the shade. He wore a loose, stained collared shirt tucked into dark slacks with no belt, and he fastened his shirt to the top button. A cane leaned against a porch whose white paint was chipped where people used it as a bench.

Latta didn't record their first meeting, but I could imagine it.

"Hi, Jeff," Mitchell said, "how ya' doing?"

Jeff uncrossed his long legs and waved. His hard, high cheekbones and sharp nose gave way to a warm smile at Mitchell's approach.

Latta offered his hand. "Mr. Mayfield, good to finally make your acquaintance."

"Please," said Mayfield, "Uncle Jeff. That's what everyone calls me."

When Latta shook his hand, Jeff was eighty-six years old and lived alone in a cabin by a cemetery, where friends brought the old bachelor food since he no longer hunted and fished. The three made small talk under the oaks; then Latta got to work trying to establish Jeff's credibility. "Is it true what they say about your childhood with the Indians?"

Uncle Jeff nodded cautiously, running his hand down his beard. "Yes," he said, "quite true."

Mike Mitchell stood beside them, fanning the shy old man with his hat to get him to continue. "Go on, Jeff. Tell Frank some more. I can vouch for Frank's character. He wants to write your story. He's a respectable historian."

"Well," Jeff said, squinting, "what have I to say?"

Mitchell looked at Latta and laughed. "Only everything."

"Well, since I moved to Visalia as a boy in 1862," Jeff said, "I haven't talked about Indians more than an hour altogether, except to the Mitchell family. They have always been good to me and helped me a great deal during the last few years." He explained that during the first six of his ten years living in the Yokuts village, he learned to speak fluent Choinumne, and during that time, he spoke little else. "Since I left the Choinumne, I have seldom talked any Indian, but I have forgotten very little of the language." He named a few things in their dialect. "*Háh-pul* means 'hot,'" he said, "like today—hot. And those pencils in your shirt pocket, they called them *we'-chet*, or 'little sticks.'"

Latta nodded. He knew this was true. Many of his interviewees had nicknamed him We'-chet. The old man even accented the correct *e*.

Standing above Uncle Jeff, studying his bony frame and thin neck, Latta realized he wasn't the interpreter he'd hoped for, but after five minutes, he knew that Jeff contained more ethnographic information than he ever dreamed of hearing.

More than fluent in Yokuts dialects, Mayfield had lived alone with the Choinumne Tribe in the Sierra Nevada from the age of eight to eighteen. They dressed him in bark and woven plant fibers.

They let him share their beds and taught him to read the weather, cook wild plant foods, and swim the cold Kings River despite the swift current. "On their large tule rafts he had traveled with them to Tulare Lake on their fishing expeditions," Latta later wrote in his book about Jeff. "He hunted with them, fished with them, and shot with them with their own weapons. Then, too, his whole life was just as interesting. He had stories of the first bandits of the San Joaquin, prospecting in Death Valley when it really was the valley of death, the Mojave Desert in the [eighteen] seventies, murder and mystery stories of the old valley settlements, and many other things of a like nature."

I'm sure Latta's gut filled with butterflies on that porch, thinking about the frontier tales Mayfield could tell and the interpreting he could do with Yokuts sources, if he could drive Jeff around the Valley soon. With the amount of time Latta spent talking to strangers, he was bound to meet interesting people. But the original settlers were dying quickly, and someone like Jeff was one in a million. Mayfield had the flu, and between his cough and light-headedness, Latta recognized the urgency of the situation. Latta spent the rest of the day and following night at home "typewriting questions for him to answer; a vocabulary such as was probably used by the Indians, questions about their life . . . and a thousand other things."

Latta returned to White River two days later at 10:00 a.m. Over coffee at Jeff's rickety kitchen table, Mayfield answered questions while Latta transcribed. Unlike Harrington, Latta used no audio-recording equipment, only pencils and paper. "Without as much as ten minutes of lost time or a stop for lunch," Latta said, "this was continued until after six p.m., eight hours or more, and at that time Uncle Jeff was as fresh and as interested as he had been at the beginning."

Latta came as frequently as his three children's summer schedule allowed—sometimes only on weekends, other times every day for an entire week—and they maximized their opportunities by talking for eight hours a day with few breaks. It took a while to loosen Jeff up. Initially, he'd talk in generalities, when Latta wanted particulars, and

Jeff would stop himself from going in depth. It drove Latta nuts, but Jeff had shared few of these details during the previous six decades.

When his father finally moved him from the Yokuts village to a Visalia school in 1862, Jeff's unusual speech drew attention:

> It may have been that I unconsciously used a few Indian words. At least the boys at school used to make fun of me. I had to whip every boy in school before they would let me alone about it.
>
> Then, too, there seemed at this time in the minds of many white people to be some sort of a stigma attached to my life with the Indians.

If he tried to talk about his life in the mountains, the games he and his adopted family played, and the members he missed, people ridiculed him. In those days, many white settlers considered Native Americans savages, part of a primitive culture. Instead of respect or curiosity, settlers treated them with pity and suspicion, because people believed they'd steal your horses and equipment and even slit your throat. People who found out that Jeff lived with "the savages" treated him like an uncivilized "half-blood" and looked down on him. "From then on," Jeff said, "I resolved never to speak of my life with the Indians. People in general had so many wrong notions about Indians and were so ignorant about their life that I was continually drawn into arguments about them. Everyone was so sure they knew all about Indians that I made up my mind I would never tell them any different."

"But as he found that someone else was as much interested as he was," Latta said, "and was willing to preserve what information he had without any changing or ridicule, he became as enthusiastic as a boy."

Over their first six weeks, the men established a productive rhythm, talking and transcribing, questioning and answering. They worked at the table. They worked on the porch. When Jeff's back ached from coughing, Latta transcribed by his bedside, where the cabin's dry boards creaked and an oil lamp burned above Jeff's bedpan and one of his two pairs of shoes. Latta often abandoned his list of subjects to let the old man's stories go wherever they took him, covering the details of Yokuts hunting, fishing, house and raft construction, manners, ceremonies, language, fights with encroaching Mono tribes, the way Jeff's father left for a year at a time, how a Mono man tried to choke Jeff in his cabin, how Jeff shot another intruder in the back with an arrow, and always stories of how his Yokuts family fed, loved, and taught him how to thrive in nature with no gun and no watch, only his wits, friendships, and the sun.

"His expression was good," Latta said, "his understanding of what was wanted complete. He had an absolutely accurate memory and the mind of a scientist. When a question was asked about Indian life he was ready with a comprehensive answer. Those things he had studied for more than seventy-five years. No one with whom he came in contact had any understanding, or appreciation, of what he knew, and he had never discussed his life with the Indians. It was interesting to observe the change that came over the man as the work progresses."

Talking was cathartic. Jeff finally felt appreciated. Sitting around the table, stuffing an oilcloth under the short leg to keep it from wobbling, both men came to life. Once Jeff started, Latta's hand cramped from writing fast enough to keep up. "Wow," Latta would say, "go on." And they did. From May into August, Jeff talked and Latta listened. To celebrate their progress, Jeanette Latta packed hot fricasseed chicken and buttered biscuits into thermoses one day, Frank picked up Mike Mitchell in Ducor and some other old-timers, and they shared lunch at Jeff's cabin. Then they got back to work.

Even when ill, Jeff had a wit that was as quick as his recall, rarely stumbling over words. So much time had passed since those Yokuts years that Latta initially questioned Jeff's clarity. He was eight years old when a lot of this happened. How much did anyone remember from age eight? But rather than blurring Jeff's stories, decades of silence had preserved details in the formaldehyde of memory. Telling stories over and over by rote often lessens their complexity and smooths their edges, leading to simplified versions too polished to be true. Had Jeff told his stories to a hostile, racist world before meeting Latta, he might have revised them to match his audience, toning down and editing so as not to elicit judgmental responses from white people. Telling them now for the first time, Jeff's stories came out crisp and clear, and Frank got them ready for permanent display.

Thomas Jefferson Mayfield was born on the family farm in East Texas around 1843. His father was a military man who had survived many battles. To avoid Apache warriors on the trail west, the Mayfields took a six-month boat trip to California. After landing in San Francisco in 1850, the year it became a state, they joined a mule train headed for the San Joaquin Valley in order to secure land.

In Pacheco Pass, six-year-old Jeff got tired of riding on his mother's horse, and he requested she let him ride by himself so that he could get a better view of the Valley when they reached it. "I remember that I proudly smiled back at her from my perch," he told Latta, "and that she returned my smile. I can see her yet. This is the last real picture I have of my mother, as she died within a year."

They passed deer in a meadow that didn't run at their approach. "Suddenly," Jeff said, "my daddy pointed over the tops of the bare hills ahead of us and exclaimed, 'Look there!' And there in the distance, until then lost to us in the haze, was our valley. A shining thread of light marked El Rio de San Joaquin flowing, as my mother said, 'through a crazy quilt of color.'" The quilt was flowers, rows and rows of "rose, yellow, scarlet, orange and blue," each species attached to a different soil type, with some colored bands stretching a mile across. "And my mother cried with joy," Jeff said, "and wanted to make a home right here in the midst of it all." They kept going, and that teenage Yokuts girl carried Jeff across the rushing San Joaquin River. They weren't the welcome committee, but their generosity knew few bounds.

Between the hills in the lower sierra, the family built a cabin on a level plot where Sycamore Creek flowed into the Kings River, immediately across from a Choinumne village. The families befriended each other. In fact, the Yokuts supplied them with so much food during the Mayfields' first three years that they quit subsistence hunting. While the new arrivals slept, the Yokuts hung deer and birds in an oak tree and set bread made from acorn meal at their door. The Mayfields reciprocated with wheat, potatoes, and corn when their fields produced it, though Jeff said, "We never in any way came near repaying them for what they did for us."

Jeff's father, William Mayfield, had fought Native Americans back east, so he was no friend of theirs. But the Choinumne were a generous, nonthreatening tribe, and as more white settlers poured into their territory, and other Yokuts bands chose to defend themselves, both groups here on Kings River likely recognized the value of a peaceful coexistence if they were going to survive. "Several years later," Jeff said, "I learned from the Indians that they kept us in meat in order to keep us from firing our guns and scaring the game."

When Jeff's mother died less than a year into their homesteading, his father and two older brothers decided homesteading wasn't enough. They needed to pursue lucrative activities. "The Indians at the ranchería had always taken an interest in me," Jeff told Latta. Some would stand behind the house for hours watching the family cook and dress, curious about their lifeways. His mother trusted their neighbors and let her son spend hours playing in their village across the river. His father and two older brothers already spent a lot of time away wrangling wild horses, searching for ore, and grazing cattle. So when the Choinumne offered to take care of eight-year-old Jeff, his father eventually accepted and took off for good.

Jeff's account of his ten years in the village is filled with stories of children's antics, wild animals, brushes with death, frequent swims, hunting expeditions, and the joys of young life. The saga of the annual fishing trips the Yokuts took down the Kings River to Tulare Lake is as vivacious and detailed as anything in Brewer's and Derby's journals, except closer to its people than its landscape.

As John Harrington said in his forward to *Tailholt Tales*, "Few readers will realize that this information which Mr. Latta has preserved lies on the very outskirts of human knowledge and that he has rescued practically all of these facts from oblivion." Oblivion is the hole both men reached into. California lost its biggest lake and many of its first people and their tribal knowledge but not all its stories. *Tailholt Tales* is a time capsule from this vanished world. It's the sort of document that Latta always aimed to create, and it represents one of Latta's two most valuable cultural contributions, which is why he considered Harrington's endorsement the highest compliment he and Mayfield could receive.

Mayfield's father and brothers would return to the homestead intermittently, and when they did, Jeff would stay with them until they left again. Jeff didn't see his dad for a year or two at a time. After ten years, Jeff said, "my daddy decided that I had been with the Indians long enough." He enrolled the boy in school in Visalia at age eighteen. That year, his father's luck ran out when he was mortally shot in a battle with one of the Paiute tribes on the Sierra Nevada's east side, where a canyon now bears William Mayfield's name. Both of Jeff's brothers died in the 1870s. One was killed as an infamous bandit; the other was poisoned after a scuffle over cattle. None of them had kids. For the rest of his life, Jeff lived alone, uncle to everyone but kin to none.

While Jeff searched for ore and herded sheep, his Yokuts family died off. Americans took over their land, cut the oaks, and crowded them out. Overhunting and grazing caused shortages of wild game, and European diseases like measles, smallpox, and tuberculosis reduced the three-hundred-person tribe to forty people. Survivors joined other tribes or moved to small towns where they worked cattle ranches, got absorbed into the population, even married into Latino families, whose language they often spoke from Alta California days, and their Choinumne identity drained away.

The construction of Pine Flat Dam in 1954 put the village and Mayfield homestead under water, though not before Latta took photographs. Water diversion helped drain the Tulare Lake that Mayfield's Yokuts once fished, so in a sense, Latta and his dam advocacy helped end the very world he was so grateful to have preserved in his books.

Tailholt remained. When he got too old to prospect, Jeff settled there. It had two cemeteries. His cabin overlooked the town's "respectable" one, the one where people went when they died of natural causes, instead of with their boots on because of gunshots, stabbings, poison, and mining accidents.

In late August, Mayfield suffered a stroke, and his friends moved him from his cabin to the closest hospital in Visalia. Jeff's health seemed dire now, but he and Latta kept talking. Such quick changes in fortune were why documentarians like Latta and Harrington did not wait to start recording; sources were here one minute and gone the next.

Jeff had no will and few material possessions. He only wanted one thing. "North of the river the dead were buried in pine boxes of lumber," he told Latta. "I want to be buried on the north side of the river, but I want to be rolled in a blanket." Latta regretted not being able to give him that. One day in late September, Latta found Jeff sitting on the edge of his hospital bed, more tired than he'd ever seen him.

When Latta sat down, Jeff stared at him. "You know I never told you how we came to this country." For two hours, Jeff filled the gaps in his narrative, starting at the beginning of his story, describing his family's trip through Pacheco Pass, their first sight of the Valley, and the girl who ferried him across the river. It's my favorite part of the story, my favorite of all Latta's work. If Latta had arrived at the hospital just a few hours later, the world would have missed it.

"By this time Uncle Jeff was becoming quite tired," Latta said. "He sat on the edge of the bed with his elbows on his knees and his head in his hands." When Latta tried to excuse himself, Jeff told him, "No, I want to finish telling you about this before I lie down." Jeff told him an incredible, harrowing story about how he and his burro survived for two years in Death Valley during a drought with no food or water. Finally, Latta felt guilty for keeping his exhausted friend awake. Visiting hours had ended, so he patted Jeff on the shoulder and said, "Goodbye Uncle Jeff."

Dow-wit-kow, Jeff said, "goodbye" in Choinumne.

As Latta descended the hospital steps, the nurse came to check on Jeff, and he "fell backwards in the arms of the nurse, dead." Or so Latta said. Like finding Jeff that one frustrating day in May, this seems too slick to be true. It made a good story, though, one he'd probably told countless times. But I trusted the bulk of Latta's account of Jeff's life. It contained a great deal of what we know about the Yokuts, and Latta preserved it in Jeff's words.

The beauty of oral history is the voices. The conversational form lets you hear the people of the past speaking as if they were right in front of you, forming an intimate connection across time that defies death.

Latta knew what a score he'd stumbled on, partly because he'd spoken to so many people with relevant but more mundane accounts: the first person to produce kerosene, the first person to plant wheat. That's why Latta published the Mayfield material so quickly, first as newspaper articles in the months after Jeff's death and then together as a poorly designed, eighty-eight-page book in 1929 called *Uncle Jeff's Story*. "This is Uncle Jeff's own story," Latta told readers in his introduction. "The writer has tried not to profane it in changing the form of expression."

Jeff told the beginning of his story last, but in his book, Latta arranged the material chronologically. Latta listed himself as editor and Uncle Jeff as author, since the book was composed almost entirely of Jeff's words. Latta loved the text but not the physical edition. "Accept my apologies," Latta wrote to the New York Public Library when he sent them a copy. "It was printed from type used in a newspaper set-up and is quite crude in composition." The next edition would be better, if he could get someone to publish it.

Latta exchanged letters with the editor at Stanford University Press, who was considering republishing the book in an improved format. But after four years of correspondence, the editor ultimately declined, hit with the Great Depression and lessening interest in what he called Californiana.

The failed plans frustrated Latta, but he shared what he called Uncle Jeff's "iron man" constitution. He also saw how tirelessly John

Harrington labored, driving village to village, dragging his car from muddy creeks, and stuffing boxes full of raw data that he rarely reread or reworked because there was always more to gather. Rather than mailing his notes to his employers at the Smithsonian's Bureau of American Ethnology, Harrington stored a lot of them in the field, because as he told Latta, "If I sent my work to the Bureau, those swivel-chair Ethnologists never would get off their fannies and go to work. There is more work here than a hundred of us can do." If no publisher would reprint *Uncle Jeff's Story*, Latta decided he'd print it himself.

For forty-seven years, he labored on an expanded, more rigorously vetted version. If it was not fact-checked in the modern sense, then it was at least checked against other settlers' accounts. As he interviewed sources for new books, Latta communicated with others to confirm things Mayfield had said, writing letters to people like Judge Atwell's son to get their versions of events that Mayfield had described. And he photographed landmarks and mining sites to add context to Mayfield's oral history. In this improved manuscript, Latta let Mayfield talk for pages about life after he left the village, including his experiences mining, shepherding, and doing various jobs in Tailholt—material left out of the first version.

A more sophisticated writer now, Latta added bits of his own dialogue between blocks of Mayfield quotes, to create the illusion of an exchange between them and, in places, to create scenes. Some of Latta's new dialogue reads like a screenplay designed to create dramatic moments that, to me, verge on fiction. But Latta had grown reflective, even nostalgic, about his past, and he wanted to amplify what he, at age eighty-four, knew was his best material, the high point of his career. In the process, he weaved a sort of memoir element into this new book, adding anecdotes from his family's research trips and the rigors of data collection and correspondence with the legendary Harrington, to depict Latta's experience as an independent researcher who'd stumbled onto Mayfield. When he printed the new 323-page edition himself in 1976, he renamed it *Tailholt Tales*, and this time, instead of "Arranged by Frank F. Latta," he listed himself as the author. It was still Jeff's story, but Latta had created a larger tale around it. And his ethnologist family were characters in the story, keepers of the flame of what happened that summer in Tailholt.

As a portal to the early California that Latta was born in, Latta wasn't just documenting Jeff's world. He was preserving his own. I was drawn to Latta partly because he'd experienced a vanished world that I couldn't access: the old Valley of flowing rivers and thick oak woods, of desert plains and vacancies, the land I sought in nature preserves that didn't always deliver.

Storytellers only get one Mayfield in our lifetime, if at all. That night in the Fresno library, it was clear that Latta was my Mayfield.

By the time the Fresno library closed, I had most of what I needed. The librarian could send the rest. A security guard walked me down the hall. I ate some tacos at a lonchero in a parking lot and headed up Highway 99.

It rained for thirty seconds on the north side of Fresno, and the drops on my windshield dried immediately. Their scent barely had time to fill the air. It was good to know that it could still rain, though it felt like a metaphor for Latta's and all life—here one second, gone the next.

Four hundred years ago a Spanish padre in a brown robe walked by the spot where you drink your morning coffee so that he could convince a Yokuts chief to give him the village children.

Where you order your breakfast burrito, William Brewer sat under a crooked oak to write his brother the letter that would become the most important record we have of the Valley's historic salinization problems.

We stand and drive and sit atop the marks of history as modernity conceals them, and I wanted to see them again. Brewer, Derby, Austin, Muir, and Latta are some of the reasons the American West knows anything about our collective past. One thing that you get from reading history is a sense of life's swiftness, how human civilizations peak and end so quickly. "Life moves pretty fast" is a Ferris Bueller cliché, but it's true. Our lives feel frenzied and slow at the same time, clogged with our ambition, our chores, our work and routines, and the trouble and drama and swirl of it all, spiraling and tightening in schedules that are all important, until one day they end and the world keeps moving without you. Your civilization will end too. Reading history shows how you become history. It shows how you fit with your tribe, how time passes until there's no one left to even forget you were here, how there's still time left to try to save it. The glaciers melt and then freeze to melt again. The mountains you loved get washed away. A sea that wasn't there will cover the site of your childhood home. Things we call drought will cycle back so many times that the future civilizations who endure them will use a new word for them, and "drought" will be locked in some regional historian's books, like pollen preserved in Jurassic bogs. Nothing's truly endangered when nothing stays the same. The outlets to the seas shift with the oceans' names, but the rivers always flow toward birth and oblivion. So maybe the smartest response is to go enjoy yourself now. Hit the beach. Ride your bike. Eat the bacon. Or climb into that car to chase your nagging questions down a highway through strangers' lives the way John Harrington did, because you won't always be able to. Get your piece of the California dream, in California or elsewhere. Things matter, but you can't get hung up on them. Leave your mark on the rocks without expecting anyone to find it. You're the tree in the forest no one hears fall. When you're done reading this history book, return it to the shelf, because when the cover closes on you, someone will have to clean your mess, and that's not what you want to make future people do. Be considerate. Take only what you need, the way the Yokuts did. Either way, you'll get replaced by a new nation, a new landmass, a new epoch, till the sun swallows the solar system and our collective memory. Amen.

At least that's how I felt driving north from Fresno. It was easy to picture people like Latta laboring alone at night in their study, long after the kids had gone to sleep, adding new material to a growing manuscript, making small corrections to the text, believing how much it mattered—this fact, that sentence's structure—and confirming things Mayfield said against things new interviewees told him. Then Latta died. What was left of his efforts? So few people knew *Tailholt Tales*, or knew him. The rest of his life's work was stored away in special collections. It was tragic. It was natural. This, I kept thinking, is my book's future. I'd hit the jackpot at the library. I was having the time of my life on the road, but the thought of Latta's legacy made me mourn for my own. If the previous generation's greatest minds were nobodies to my generation, what chance did anyone have?

The people whom I mentioned Latta to often viewed him as just another obscure dude who did some scholarly stuff with dead people in the olden days, and that was exactly how future generations would view my San Joaquin Valley book, just one more shark tooth buried in the sediment of scholarship, if they discovered it at all.

I wondered if Latta's energy flagged—if he sat in the punishing sun one day, nursing his injured back, and considered catching a car to Stockton and San Francisco instead. Did he question his boat trip's value? Did he wonder why he bothered to gather all that oral history? Or was he more possessed than that, convinced that one day, some curious stranger would sit in a library just as I had, reading and appreciating his material?

We reach the end of our lives and question if our days added up to something. Did we leave a mark on our children? On the world? That's what people often talk about with writers: *At least people will read your stuff a hundred years after you die.* To which I say: not necessarily. More than the enduring works, literature is composed of the people whose names we do not know. It's a canon composed of books few have heard of, written by people whose voices grow quieter each year.

It's delusional to expect your work to live on in subsequent generations. You do the work for yourself and for the people who walk the earth now. You do it because if you didn't, no one else would. You do it because it's your duty as a citizen to record your world as it is, so that those who live after you can know where they come from and how their world got this way and so that they can appreciate the sacrifices and efforts that helped build the world they inhabit. That's why history matters, and that's why we stare into the void, to rescue stories from oblivion.

5

Through the Swampy Center

Strange, *all* dreamed of *water*.

—William Henry Brewer

When Latta's crew entered Fresno Slough on Thursday afternoon on June 23, forty miles of swamp lay between them and the San Joaquin River.

The winds were calm here and had left the water glassy. Calm conditions fit the mood; the crew had conquered their route's most challenging sections. Looking at a map, you can see that the second half of their journey would be very different than the first. Even in flood, the San Joaquin River offered a more defined course than Tulare Lake. Small roads were closer to shore in case of emergency, and the shore was usually in sight. Granted, many of those roads lay underwater. And submerged fences and vegetation still posed dangers in shallower sections, but the crew's primary concerns now were sun exposure, their schedule, and getting stuck in mud.

All Thursday the *Alta* floated north toward the junction with the Valley's namesake river. There were no towns. This was ranchland cut by old cattle trails and the train tracks that carried freight toward San Francisco. The smell of hot tar and greased railroad metal mixed with the smell of murky water, as the *Alta* drifted mile after mile through flooded prairie, enduring hours of the same simmering heat that had tormented nineteenth-century travelers with mirages and that had littered the plain with dead cattle. Forty miles is a long way to boat in ninety-degree heat.

In 1852 Lieutenant Derby traveled through here with the U.S. Army Corps of Topographical Engineers and wrote that the land "between these sloughs was miserable in the extreme, and our animals suffered terribly for want of grass." Derby tried to cross the swamp, but it stretched ten miles wide. The mud made that impossible, and one deep channel even required a member of his party to fetch a boat from a town nearly forty miles away to ferry their horses across. In 1863 Brewer rode thirty miles through this "tedious and monotonous" land and saw only one small willow. "[It] was visible for two hours," he said, "but we passed nearly two miles from it; it was a mere speck." In 1938 Latta's crew suffered too.

The current was slow. In some years, the direction flowed south, pulling the water back into Tulare Lake. This year, it was sluggish, so the boys probably had to paddle. And paddle, and paddle. Their arms tired. When they needed a rest, I imagine Latta fired up the motor. He wanted to reach Tranquility by nightfall, but he also needed to conserve gas in case of emergency.

Multiple sloughs branched out from Fresno Slough's main chan- nel, striping the land with bands of muck and inlets. As the waters stopped at various points, the crew had to drag their fifteen-foot skiff onshore to ford the breaks. It was a dismal, grueling process that required sloshing through thick reeds to drag the boat onto dry land. Water would have reached up to the crew's waistline in places. Loaded with two motors, food, cameras, fuel, and camping supplies, the boat would have tugged at their tired arms. Once they hoisted the boat on their sunburned shoulders on solid ground, summer heat dried the mud on their pants and boots, adding a horrendous weight that they had to tolerate until they stopped someplace to scrape it off. If they tried to walk too far in any direction, they got stuck. As Derby had said, this was miserable country. Imagining the *Alta*'s struggles made me grateful for roads and my air-conditioned car.

At the end of the day, close to the north end of the Slough, the *Alta* reached Tranquility. Founded at the turn of the twentieth century, this eight-hundred-person farm town was originally an isolated, sparsely populated outpost in an area more taxing than tranquil.

To the east, 14,494-foot Mt. Whitney, the tallest peak in the Lower 48, pushed into the cool dry air, a startling contrast to Tranquility's muggy 164-foot elevation. The Southern Pacific Railroad tracks crossed the slough here, and this time, Latta didn't hit the bridge while passing under it. The crew camped on high ground. When they woke up Friday morning, they floated the slough's last fifteen miles to the San Joaquin River.

One of the Valley's oldest Spanish towns, Pueblo de Las Juntas, once stood nearby. At its peak, 250 Spanish-speaking residents lived here in adobe houses made of mud and straw, as well as tule reed houses modeled after the Yokuts'. Spanish frontiersman who tired of living alone on the barren west side moved to the Pueblo by the water. I imagine that the air smelled of warming tortillas and beef stewing in red chile, but the town's namesake is uncertain. Many details of local life went unrecorded before statehood; if the Valley's first Spanish settlers did write down their history, few accounts survive. We know that *las juntas* literally means "meeting place" and "junction." The meeting could have been the meeting of Fresno Slough and the river. More likely, the name comes from the location's popularity as a meeting place for bandits and outlaws.

Like Yokuts hiding in the tules to escape the coastal missions, fugitives rendezvoused at Las Juntas. Protected by its isolation, outlaws came here throughout the 1850s and 1860s to get sauced. They gambled, stole horses, and got in fights that ended in murder. The place had a rough reputation. Joaquin Murrieta, California's most feared and mythical bandido, reputedly stocked up on supplies here between raids, maybe had a drink, and then ducked back into his hideout on the Valley's mountainous west side, since the east side was crawling with gold rush miners.

Murrieta's life is a mix of facts and folklore, built of details that can no longer be verified and weren't all verifiable back then. People agree that Murrieta moved from Sonora, Mexico, to the Sierra

Nevada around 1849 to try to find gold. One of many versions of his life says that a group of white American miners raped and killed his wife, stole his mining claim, and beat Murrieta close to death. After recovering, Murrieta picked those men off one by one, dragging many behind his horse, and he spent the rest of his short life stealing livestock; robbing farms, towns, and travelers; and exacting revenge on the gringo aggressors who had stolen California from Mexico and stolen his love from him. Authorities put a $1,000 bounty on his head, but Murrieta's gang had multiple hideouts. Their preferred hideout was a mountain fortress of boulders and caves north of Coalinga, where they could perch atop three sandstone rocks and see anyone approaching in the Valley. From there, Las Juntas was an accessible place to get supplies. When a posse of California rangers finally killed Joaquin and one of his sidekicks, they cut off his head as proof and collected the ransom. Murrieta's head was displayed in San Francisco for years, preserved in a jar of alcohol. The grizzly $1 exhibit attracted many visitors, but some who had seen Murrieta in life claimed that this head wasn't his, including his sister. For decades after his supposed capture, people in the Valley told stories of the bandit riding his horse, still robbing settlers.

To finally separate history from legend, Latta wrote a whole book about the fabled bandit, titled *Joaquin Murrieta and His Horse Gangs*. For a book that turned out to be decades in the making and hundreds of pages long, Latta dug through newspaper archives but didn't use any secondary material. Instead, he made multiple trips to Sonora, Mexico, to study Murrieta's family records and interview the bandit's relatives and friends to confirm existing details and gather new information. He located Californians who claimed to have run into Murrieta or whose families had told them stories. He interviewed a ninety-four-year-old Merced settler named Mrs. Ann Elizabeth Hardwick Ruddle, who had an uncle whom Joaquin supposedly shot on the Merced River in 1852; as it turns out, another bandit shot her brother, though Joaquin might have shot her brother-in-law, Allan Ruddle, on the Tuolumne River. Latta recorded a story by Joel A.

Whiteside, who cornered Joaquin's ruthless nephew Procopio in a mountain cabin in 1878 and still couldn't capture him. As he escaped, Procopio shot Whiteside's young friend, killing him a week before his wedding. "My experience," Whiteside told Latta, "has always been a tender spot with me and it is only to record the right account of the incident that I am telling about it."

During this research, Latta met people who sold him items that supposedly belonged to the Murrieta clan: Procopio's pistols, one of Joaquin's daggers, the hooded tapaderos stirrups on Joaquin's last saddle. But it's his conclusion that separates his from other Murrieta books: he claimed that the rangers never captured Joaquin. The dark-haired, dark-skinned severed head didn't match the many descriptions of Murrieta's "blue eyes, light brown hair and fair skin." The head, he argued, was a Native American's. Joaquin was *güero*, meaning "blonde." Some historians question Latta's main sources—a known liar named Avelino Martinez, who claimed that he rode with Murrieta but whose dates don't line up, and the diary of Sheriff Ben Marshall, which was lost, later transcribed by Marshall's son, and then shared with Latta—and Latta's lack of secondary confirmation and bibliography. By relying on oral history, they said, Latta did little to verify interviewees' accounts. This was a weakness with the form. Latta disagreed. "Some authors just quote newspapers and think they're finished," he told an East Bay newspaper. "That's where I begin. Newspapers are interesting to start from. I quote very few newspapers, for the participants themselves are my authorities." He used sources he felt were reliable and delivered their version of the truth. And while Latta aimed for a verified account, frankly, most people prefer a good story. Latta's book settled nothing, mostly because nothing about Murrieta can be settled, but the anecdotes make great reading.

The state's other legendary bandido Tiburcio Vásquez also visited Las Juntas. Vásquez robbed towns and stole cattle in the 1860s and 1870s but claimed that he never killed people. He presented himself as a Latino Robin Hood, putting fear in gringo hearts in order to liberate Alta California and return it to Mexico. "I had numerous fights in defense of what I believed to be my rights and those of my countrymen," he told a newspaper before his hanging in 1875. "I believed we were unjustly deprived of the social rights that belonged to us." His fight for justice and his refusal to tolerate racism and American incursion make him a beloved figure in some Mexican American circles to this day. His last robbery took place in the mountains west of town.

Two big ash trees grew on the river at Las Juntas, so people also called the village Fresno. *Fresno* means "ash" in Spanish. Early settlers often named towns for physical features: Oakland, Red Bluff, Tree Valley, Los Banos ("The Baths"), Tres Piedras (Murrieta's "Three Rocks"), El Arroyo de las Polvarduras ("Dust Cloud Creek"). Pioneers named one local town Lone Willow. This was the first Fresno. When an American company bought the land in 1879 to build a canal, the residents relocated north to Firebaugh's Ferry. The massive Miller-Lux company eventually bought the property to raise sheep, mashing it into the cud of their giant meat-rearing nation-state, erasing the town from the map and almost from memory.

After the first Fresno, a second one sprung up to the east. Because wet years allowed shallow boats to travel all the way up the San Joaquin River and float part of Fresno Slough, entrepreneurs built a pier here in 1858. Placed among the ash trees, investors believed that the site would generate enough commercial boat traffic to grow this new Fresno City into a thriving shipping center and that its location on the Butterfield Overland Stage route would guarantee visitors and commerce. People built houses, a hotel, and a warehouse. The boom never came. Trains superseded the Butterfield. The water was too unreliable, dropping from twenty feet deep to two, in a season. When William Brewer visited on April 8, 1863, he found "one large house, very dilapidated, one small ditto, one barn, one small dilapidated and empty warehouse, and a corral." Brewer visited again the following year and found that "a *city* was laid out in early speculative times, streets and public squares figure on paper and on the map, imaginary bridges cross the stinking sloughs, and pure water gushes from artesian wells that have never been sunk."

Fresno City did have something going for it: color. "It is surrounded by swamps," wrote Brewer, "now covered with rushes, the green of which was cheering to the eye after the desolation through which we had passed." By then, residents had taken their hopes elsewhere. As the buildings fell apart, a small settlement to the east, built on the harsh desert land between rivers, far from piers, inherited the Fresno name and grew into a real city, defying expectations.

Back on the slough, Latta's crew found Mendota Dam blocking their way into the river. Beginning in high mountain lakes above Yosemite National Park, the San Joaquin River flows over bare granite rock, through thick evergreen forests, and past some of the world's largest trees. After it passes Fresno, the river curves north at Mendota, once and for all, and heads toward the sea. At 330 miles, it's California's second-longest river; measured by agricultural commodities, it's one of the world's most important.

If you control water, you control wealth, and Americans started controlling water ever since we moved into the Valley. Settlers built the first primitive dam at Mendota in the late 1800s using brush. Later versions used sacks of dirt, earth, and wood to catch San Joaquin River and Fresno Slough water in what's called Mendota Pool, allowing irrigation ditches to redistribute it to farmland. In 1919, people replaced the dam with a concrete version. This is the one the *Alta* encountered. When Friant Dam began collecting irrigation water upstream in 1944, downstream flows diminished and Mendota Pool dropped. Water levels dropped further in 1951 when the new Friant-Kern and Madera Canals started diverting the rest of the river water to distant farms. The smaller Madera Canal waters about 150,000 acres around its namesake town. The 152-mile-long Friant-Kern distributes most of the San Joaquin River to fifteen thousand farms along the Valley's east side in Kern, Tulare, and Fresno Counties. The system is part of the massive federal Central Valley Project. As Secretary of the Interior Harold Ickes said at the Friant's formal dedication in 1949, the dam is "but a lifeline to preserve and enhance our American civilization. This is a line of creation, built to unlock the fertility of the rich soil, to resist drought, to overcome floods, to provide outdoor recreation, and to generate cheap power that will improve the living conditions of millions of our citizens." It certainly does much of that. Canals siphon nearly all of the river away at Friant Dam, so when the channel reaches the Valley's floor, it runs dry for approximately sixty miles between the Friant and Mendota Dams. Ickes's words ring with manifest destiny, and it's clear he didn't extend that "line of creation" to all God's creatures, because the dam deprives farmers of water downstream and keeps thousands of salmon and steelhead from migrating here, killing the fishery. People call this "dewatering."

Downstream, an estimated eighty thousand salmon ran up the river in spring and fall, while twenty-one thousand made it upstream around Fresno. People once camped on the shore of the San Joaquin River to fish. Some spearfished from boats at night, while a few dropped dynamite in the water to kill hundreds at once. "The San Joaquin was probably the finest salmon spawning area in the state," said one retired California Department of Fish and Game employee in Gene Rose's book *The San Joaquin: A River Betrayed*. "It was a tragedy that we lost it."

In 1951 the Central Valley Project completed a new, taller Mendota Dam. To replace what the Friant system diverted, the federal government built the Delta-Mendota Canal, which moves water 117 miles from the delta, south to Mendota Pool, and sprinkles water back in the river channel. This means that the federal government built a canal partly to replace the San Joaquin River water that other canals divert. It's an incredible feat of engineering, and it's as crazy on paper as it is in operation. Would Latta have seen it the same way?

Since the construction of Friant Dam, locals have been fishing in canals for bass, not for salmon. The town of Mendota is officially the Cantaloupe Center of the World, and coyotes travel the dry riverbed like any other piece of desert. I stopped at a low bridge on the river once where a sign said No Diving. The bed was sand. Many nonprofits have joined forces as the San Joaquin River Partnership, to put water back into the channel. But in the Valley, the river reappears inside canals and in the form of citrus, melons, and nuts. So many growers, recreationists, and wildlife depend on this one river that it has been impossible to reach an agreement between conservation and commerce that satisfies all parties. It does seem appropriate that the Delta-Mendota Canal cuts across the old site of Las Juntas, since many Californians believe that the state has reached a critical junction about how to manage its water and whether its complex distribution system can continue to work. Until these concerns are resolved, people will continue to dump their tires in the dry riverbed. They dump mattresses and couch cushions, diapers and bags of trash. Whole cars lie rusting among the weeds beside the reinforced banks. As an empty channel, it has been treated like a vacant lot, dead to the world and never coming back.

On Friday morning, Latta's crew had more water than they could handle. Heaving their boat ashore, they walked it around the dam and slid it back into the water. The *Alta* was now officially in the San Joaquin watershed. From here, they could briefly put down their paddles as the stronger current carried them north toward Firebaugh. For once, they were on schedule.

Various California towns claim to lie halfway between the state's top and bottom. The state's true center lies thirty-five miles northeast of the Valley town Madera, in North Fork, and Highway 99's halfway point lands in Fresno. But one halfway point that people have claimed lies south of Madera. Two trees grow there on the median of Highway 99, marking the symbolic middle of California: a palm to represent the southern half and a pine to represent the north.

Located between Avenue Ten and Avenue Eleven, the trees stand like any other highway decoration, surrounded by orchards and vineyards, blending in so well that drivers easily zoom past without noticing. The trees aren't natives. One is a canary palm from the islands off Morocco; the other, a deodar cedar from the Himalayas. But they have been planted widely enough throughout California to now seem native. People agree that the trees predate Highway 99, but theories abound on their origin. Some people credit Fresno agriculture students for planting them in 1915, after which engineers laid the lanes around them. Others say that the Leyh family planted them in their yard as part of their motor camp and market; when the federal government seized the Leyh's land with imminent domain to establish U.S. Route 99, then the main highway between Canada and Mexico, the family demanded that the highway be built around their trees. Others speculate that the early engineers who paved the old road through here also planted the trees to mark the halfway point, before they had more advanced surveying technology. Whatever the truth, locals have grown protective. When CalTrans planned to remove the trees to update the highway, locals and CalTrans employees convinced them to build around the trees, just as engineers always had. After a 2005 storm blew over the original cedar, it was CalTrans that planted the replacement.

Even though the trees don't stand exactly center, they offer a profound visual representation of the division between California's wet north and dry dependent south, as well as a cultural divide—not just one area being fancy and beachy and the other being rural or mountainous. It emphasizes how residents feel disconnected from each other. The state is so huge that entire countries could fit inside its borders. Many inner Californians feel as removed from San Franciscans as they feel from Angelenos and Oregonians, but they have strong feelings about the others, viewing coastals as people who hang on the Valley's coattails, tug at its farmers' sleeves, and only give back grief about their impressions of the Valley's land and people. Coastal folks take the Valley's food and water and only give back attitude. And how would these regions feel connected when so few things unite them. What are Californians' shared values and goals? The struggles that shape their larger identity? Or even unite people in Bakersfield with people in Fresno? Palm trees and pine trees; redwoods and beach sand. Across those hundreds of north-south miles, allegiances fall apart, a sense of connection frays, and bitterness forms as one side feels drained and disrespected by the other. Water issues divide California, but from another perspective, water issues should unite the state. Water is one of the main themes of their whole narrative, and many nonprofits propose water sharing as a solution to help California.

Highway 99 runs parallel to the old Southern Pacific Railroad tracks and connects the Valley's largest cities on the densely populated east side. Leaving the spacious middle felt both invigorating and unnerving. Latta had the river. I had the 99.

Traffic. Chain stores. The impatient drivers riding your bumper, and that worthless urge to weave between the cars in front of you to jockey for first place in a race to Heart Attack City. The cortisol surges, and once again the highway becomes an irritation, an intrusion, an obligatory space you must endure to get to where you're really going. This is the experience most people have of the Valley.

So much of Valley life is highway life. Hours-long drives are the quintessential experience. When they interviewed elusive cotton magnate J. G. Boswell for their book *The King of California*, journalists Mark Arax and Rick Wartzan zigzagged for 150 miles without ever leaving his property.

On the highway, the air can go from heavenly to horrific in seconds.

By the huge Halos citrus plant in Delano, the air smelled intensely of fresh fruit—one of the best smells I've ever encountered, a perfume of pollen, citrus skin, and freshly squeezed juice. Sixty seconds down the road, the smell of burnt hair overtook it.

As I passed a building paradoxically labeled Freshko near Fresno, the air smelled of chemicals and pine. Thankfully, the scent soon gave way to the clean smell of clipped lawn grass, something actually fresh.

Rather than rotting plants or corpses, some of the Valley's stink comes from the chemicals sprayed on crops. Those come and go with the season, but some of the smells that stay yearlong come from facilities processing cottonseed oil and from rendering plants, where workers turn animal carcasses into the raw material for products like gelatin, fertilizer, and soap.

Highway 99 can seem monotonous, but its appearance changes as much as its smells. Sometimes it's a corridor of oleander and orchards. Sometimes it's a flat, naked strip laid out across a boundless sea of fields. When you get up on raised overpasses near the towns, the view is spectacular, farther and wider than anywhere else you'll see here. But it's brief.

Despite it all, I've come to like the 99. Intimacy improves appearances as you see past the warts. I've seen roosters running on this highway. I've seen coyotes. I've seen a peacock pecking the dirt right outside downtown Fresno, and a mess of plastic trash bins strewn across three lanes after they fell off a truck. I've seen brown paper bags scoot in front of traffic in a way that looked like groundhogs running, and I've seen a groundhog scoot into my lane before it was stopped with a thump. After a car accident, the shattered glass twinkles like stars, and the husk of a burnt car looks especially morbid parked on the shoulder beside a tilled field. On one trip, I spotted three colorful chickens walking the oleander divider, unaffected by passing traffic. I feared for the lives of the two nipply dogs trotting beside that same divider farther south.

Sometimes Highway 99 is too crowded and deflowered, too cluttered with fast food, look-alike towns, and all the greedy fruit of resource extraction. Certain sections seem doomed. Mostly, I like driving it. I love its empty stretches. They're meditative, especially between Kingsburg and Delano and between Turlock and Madera. The air is cool and fresh there; the night, particularly black. South of Chowchilla you can see a blinking red light on a lone cell tower and the glow of an approaching train for miles. A solitary Chevron station floats in the darkness, eerie and welcoming at the same time.

Driving Highway 99 at night is a different experience. In places, you only see what's in your headlights. The darkness plays with your mind. An occasional dome of light will rise in the distance. The night swallows the horizon, but the dome glows out on it, suggesting some city on the plains, a big town or agricultural operation that you, as a civilian, would know nothing about if you saw it. The light's intensity astounds you, the severity of its brightness. The way it comes out of what seems like nowhere is weird. Everything else is pitch black. Just farms, side roads. Then this crazy dome of light in an otherwise unpopulated land. But that's the thing you don't understand; it isn't unpopulated. It's the fastest-growing part of America's most populous state. The Valley is so huge that it absorbs all those people, and you can drive the empty spaces between towns for so long that you think no one lives here.

On my night drive from Hanford, my tires hit Highway 99, and something else kicked in. I had missed the rural interior's views and aromas. I had missed its vacancy. But I couldn't deny that it had been nice to reunite with modernity. As comfortable as I feel amid farms and on parklands, I'm partly a city person, and I'd come to miss the energetic trappings of city life. From a campsite near Benicia in 1862, William Brewer wrote, "The crowds of the city make me feel sad and lonely. I feel restless and long for the quiet of camp life—quiet, yet active—rich in that excitement that arises from the contemplation and study of nature." I used to feel that way. Now I like bustle. I like sidewalks on my streets and pedestrians on my sidewalks. Bakersfield was no Fresno, just as Fresno was no Berkeley, but Bakersfield was more comfortable than Lost Hills. At least I could get a matcha latte at a local coffee shop in Bakersfield and shop a natural-foods store. The Valley is big enough to contain both worlds. I am too.

On Highway 99, on the opposite side of the Valley from Latta's route, I continued north toward Madera, letting Fresno's pavement fade in my rearview as it turned the land back over to food. Madeira is a kind of Portuguese wine, but the California town of Madera takes its name from the Spanish word for "lumber." It was founded in 1867 to process Sierra Nevada logs.

As fertile as the Valley is for farming, the sierra was equally rich in timber. One of the world's largest and oldest tree species, the giant sequoia, grows only here. The biggest tree there has grown over three hundred feet tall, one hundred feet around, and three thousand years old. Enormous sugar pines, ponderosas, and Douglas firs towered among them, creating a landscape that enchanted naturalist John Muir enough to devote his life to exploring, recording, and protecting part of the Sierra Nevada. It was in Yosemite in 1903 that Muir convinced President Theodore Roosevelt to expand the small park's federal protections and in turn create a more unified National Park System. But with trees that tall and that straight, the Sierra Nevada were also a logger's dream. A third of the sierra's virgin timber was cut by the 1870s. Loggers hauled trees out of the mountains on horse-drawn wagons and by floating them down rushing rivers. They were processed in towns like Madera.

Logging only provides a small part of California's modern economy compared to farming, technology, and outdoor recreation, and Madera is now a growing residential community of sixty thousand. Latta's ethnological work frequently took him into the Sierra Nevada's foothills, but because the Yokuts didn't inhabit the elevations where the sequoias grew, Latta's books rarely range that high either.

As I sped north with the windows down, a white haze formed a ring around the moon. Even an outsider like me could tell that tule fog was forming. I hadn't dealt with much fog on this visit, but some had blindsided me outside Madera years earlier.

I had been driving sixty miles an hour in a ten-foot U-Haul, towing my small Toyota sedan on a rattling trailer hitch from Phoenix to Oregon. I'd read about tule fog, how it cut visibility down to a few hundred feet, even a foot, in seconds. When fog struck Highway 99 that night, it swallowed the world.

The shoulder disappeared. Lane lines disappeared. I squeezed the steering wheel and leaned so far forward that my forehead nearly touched the windshield, and I could still barely see past my hood.

Adrenalin surged through my chest as I released the gas and held my foot above the brake. My headlights turned the moisture into a flat iridescence that smeared across my windshield like dirty wiper fluid. No mile markers. No trees. No sign that I was moving except for my speedometer's fall. What was fascinating was how the fog first appeared as a wall up ahead, stretching straight across the stubby fields and highway from right to left. By the time I realized what it was, I was in it.

I unrolled the window. Somewhere, an eighteen-wheeler rumbled. Cold wind wet my face as my speed dropped from fifty to thirty to twenty.

In extreme tule fog, the National Weather Service suggests that travelers postpone their trips until it lifts—usually by late morning—but I was only a few miles from my hotel. I'd driven nearly seven hundred miles from Phoenix, Arizona, and I wanted to sleep. I coached myself: Be brave. Hang in there. Then the competing voice weighed in: Driving without visibility—that's not courage; that's recklessness. Pull off the highway. Wait it out.

I coasted, slowed. A faint halo appeared beside me, and a single car emerged from the mist. Materializing like a hesitant phantom, the car braked and then sped up, flashed its high beams once, and fell back into the mass of undifferentiated white.

My exit sign appeared before I could react. Riding the brake, I drove on toward the next exit, watching for it carefully. After two white-knuckle miles, it emerged. I eased onto the off-ramp, squinting for the stop sign. I looked both ways countless times, but it was pointless. I couldn't see either direction. So I honked and pulled out, hoping for the best.

On the opposite side of the Valley from Madera, along Latta's route, is another town few outsiders talk about called Firebaugh. Squeezed into a narrow strip between the San Joaquin River and Helm Canal, this 7,500-person town of feed stores and packing sheds has two quaint Main Streets running parallel to each other, graced with nice houses, dirt lots, and low midcentury storefronts filled with restaurants and barbershops. With its blue sky and dusty horizon, Firebaugh reminded me of small-town southeastern Arizona, without the cactus.

In 1985 the LA punk band Circle Jerks released a song about it.

The band's bassist, Zander Schloss, broke down in Firebaugh once driving to a show, and they had to wait for a mechanic to fix his van. He and drummer Keith Clark cowrote this song. It's a simplistic, adolescent take on small-town America, but it's the only song that mentions Firebaugh. A punk wearing cutoff camouflage shorts and skate shoes with no socks probably attracted funny looks here in the early 1980s, before alternative music went mainstream, and this song captures the author's feeling of displacement, of being unwelcome, of perceived judgment and urban superiority, as well as his larger perceptions about the whole Valley: rednecks, racism, hatred, insularity, xenophobia. After spending so many years around here, I knew that was only part of the picture.

The rivers that flowed from the sierra caused travelers many problems, so early American settlers built their roads along the Valley's far east side. The soil didn't turn to mush at the base of the mountains, and the waterways' narrower upper channels were easier to swim, cross on horseback, and build bridges across. Farther east, the waters spread in marshes, and poor drainage left standing water in inlets like Lone Willow Slough. The discovery of gold in 1848 sent a stream of hopefuls through here trying to reach the Sierra Nevada. Water stood between miners and their fortunes, so businessmen sold them ferry passage at places like Firebaugh, just like San Francisco outfitters sold them picks, rope, and tack. What's more American than a business opportunity?

The Sutter's Fort–San Jose Trail crossed the San Joaquin River outside modern-day Manteca, creating a steady supply of customers, so that's where John Doak and Jacob Bonsell launched the Valley's first commercial ferry in 1848. Doak and Bonsell shuttled people across for a dollar a head, three for a horse. Wagons cost eight. Those prices were expensive, and the two men made a killing. Ferries popped up everywhere after that.

During the 1850s and 1860s, Whitmore's, Smith's, and Jones's ferries crossed different points along the Kings River. Twelve operated on the San Joaquin River. Some ferries were repurposed rowboats. Some were flat, wooden platforms with no railing. Sophisticated operators used metal cables to keep their direction straight. Sometimes the current tore the docked boats free and sent them downstream. Travelers didn't always need the ferries. During dry years, people could simply walk across. Ferry passengers and outlaws were the Valley's first commuters, moving east and west across the area between their wilderness jobs.

A businessman named Andrew D. Firebaugh started operating a ferry here in 1853, during the second to last year of the gold rush, and the town grew around it. As the railroad laid more tracks and the Valley's rivers got drained, private landowners built bridges across the rivers, making the Butterfield Overland Stage and ferries like Firebaugh obsolete by the 1870s.

The ferry had stopped running when William Brewer visited in the spring of 1863. Instead, like Las Juntas to the south, outlaws, violence, and booze had roughed the village's edges. "When we got to Firebaugh's," Brewer wrote, "we found more excitement. A band of desperados were just below—we had passed them in the morning, but luckily did not see them. Only a few days before they had attempted to rob some men, and in the scrimmage one man was shot dead and one of the desperadoes was so badly cut that he died on Monday. Another had just been caught. Some men took him into the bushes, some pistol shots were heard, they came back and said he had escaped. A newly made grave on the bank suggested another disposal of him, but all were content not to inquire further."

Joaquin Murrieta was supposedly dead by 1863. Various outlaws claimed to be part of Murrieta's clan, using his name to generate fear and respect, though they had no real affiliation. The bandits Brewer heard of could have been a group that went unrecorded, or they could have been Tiburcio Vásquez's compadres. Vásquez's group descended on Firebaugh in the early 1870s, robbing people and killing residents for, stories say, no reason. On December 26, 1873, Vásquez's gang raided Whitemore's Ferry, northwest of Hanford. At night, the bandits tied people up and robbed them and three stores of over $2,000 in cash and property. Then they ran across the new bridge on the river and escaped on horses they'd stashed in a corral. It was the very bridge that permanently diverted the ferry's customers. When Latta came through, all that was left of the ferries was their names.

On Friday morning, July 24, 1938, Latta called Kern County Chamber of Commerce secretary Gary Hoffman to tell him that the *Alta* had safely reached Firebaugh. Beyond Firebaugh, the *Alta* passed Dos Palos. *Palos* means "timber"—particularly, tall, straight trees with trunks like poles. When Spanish explorer Gabriel Moraga came through here in the early 1800s, he found two big poplar trees growing alone on the plain and named the site Dos Palos. Most of the Valley's well-known Spanish names came from Moraga: the Kings River, the Merced, Mariposa, Calaveras, and, of course, the San Joaquin. Add to that list this dinky little town.

Moraga's two sticks stood near the southern edge of the 48,823-acre Rancho Sanjon de Santa Rita. One of less than twenty Mexican land grants in the Valley, this was one of the biggest and wettest. It stretched for miles along the west bank of the San Joaquin River and was well irrigated with sloughs and often covered with seasonal floodwaters and all their attendant waterfowl. The word *sanjon* means "slough." The sanjon in question is Fresno Slough. It's the sanjon that drove Derby nuts.

The original owners did little to develop this swampy, out-of-the-way property, so they sold the ranch piecemeal to Miller and Lux by 1865, along with their 7,500 head of beef cattle. "The grass [was] green there nine months out of the year," Miller once said. "I thought it was the most favorable place that I had struck yet."

Always the expansionistic opportunists, Miller and Lux immediately started buying public domain swampland on the ranch's north and south sides, often gaming the system with fake homesteader names. By 1881 they owned sixty-eight miles of unbroken riverfront along the San Joaquin's west bank; in places their land stretched forty miles wide. Miller established the original Dos Palos Colony and built the company's regional headquarters nearby. Before then, this stretch of land between Firebaugh and Los Banos was so dark and lonely that a Dos Palos settler named David Mortimer Wood also used to hang a lit lantern in his cabin window for Butterfield Overland Stage drivers. The light oriented them on the plain and offered a welcome nod in the deep frontier night.

I know how lonely you can get, traveling for hours alone. So far, on this trip I'd driven 289 miles from Bakersfield chasing Latta, plus about 170 miles of side roads and backtracking. But I can barely imagine how good stage drivers felt seeing that solitary lamplight emerge up ahead, because it's difficult to imagine the depth of night that cloaked nineteenth-century eyes before modern-day light pollution.

Back on the other side of the Valley, the lights of Chowchilla appeared ahead of me on Highway 99. There weren't many, but they provided the main glow on the horizon, as comforting as a lantern in a window.

The stretch between Madera and Merced is one of my favorite pieces of Valley road. It's empty, quiet. While it's green by day, its night immerses you in darkness as deep as the back of your eyelids. Highway 99 travels long distances between towns in one of the mid-Valley's more vacant quarters. It's the kind of place people mean when they say, "I grew up in the country," a place where people have opinions about water rights and holding the door for strangers, where people love trucks and mention Jesus and will show you a good time on the river if you join them fishing. It's not a Whole Foods kind of marketplace, though it is bookended by them on two sides and could become one. For now, I stood in line at a Chowchilla taqueria beside a cowboy in silver spurs.

Tacos El Grullense No. 2 was your usual quickie place with sweet powder-mix horchata and hard plastic seats that felt comfortable after a long workday. I got in line next to the cowboy. We both leaned against the railing, studying the menu. "Go ahead if you know what you want," the cowboy said. He wore a huge battered hat, dirty jeans, and a dark vest over a white western shirt. I said thanks but I was still figuring that out too.

While Portugal's soccer team played Argentina on the corner TV, the cowboy and I talked about choices. "I've had that super burrito before," he said. "It's pretty good. Had their tacos. They're good." His breath smelled like beer, and he talked slowly, using his tongue to adjust a tobacco chew in his lip between sentences.

On the other side of the room, a group of sixteen middle-aged, tan white people took up multiple tables, filling the tiny restaurant with chatter and laughter. They were part of an RV club staying at a nearby RV park. Members had come from all over, including the Bay Area, Hayward, Modesto, and Grass Valley. When they left, they danced outside by the door, and as one lady slipped out, she told me, "And we haven't even been drinkin' yet!"

The cowboy's spurs clinked against the white tile when he approached the register, the way I imagine cowboys did to a saloon back in 1860 Firebaugh. He ordered in such a low, deep voice that I couldn't hear the words. The cashier asked, "Here or to go?"

He said, "To go, please."

She said, "Need anything to drink?"

"No," he said, "I'm gonna go home and have myself a cerveza." They laughed. "That's gonna be alright."

I ordered my usual: two tacos and a side of refried beans. Instead of my usual carnitas and al pastor, I got chilé verde tacos this time, which I didn't often see. The cowboy sat down. He was number 80. The cashier called my order first, and when I carried my tray past the cowboy, I said, "I feel rude eating before you get yours."

He smirked and nodded, dipping his big hat low to block his eyes. "That's alright. Yours is smaller."

I sat down to eat as the lights of Main Street Chowchilla loomed to my left. Like a painted line, they ran straight west from here across the highway, on down through the central part of this eighteen-thousand-person town.

Chowchilla. The name conjures images of fur-bearing Andean

mammals. It lends itself easily to jokes: *What are you doing tonight?* Answer: *Chowchillin'*. *What are you drinking?* Answer: *A Chowchiller.* The people who originally claimed it were no joke. They were warriors. They lived on the Chowchilla River and stole settlers' horses. Local folklore says the name means "bravery" in their Yokuts dialect. Others claim that it means "murderers." However many people the Chowchilla Tribe killed, it could never compare to the thirty thousand to eighty thousand Yokuts that American settlement killed and displaced in the Valley to build our agricultural empire. The cowboy I joked with is part of a long tradition of local cowboys, some of whom ran the Chunut people off Atwell's Island when they decided to use it for cattle. Chowchilla's local tribe were originally the Chaushila, but settlers anglicized it into something that we could pronounce or transcribed it the way they misheard it. History is filled with transcription errors and modifications. Unlike the Chunut and other peaceful Yokuts to the south, the Chowchilla were tough, dogged fighters. When American settlers started encroaching on their territory and trying to run them out, a militia led by local entrepreneur James Savage chased the Chaushila into the Sierra Nevada in 1851. Savage spoke Yokuts dialects. He'd married Yokuts women and even fought battles with them against other tribes. Local legend says that his militia followed the Chaushila into a spectacular valley whose soaring granite domes hung thousands of feet in the air and were cut by waterfalls. Everyone knows Yosemite. Few know Chowchilla. White people would have found the Yosemite Valley eventually, but the Chowchilla connection is stitched into the fabric of history.

On Robertson Boulevard, the main drag through downtown named after the town's founder, teenagers ate at Pedro's Pizza, and a middle-aged man walked his BMX down the sidewalk. Main Street businesses, like Miss Kitty's Mercantile, occupied low, midcentury brick shops with wooden-shingle awnings. It wasn't the frontier architecture of Hanford, but it had a nice *Leave It to Beaver* look amplified to that California pitch by towering palms whose swaying fronds are now as iconic as a Valley oak. Chowchilla's wayward location has so far placed it outside the sphere of gentrification and suburbanization shaping Fresno and Modesto.

Chowchilla didn't form along the railroad tracks or because of choice geography. It wasn't a ferry or stagecoach stop. One speculating Pennsylvania land developer saw an opportunity for a planned community. On May 22, 1912, the friendly, well-liked Orlando Alison Robertson bought a large ranch from the California Pastoral and Agricultural Company. He split half the ranch into small lots to sell to farmers, and he laid a grid of city streets on the land's northeast corner, including Robertson Boulevard, which he lined with palm trees. He built commercial buildings and a hotel, installed the water supply, and even got the Southern Pacific Railroad to build a twelve-mile spur line into town. Somehow, he chose to honor the local Yokuts by naming his town after them. Most modern advertising agencies would have likely advised against that. I applaud Robertson's choice.

Unfortunately, when the town is known at all, it isn't for its pistachios and dairy cows. It's for the Chowchilla incident. California is a state plagued with bizarre crimes, from the Charles Manson murders to the Zodiac Killer to Patty Hearst's kidnapping by a left-wing Berkeley guerilla group. But the Chowchilla incident still counts as one of California's strangest.

On July 15, 1976, a yellow bus full of twenty-six kids stopped on rural Avenue Twenty-One outside Chowchilla. They were coming back from the second-to-last day of summer school at Dairyland Elementary, where they had balloon tosses and made arts and crafts. A van was parked in the middle of the road with its hood up, seemingly broken down. When the bus driver, Ed Ray, went to help, three masked gunmen stepped onto the bus and pushed Ray to the back. Kids hid under their seats. The gunmen transferred them to vans hidden in a ditch and drove one hundred miles west to Livermore, where one of the kidnappers' fathers owned a rock quarry.

Before the heist, the men had built a holding cell by burying a moving van six feet deep in the dirt. After dark, they forced the kids and bus driver inside. It was a one-hundred-degree day. There were mattresses on the floor, along with some food and battery-powered fans. As Ray later recounted, "The ceiling started to cave in and everything else. We thought we were going to have it right then, but kept begging to let us out."

Ages five to fourteen, the kids cried for their parents. They comforted each other, threw up from fear, and peed into a small box with a hole cut in it, and the van filled with the stench of bad breath and vomit. The fans the kidnappers installed ran out of batteries. The hostages thought they were going to die.

The three twenty-year-old criminals with pantyhose over their faces had hatched a plan to get rich. They'd seen a newspaper headline about how the state of California had a billion-dollar surplus. "I kept thinking the state's got more than it needs," one of the kidnappers told the parole board. "They won't miss $5 million."

As parents reported their kids missing to the Chowchilla Police Department and journalists called for information, all the activity jammed the switchboard, and the criminals couldn't call in their $5 million ransom. After struggling to get through the phone lines, the kidnappers took a nap. By then, the kids had stacked the mattresses to reach the buried van's roof, which allowed Ray to pop the hatch and push away the dirt and heavy truck battery that weighed down the lid, and they ran to the one quarry employee on the premises. The man recognized the kids from the news. "This world's been looking for you," he said. They had spent sixteen hours down there in the dark.

The three criminals were sentenced to life in prison. The victims returned to school in Chowchilla and grew up, but their trauma remained. They suffered from anxiety, claustrophobia, depression, and post-traumatic stress disorder. Some couldn't sleep. They had nightmares. "It's not normal for someone who's almost 50 years old to be afraid of the dark," one victim told CNN decades later. The trauma made her overprotective of her kids, even following her oldest son's school bus from kindergarten to his babysitter's house one week. Who can blame her? I doubt I could even put my kid on a bus. Forty years later, two of the kidnappers got out of prison early, and some of the survivors sued them for emotional distress. These unlucky kids were just trying to ride home from school. Their Chowchilla is an incident without end.

But not everyone I talk to knows that story, or even the town's name. For all the ways America has erased Native American culture, indigenous linguistics still color many regions. Washington State has its -ish suffixes in singular names like Duwamish, Snohomish, and Stillaguamish. New York has -ogue and -ioga in Cutchogue, Onondaga, and Ticonderoga. To me, Spanish names like Fresno define California more than Anglo ones like Bakersfield and Webb. Having grown up in Arizona, my tendency is to turn everything into Spanish, and it doesn't matter if it's French or Italian, which in this case makes me want to turn the double *l*'s into a *y* to make it "Chowcheeya." Chowchilla is just one of the Valley's many memorable names that make travelers pause before saying them out loud, and that sometimes seem less Spanish, English, or Native American than rural Californian.

There's Biola, Planada, and Orosi.

There's Ceres, which is pronounced "series," instead of "ser-ehs."

There's Lathrop, often pronounced "lay-throp," with a long *a*, though it's supposed to be "lah-thrup," with a soft *a*.

There's Manteca, which for years I mispronounced as "man-teh-kuh," assuming it was the Spanish word for lard. No one ever corrected me, though I would've welcomed it. Locals pronounce it "man-tea-kah," and it wasn't named for lard. Some people will tell you that the area was settled by people of Portuguese descent, and in Portuguese, *manteca* means "butter." In fact, the name is a misspelling of the train station's original name, Monteca, which locals came up with at random in 1873 because their first choice, Cowell Station, was taken. Lard is still a local joke. I'm sure city officials aren't laughing.

Nearby, there's Ripon. Not "rih-pawn," as I've always pronounced it, pretentiously: "Pass the Grey Roupon mustard." Locals call it "Ripp-in," as in, "I'm rippin' through town," which sounds super country when you say it out loud. It's a similar situation to tiny Tipton by Bakersfield, which people pronounce "tip-tin," not "tip-tawn."

Then, of course, there's Tulare. I'm not sure if there's a right or wrong way here, but my urge has always been to pronounce it "too-la-ree." Locals mostly say "too-larry," as in, "I knew a guy named Larry," and as they're residents, I would defer to them.

The clerk at the Dollar Mercado didn't know why the town was called Chowchilla. "What does it mean?" she said shaking her head. "I don't live here." She commuted sixteen miles away from Madera. Robert the trucker didn't know either.

In a long parking spot at McDonald's, Robert ate in the front seat of his semi. It was 8:00 p.m., but his shift ended at 3:00 a.m., so this was lunch. The smell of french fries and manure from nearby stockyards filled the air. Robert ate with the door open, because he liked the cool breeze, and he'd be sitting for the next seven hours. "I haul nasty stuff," he said, "rendered animal byproducts," meaning organs, bones, blood, and fat. He did two runs a night between Fresno and Turlock, a total of four hundred miles. When he finished at 3:00 a.m., he crawled into bed beside his wife, who woke up a few hours later. She stayed at home. "That's her job," he said. I wondered what she thought about his sexist description. They didn't have kids and had no plans to have any. His work was exhausting enough. At least the night shift gifted him clearer roads and cooler temperatures than what daytime drivers dealt with, definitely better "than that mess near Fresno at any time of day." He lifted a tall cup of McDonald's coffee, showing me the secret to his nocturnal power. Empty packs of cigarettes sat in multiple cupholders and on the passenger seat. A souped-up pickup splattered with mud raced out of the lot, and Robert looked at the clock. Lunch had ended, so he swung his legs inside the cab and headed south on the 99.

A freight train barreled across Robertson. Eventually, the high-speed rail will too. The state selected Chowchilla as the site to build the Y-shaped train junction, called a Wye, where the track's main line will break into two—one running up to Merced, the other to the Bay Area. Soon, isolated Chowchilla will be more connected to the rest of California; the space and distances that once sheltered it will collapse, along with the wall between the interior and the coast. Would the train change the town? Would commuters just make more jokes about the name?

Across the street at Starbucks, a preteen tried to steal bills from the tip jar. A customer caught him and told him, "That's the kind of thing that'll get you locked up." The kid dropped the bills back into the plastic bin, but he didn't like it. By the front door, the man kept schooling him: "You better watch out, son; what you're doing's no good." The kid ignored him, running his finger across a black metal table and then following his two friends west across the lot toward the Shell station. The man put his phone back to his ear and told the person on the other end, "Oh, some kid who's obviously never worked a day in his damn life."

In the vacuum left by Robert's rattling truck engine, birds chirped in the trees. The air felt clear, free of summer's heaviness. Somehow, even a fast-food parking lot could be beautiful in the right weather and if, for a moment, you could appreciate how fragile life really was. This damp part of the Valley felt alive to me, more like grass than wet dirt, more secure and vivacious than the parched desert lands south of Fresno. If I had to settle in the Valley, it would be here.

Thirty miles to the west and nearly a century earlier, Latta's crew floated winding river miles where the only ones to witness their journey were the sort of cows that would one day end up in Robert's truck. As I headed back toward the highway, signs reached out for my attention. Signs for an antique sale, signs for $1 coffee, signs warning Caution: Vehicle Clearance 15'4", and one sign listing

<= North

99

South =>

The sun set on Chowchilla, and when it rose again, I kept driving. Next to the Chowchilla River by the Merced County line, a sign said Pray for Rain. In a land most people see from their cars, drivers are a captive audience, and businesses use signs to turn drivers into customers or political allies.

Signs were especially dense on the dry west side, but all along the Valley's roads and highways, agricultural interests run ads warning drivers about the tenuous relationship between water, jobs, and their food supply. Food Grows Where Water Flows is the most familiar roadside slogan, but the attempt to change drivers' minds takes many forms.

Farm Water Feeds the Nation.

Farm Water Cut No Water | Higher Food Cost.

No Water = No Jobs.

Stop the Congress Created Dust Bowl.

Solve the Water Crisis.

These messages appear on traditional billboards. Some hang on huge banners draped on rusty semitrailers parked beside fields. Once used to carry cattle or tomatoes, the trailers now carry a new crop: public relations.

With simple slogans, the signs try to change voters' and taxpayers' minds by connecting local water regulations to passersby's wallets, to connect the dirt to drivers' families and to dissolve the psychological distance between the coast and the interior, which has long made the region's problems seem like only farmers' issues. Many of us struggle to reconcile our concerns over agriculture's environmental impact with our empathy for struggling farmers and with our love of ice cream and avocados. As Rene said at Starbucks days ago, it's complicated. Marketing campaigns try to simplify everything, smoothing the big issues' rough edges to make gray areas black and white. They tell us who the enemies are (Congress) and appeal to our sympathies (Do you really want to take away people's jobs?) to convince consumers of the necessity of farmers' enterprise to everyone's livelihood. It's not just farmers who need water, see; it's you and your kid and your dog, which is true. These slogans use a type of implied modus ponens argument: *Farmers grow food. You eat food. Growing food requires water. So you need farmers to keep their water.* If A, then B. If B, then C. Because A, therefore C. The message might as well read, "Hey, do you want to live? Then give farmers their water." The question is whether these marketing slogans change people's minds. Concise as they are, it's hard to ingest messages at eighty miles per hour, especially when you're scrolling through your device for songs and reaching into a bag of chips.

I tried to analyze the signs' rhetorical strategies while I raced past them. On the I-5 north of Lost Hills, one sign said, "25 million Californians pay millions for State water that's not delivered!" That was too long. The best ones were short and sweet and humanized abstract issues: "Do you want your ice cream to be expensive?" "You will lose your jobs." "Do you like to eat?" Some signs try to scare drivers. Some try to persuade. Some use catchy phrases and pretty pictures to evoke pleasant feelings, showing farms not as agribusiness filled with stinking manure pits but as charming old-world enterprises run by families who are in touch with the land. One very effective strategy involves cost.

Few American consumers want higher prices, and we fear scarcity. So farmers use signs to convince us that unless they get cheap, reliable water, their productivity is threatened, and prices will skyrocket. The thing is, productivity has always been threatened, because if food grows where water flows, then in the Valley's case, that water often flows salty and there's not enough room to store it.

Farm slogans try to connect the dots for consumers, to connect our lives with the lives everything around us, to make us think just a little about this land we're speeding through. *We work hard here,* the signs are saying. *We're trying to get by just like you. Don't vote against us. You need us!* They try to put a human face to the abstractions like "drought" and "farm crisis" we hear in the news, to humanize issues. *You want to eat? Fine. You want to pay more for food? Fine. If not, listen up. Pull the frozen peas from your freezer,* the signs try to say. *Look at your kid eating toast at the table. See the slippers on your feet as you eat an ice-cream bar at 10:00 p.m. in your kitchen. We made you. This soil is you. Don't forget it.* Then your car passes, and the message is gone. The billboards have to serve strong medicine to reach an oblivious driver whose only point of contact is a few seconds' approach. The signs shoot through the car window and barb the words so that the message stays after the sign has passed, like a fishhook or an exploding bullet.

Who wrote these slogans? Did irrigation districts pay advertising agencies, or did the California Farm Water Coalition pay them?

On Highway 99 outside Kingsburg, a small sign on the side of a fruit car said Drivers Wanted, near a large sign that said Jesus Is Lord. If that were true about Jesus, then why had he shown no mercy with rain? At this point in the drought, even people in the wine industry would be fine if Jesus turned wine back into water.

Pray for Rain the sign on the Chowchilla River said. What was missing was a sign that said The End.

After Chowchilla, one of my favorite signs appeared. Maybe too many adolescent things still amuse me at my age, but after years of driving by Sandy Mush Road, wondering about its origin, I couldn't shake the fact that Sandy Mush is one of the most suggestive street names in America. And that's compared to Arizona's Bloody Basin Road, Connecticut's Roast Meat Hill, and North Carolina's Puddin' Ridge Road. My California atlas showed that Sandy Mush Road bisected a large area named Sandy Mush Country—a whole land of mush— before it ended twenty-one miles later at its juncture with the San Luis National Wildlife Refuge. How did anyone plant crops in this place? Or build houses? Didn't the road sink? I decided to finally drive its entire length to find out.

Before I headed west on Sandy Mush, a gas station attendant admitted he wasn't sure about the name. He said, "I've never thought about it." Really? Those thirteen letters contain entire worlds. A hotel clerk nearby told me, "I think there's, like, a juvie that's called Sandy Mush, and it's on that road, so maybe they have to do with each other." A customer at a Wendy's thought the name had to do with the fact that it was out in the country, far from civilization, so that "mush" was slang for "the sticks."

I flipped a U and cut across three lanes of Highway 99 traffic to reach Sandy Mush Road. Bumpy and uneven, it had more cracks than the usual small rural road and was riddled with warps that kept me thinking of Duane Eddy's song "Forty Miles of Bad Road."

CalTrans had started building a new overpass to funnel cars east and west over Highway 99. Thirty-seven thousand vehicles passed Sandy Mush Road every day, with eighty thousand projected by 2024, yet it was the last road in Merced County to cross the highway on ground level, or "at grade." That meant cars had to cross three lanes, as I did; stop in the center, in the wide median; and then dart across another three. There was no on-ramp. To turn right, you had to turn into southbound traffic near the caution sign. The overpass would cost $77 million and was part of CalTrans's long-term plan to widen all of Highway 99, from the top to the bottom, to six lanes. For now, a huge mound of dirt awaited paving in a green field beside me. Behind me, a small black pug chased my car for a quarter mile before stopping in the center lane to bark. I wanted to drive to the first houses I saw to ask the residents about the name, but locked gates blocked each dirt driveway. Instead, I found Adam.

Adam was sitting on bags of wheat seed stacked on the back of a flatbed trailer. He sat exactly the way men had in the black-and-white nineteenth-century photos of barges moving grain along the San Joaquin River: back straight, legs dangling, one hand on his hip. He was the kind of local whom Latta would have interviewed, and this was the kind of moment that I imagine Latta frequently had. Age twenty-six, Adam lived in Le Grand, a town of 1,600 to the east where the bus from the Chowchilla incident was stored in a museum. When I asked what today's work entailed, he pointed to the tractor driving back and forth in the field. He said, "Sowing wheat."

Adam tore the tag off the bottom of the seed bag, leapt from the truck, and handed me the tag. "It's certified," he said proudly, assuming I knew what that meant. He had a wide, warm smile and worn jeans. As we talked, he kicked the side of the tire to get dirt off his shoe and popped a few kernels of wheat in his mouth as though they were M&Ms. "Patron brand wheat," the bag said, "certified for human consumption."

He and his friend in the tractor had worked before for these ranchers, J. Marchini and Son, who used the more costly flood irrigation for their crops, not drip. "Maybe they got a lot of money," he said, "I don't know." What did he know about this road's name? "Everybody used to call it the Mush," he said grinning, "'cause of the prison." He studied my face and smiled. "The Mush. I just know it as a crappy road." It was crappy, one of the most rutted I'd driven. Once that overpass was finished, the road might not be that way for long. From the satellite view of history, you could see that overpass as preparation for the area's coming suburbanization, a preemptive measure for a time when more cars than tractors would need to cross the 99 from their cul-de-sacs among the wheat. Adam nibbled kernels and gave me some to chew as I drove west.

Small birds in the middle of the road leapt into flight at my approach. A Hispanic man with his cotton hoodie on his head walked along a field's edge, checking something, irrigation maybe, making the whole local economy function. The air was chilly. Dairies to the south released the tang of manure, but in the crisp fall, even shit smelled invigorating.

A large tuft of sacred datura grew on the shoulder. Called jimson weed, the beautiful white silken flowers produce seeds that the Yokuts made into tea to induce psychedelic visions in puberty and other ceremonies. It can kill you if dosed incorrectly. Kids in the Valley took their chances, sometimes embarking on memorable trips, other times ending up in the hospital on dialysis or in local police stations, talking to people who weren't there. Even experienced Yokuts shamans occasionally killed people by mixing the wrong dose.

Finally, I found a house. It stood beside a small band of willows, all stucco and red tiles, like something plucked from the outskirts of Modesto and plopped in this pasture. A large pickup was parked next to the garage, and the front door faced a horizon without end. Its owner met me in her large circular driveway, cradling a newborn. Born in Madera, Julie had lived on Sandy Mush Road for twenty-five of her twenty-seven years. The road's name never struck her as unusual enough to ask anyone about it. "It was always just Sandy Mush Road," Julie said. "It's just been the name of the road." The baby slept. Her young daughter was inside waking up from a nap. "I mean, yeah, it's a different name, but I'm just used to it, I guess. It's not funny to me." I assured her I wasn't mocking the name, only trying to explore its roots. My investigation struck her as stranger than the road's name. She offered a tired smile. "I just had my baby, so—"

I drove on, past a large stinking dairy, to a point where the pavement briefly turned smooth and unblemished. The fields were bare of crops. Cows nibbled it as pasture. Although drought had baked the land, the soil remained mush underneath.

The noun *mush* dates back to the late 1600s, where it derived from the word *mash*. Defined as "something that is soft and wet and often shapeless," mush originally referred to "cornmeal boiled in water or milk," which was always what I pictured in the bowl when Oliver Twist asked for more porridge. The road's name was not flattering. It did the land no favors. Instead, it acted as a warning for travelers or potential settlers: tread lightly, bring a boat and rubber boots, or find more solid ground.

Before modern road technology, it was hard to build roads through here. Even with improved technology, it's hard to build roads here. Sandy Mush Road buckles; the land beneath it shifts. So much of it worked better as pasture than as farms or settlements. Now the name acts as a reminder that this place had a life before we arrived, evidence that as civilized as the wine bars of nearby Modesto are, part of this plain remains undisciplined and unreliable. For all the Valley's incredible engineering, it couldn't correct the mush, and this region preserves something of an outside force, where the land raises its middle finger and mutters, "Come try." I respect that independence.

I passed a couple more houses. One had too many half-built cars in the yard to feel welcome to solicitors, so I stopped at the Yosemite Valley Beef Packing Company.

Inside the office, a man named Raul Navarro sat at the front desk. "Hi," he said. "What can I do for you?" He was watching funny videos on his computer, slumped in his chair, with papers strewn around. He silenced the TV and stood to shake hands. I felt bad asking my weird question. He didn't know what the name meant, but it wasn't a mushy road anymore. "It was fixed," he said. "It was really bad." Worse than this? "Much," he said. Did anyone call it the Mush, as Adam said? Had he heard that? He sat back down and draped his arms on the desk. "No one calls it the Mush around here." He seemed annoyed that I had interrupted to ask this.

Born in Mexico, he and his wife lived in Merced now. He did admit there were some weird local street names in different Valley towns. In Delhi, northeast of here, there was a Shanks Road. Even saying that out loud made him laugh: *Shanks* Road. "People must not live long on Shanks Road," I said. He didn't think that was as funny as I did, though he did laugh. Maybe he was laughing at me.

Driving east beside fields of hay and dirt, I got stuck going twenty miles an hour on a fifty-something road (I hadn't seen a sign for miles), behind some sort of utility truck towing some sort of enormous motor with the name Doosan on it. Then a Merced police officer raced by going seventy miles an hour, because there was no one around. The vacancy tempted me to follow suit, though I knew somehow I'd get ticketed if did, maybe by some sort of aerial patrol.

Past the Merced Power Plant, I stopped at another dairy, where a black lab trotted out of nowhere and jumped up against my driver's side window, panting and smearing it with mud. A door on the gray cinder block building was open, but nobody was inside with the milk-processing equipment. Farther down, norteño spilled from a smaller open door. Beyond it, large pens filled with cows released occasional moos.

Past the John Latorraca Correctional Facility; past 3 Machados Dairy Inc.; and past Homen Dairy Farms and Homen Custom Chopping, whose entrance sign said Please Drive Slowly / Cows at Work, the road passed the Merced National Wildlife Refuge and curved sharply south where a sign warned drivers to slow to fifteen miles per hour. A series of nine reflective black-and-yellow arrows marked the bend at Nickel Road. At night, without the signs, you'd drive straight into a field and an irrigation ditch.

Before the bend, a huge great horned owl dropped from the sky. I swerved to dodge its massive wings, though I didn't need to. The bird veered at the last moment and then soared low over the fence to my right, coasting without a flap of its wings, and that was that.

Past the Merced National Wildlife Refuge, my route toward Interstate 5 led me between other sodden wildlife refuges, south of Kesterson's infamous toxic wastewater evaporation ponds, along the northeastern edge of the old Rancho Sanjon de Santa Rita, on down to where Henry Miller Avenue passes the town of Los Banos—a company town Miller founded, with a store that sold goods to his employees. At one point, Miller and Lux owned all of this. After Miller died and the price of beef plummeted in the 1920s, his heirs sold land to ranchers and private duck clubs, breaking up the Rancho Sanjon de Santa Rita into the smaller private parcels that we see today. Thanks to floods and unstable soil, the river left an enormous amount of standing water in this part of the west, which hosts thousands of migratory Canada geese and sandhill cranes annually. Now the area has the Valley's densest concentration of wildlife refuges, and its single-largest state park, called Great Valley Grasslands. It's the kind of statistic that helps set apart what, to most passersby, looks indistinguishable from the rest. When you make it this far and deep into the Valley, you see the truth: the flat, massive Valley has as many distinguishing marks as your lover's cheeks.

Henry Miller Avenue meets I-5 at a cluster of roadside restaurants and gas stations called Santa Nella. I'd eaten at the Denny's before.

The restaurant was packed. Men in mesh John Deer hats with brown glasses cases in their front flannel pockets filled nearly every table, alongside families dressed for the Southern California beaches they were driving to. I spread out my atlas and notebook and ordered an omelet. Then a twenty-something walked through the front door.

Dressed in a purple zip-up soccer sweatshirt and baggy brown corduroys that folded in frays under high-heels, the guy spoke frantically to the confused hostess. He tugged on his long brown hair and nervously rubbed his head, and then after a few anxious minutes, he spun around with ballerina precision and slipped out the door.

When I asked what had happened, the waiter refilled my water and shrugged. "Said his friends just drove off without him."

"Wow," I said, peering through the shutters to watch him shuffle through the parking lot. "Ditched, huh? Poor kid."

The waiter just nodded. "You see all sorts of weird stuff working here."

Twenty-three and carrying pancakes on arms thick enough to throw serious touchdowns, Alan was born and raised in San Francisco to a Mexican mother and Guatemalan father and had moved to nearby Los Banos a few years back after getting into some trouble. Drugs, he implied.

Studying my map and notes, Alan asked, "You on a road trip?"

"Yeah." I told him that I'd hoped to be out in the marshes right now watching ducks before they flew off to hide in the fields for the day, but instead, I'd succumbed to the joys of warm food.

"Where'd you stay?" He said someone was killed at the nearby Motel 6 two weeks back. He collected the condiments from the next table. "That's why rates went down five bucks." That explained the sheriff prowling the parking lot. I'd spotted him ticketing a man who, dressed in full camouflage, had illegally parked his aluminum duck-hunting skiff.

It was duck-hunting season, and Alan advised that I drive the speed limit on all local roads. "See, if you're on pavement, you're fair game," he said, "and they don't like newcomers in their town. Especially if you're from the city, or Hispanic." He laughed. "And I'm both. You get pulled over Hispanic," he said, his head shaking side to side, "get ready for twenty questions."

He warned to watch out for tweakers. Around Los Banos and Santa Nella, Alan said, people call meth "shit"—Got any shit?—and manufacture it in houses way out in the country where, buffered by vast farm fields, there's no one around to smell it. Alan described a local Los Banos cop who had pulled him over a number of times in the last year and was definitely a meth addict. "Anyone with any sense knows he's on it," Alan said. "It'll be cold and rainy outside, and he'll be all hot and sweaty." He returned everything to his wallet before returning a plate of fried shrimp to the line cook: "Santiago, mashed potatoes sin brown gravy, por favor."

Los Banos had a lot to watch out for. Half the city news posts on the town's homepage were unsettling:

Mosquito Warning
Important Information about Los Banos Drinking Water
Hexavalent Chromium White Paper
Storm Preparedness—Where to Get Sandbags
"Check before You Burn" Kicks off 14th Season
Storm Drain Improvements

"The City of Los Banos cannot comment on the effects of hexavalent chromium consumption on human health except to refer citizens to the California's published Public Health Goal, which is 0.02 ppb," the city's white paper said. "It is worth noting that the water being served in Los Banos would meet all drinking water standards anywhere else in the World except for California."

Before leaving town, I stopped at the Rotten Robbie, one of Santa Nella's four gas stations. In Oregon the law states that paid attendants must pump your gas, so it was nice to stretch my legs in the cool California air and fill my own tank.

Inside, above the gray-haired gas station cashier and over the entrance, a thick layer of photos of military men stationed in desert places decorated the wall. "These all people you know?" I asked.

"They're all local boys," she said, and pointed over the beeping register. "That there's the manager's son." A tall blond twenty-something wearing a belt of fifty-caliber bullets over his shoulder held up a handwritten sign that read, "Live from Iraq."

As the cashier handed me change, the door flew open, and the ditched kid from Denny's barreled in, one hand over his mouth, the other cupping his chin. Frantic, he moved with plenty of swish in his step, which made him stand out in this conservative land of farm boys in mesh caps. "Did anyone come in here looking for me?" he asked.

"Asking for you?" the cashier said. "No, honey, no one has. Is someone looking for you?"

"Um." The boy tugged his lip. "I was sleeping in the back seat, and when my friends stopped here for gas, I got out to use the bathroom. Then, when I came out, the car was gone."

A man at the next register laughed.

"They left you here?" the cashier asked. "Where were you going?"

"From San Francisco to LA."

The cashier's narrow gaze shifted between me and the kid. "Well, surely they'll turn back for you." Pale faced with dark rings under his giant emerald eyes, he stared at us with a sad pout. Each blink looked painful. "Right?"

I asked if he needed to use my phone. "No, my boyfriend has one but isn't answering it." Okay, I said. But didn't he think they'd eventually notice he was gone and turn around? "I don't know if they even know where they stopped."

It turned out that he had no wallet, no phone, only a calling card and a wad of crumpled bills, part of which he quickly offered to the clerk. "A pack of Black and Mild, please."

"I can't sell you anything unless I see an ID, honey."

He stared at the clerk with eyes too wide to be sober, and I gave him one of the machine-rolled cigars I used to smoke back then. "You too?" he asked, as if the odds of two different people being abandoned in the same tiny town at the same time weren't infinitesimally slim.

"No," I told him, "I just wanna make sure you're alright."

He pulled his hair into a single brown braid. Despite his fidgeting, his tone wasn't as fevered as you'd expect of a person abandoned at a truck stop with no money. I searched for worry behind his huge eyes, but they only seemed empty and green. I wondered if he'd gone into that bathroom to shoot up or was maybe manic. Maybe his friends meant to leave him; a hundred-plus miles with a loudmouth can do that to you. "Okay, well," he mumbled, "I'm going to use the payphone again," and slipped like a fence lizard out the door.

A silence fell over the store; then the cashier snickered. "Did he say boyfriend?" When I said yes, she laid her wrinkled forehead on the counter and laughed. I told her to be polite and followed him out.

Back outside, washing my windows, I watched a squadron of ducks pass overhead. Squawking as they soared, they flew low enough that the whoosh of their wingbeats was audible over the idling semis' engines. I turned around, and there behind the building, arms folded across his chest, was the kid, sitting at a table beside the old phone booth, smoking his cigar, waiting as the sun went down, waiting to somehow go home.

In 1935 Latta interviewed a Los Banos settler named William J. Stockton. The son of an Illinois miner and rancher, Stockton moved here with his family in 1859 and became Los Banos's first blacksmith.

"There was always some internal strife at Old Los Banos," the eighty-seven-year-old told Latta. "The Thornton Hotel was a short distance away from the store. Harry Thornton made fun of the storekeepers for keeping so many dogs and called the place Dogtown. As such it became well known on the West Side as far away as Hill's Ferry. [Shop owners] Korn and Hirschfelt were not slow to retaliate and because Thornton kept hogs to eat the kitchen refuse from the hotel called his place Hogtown. So Dogtown and Hogtown they were."

Two of Latta's strengths as a writer were that he knew how to find good sources with stories to tell and that he knew when to shut up and let his sources talk. He was, first and foremost, a collector of stories, and he knew that a good story is more compelling than a bunch of facts and figures. Stockton's was the kind of voice that oral history preserves so well, letting it echo from the grave to bring life to a place that doesn't always seem to have any.

When President Grover Cleveland gave away public land, Stockton and his wife and daughter camped on a small claim until they could build a house and plant some crops. Things didn't go well at first.

> All we had to contend with were coyotes, rattlesnakes, skunks, horned toads, grasshoppers and kangaroo rats, north winds and dry years.
>
> We planted grain out there on the plain until we were so poor I hadn't a friend in the world. I would go a mile and a half out of my way to avoid meeting a man I owed a couple of dollars and who needed it as badly as I.
>
> After it seemed that I had lived there beyond all hope, I used to gulp about three times before I would ask a man to trust me for four bits' worth of beans.
>
> When it seemed things had gotten so bad I couldn't stand it anymore a man came along and said, "How are you getting along, Mr. Stockton?" I answered, "Poor enough." Then he said to me, "Mr. Stockton, I am going to dig a canal right above your land." Talk about the voices of angels, they are nothing compared to those words.
>
> Then Henry Miller told me I could have credit at his store. About fifty of us held a meeting to agree about taking water from the proposed canal. All of us could not have raised a thousand dollars to save our lives. And no bank would have loaned it to us either.
>
> Miller went to work and dug us a canal forty miles long and 100 feet wide. He filled it with water and told us to go to it. Not a man of us who owned an acre of land that he did not make a rich man. Henry Miller was the finest man I ever knew in my life.

As Stockton said in his rags-to-riches story, "I often wonder if people really know what poverty is." Having seen Alpaugh, Fowler, and Fresno's shantytown by the freeway, I think they do.

High above Los Banos, overlooking the perpetual stream of cars passing on 1-5, the Coast Range opens into a wide valley. This is Pacheco Pass.

Pacheco is the pass that John Muir walked through when he first laid eyes on the Sierra Nevada in 1868. It's the pass that Thomas Jefferson Mayfield's family traveled through when they moved into the Valley in 1850, the place where eight-year-old Jeff rode with his family in a line of packhorses when his father yelled, "Look there!" pointing to a plain beyond the hills where a purple haze of pollen and dust hovered above endless rows of flowers—"rose, yellow, scarlet, orange and blue"—each species attached to a different soil type, with some bands stretching a mile across in what his mother called "a crazy quilt of color" before she stood and cried among the blossoms, asking that they build their cabin "right here in the midst of it all." When William Brewer's crew camped in Pacheco Pass in 1862, they found that "the wind was so intense that [their] mules at times were blown out of the train several feet—they could scarcely stand. The oak trees often lay along the ground, in the direction of the wind. They were not uprooted, but had grown in that way in that perpetual wind." Two years later, in ninety-two-degree heat, Brewer ate breakfast here at San Luis Ranch. "The wind is so high that we can build no fire," he wrote, "so we cook in the dirty kitchen. Dust fills the air—often we cannot see fifty yards in any direction—it covers everything. We cook our dinner, but before it can be eaten we cannot tell its color because of the dirt that settles on it. Our food is gritty between our teeth, and as we drink out our cups of tea we find a deposit of fine sand in the bottom. Dirt, dirt, dirt—eyes full, face dirty, whole person feeling dirty and gritty."

Now around two hundred turbines line the hills above the pass, harnessing the wind for power. A temperature differential between the cool coast and hot valley creates a convection current, which generates winds up to thirty miles an hour. The windy season runs between March and October, though winds still blow through the winter. People consider wind power another agricultural product, hence the name *wind farming*. The old dry wheat growing technique of skyfarming here takes on a new life, drawing a commodity from the air. Unlike solar farms, which sit low on the ground and take up a lot of space, farmers can add wind turbines to their land without interrupting existing cattle grazing and crops. Most of the activity occurs high above the surface. Pacheco's wind farm is small. One of the largest wind farms in the country is in Altamont Pass to the north. It generates some of the largest amounts of wind energy in the world, though its old turbines are being replaced because they kill thousands of birds each year, including federally protected golden eagles, which have quit nesting in a twenty-square-mile area around the farm. Besides generating electricity, the Pacheco Pass is an important storage site for Southern California's water.

In 1960 the state and federal governments teamed up to build the enormous San Luis Dam at the base of Pacheco Pass and collect water in San Luis Reservoir. Its namesake, San Luis Creek, is too small and fickle to fill the broad valley; instead, the federal Delta-Mendota Canal and the state's California Aqueduct carry Northern California water along the Valley's west side, parallel to I-5, and fill the O'Neill Forebay below the dam. In the complicated, gravity-defying way typical of California's water-transport system, O'Neill Forebay then pumps its water uphill into San Luis Reservoir, where it's stored and redistributed to farms and cities on both sides of the Coast Range and as far south as Los Angeles. Of the 154 large reservoirs that the California Department of Water Resources monitors, San Luis is the fifth largest.

A busy highway runs right above the water, funneling people between the interior and the coast just as the system does water, and pleasure boats drift atop the reservoir's ruffled surface. In a large paved lot overlooking the shining waters, a Chevy Astro minivan was parked alone. A muted thudding beat from inside it, rising above the wind like a broken metronome: Boom boom bada bada bada bada boom. Boom. Boom boom boom boom. Alongside the revving boat engines and distant construction noises, it was hard to identify the hollow beating as a bass drum.

Spotting a set of backlit arms swinging behind the grimy windshield, I questioned the wisdom of approaching this sweaty stranger, but I couldn't contain my curiosity any more than he could keep a beat. "Hey," I said, stepping to the van's open side door. "Nice setup." Behind the front passenger seat, on a floor covered with clothes, stood a ramshackle drum set: brittle snare, dented floor tom, loose hi-hat, cracked crash symbol, and a bass drum with a double pedal for that heavy metal sound.

A lean young man, dressed in blue board shorts and a white tank top browned around the armpits, sat behind the drums. He hung a set of stereo headphones on a cymbal and said, "Yeah, man, it's my kit." Cool, moist breezes flowed east through Pacheco Pass, shaking the brown grasses, and the hot Valley air pushed them back. Fat black flies converged on the drummer's forearms and neck. The van's rear bench seats were all missing. In their place sat three yellow milk crates overflowing with T-shirts, cassette tapes, and empty packs of Kool cigarettes, making it unclear whether he lived in the van or never cleaned.

The man slipped on a pair of red flip-flops and leaped from the van. The sun made him wince as he lit a smoke. He had come out here to practice, because it was quiet and nobody bothered him, unlike back home. His eyes showed the kind of intensity you see during bar fights—darting nervously back and forth, scared and vengeful.

The man said, "Pretty badass, huh?" In one unbroken stroke, he reached into the van and thrust two sticks in my face. "Can you play?"

I could. Two friends had drum sets growing up, so I taught myself the basics.

Trying not to seem unnerved about trapping myself in a stranger's van, I took the sticks and climbed inside. Metal springs poked my ass as I straddled the stool. My arms, fly covered and anxious, found their place as naturally as a snowboarder's legs after a season off the slopes.

"Do it, man," he said, "rock out." With an intensity bordering on entrancement, he watched me inch up to the tom. "I'm Bae, by the way."

We shook hands as I tested the bass pedal. "I'm Aaron," I said. "Nice to meet you."

The van smelled sharp and musty, like rancid cheese and ashtrays. But the setup was too cool to be ruined by the stink. Park anywhere, crawl in back, and jam—a mobile drumming unit.

"Here," Bae said, flipping over the snare to tighten the bolts. He pulled a pillow out of the bass drum—the reason it had sounded so muffled from across the lot. "That'll sound more rock and roll." Smiling, he swung two imaginary sticks in quick successive jabs. "Rock hard."

Bae leaned against the doorframe, grinning and puffing his menthol. He was friendly, but he seemed amped. I drummed a paradiddle on the worn snare, rolled across the tom, and slid into a tight, frantic beat. For an unbroken two minutes, I bounced between Bad Brains' "House of Suffering" and Art Blakey's "Moanin'," the whole time staring out at the dry golden hills and the distant flecks of interstate travelers passing along the shore.

Afterward, I set the sticks on the passenger seat, near a bundle of old sweatshirts and a Sudafed box.

Bae screamed with what now seemed an ephedrine energy. "Yeah, man, you can play. Hell, yeah, you can play!" His lips peeled back to reveal straight, clean, white teeth. He pointed to an opened case of Milwaukee's Best and offered me a can. When I told him no thanks, he admitted how he hadn't been able to sleep well lately from all the worry. Born and raised in San Jose, he'd taken a job in Modesto after three years in dental school. Then, two months in, barely long enough to know all the nurses' names, cops arrested the whole office, twenty people total, for medical fraud. "I was in the paper and everything," Bae said. "I spent two weeks in jail with a bunch of junkies. The cell smelled like shit. Toilet was in the corner."

In the meantime, Bae couldn't find another job, and as long as the fraud case was pending, he couldn't lie on the application about his felony. After investing all that time and work and dental school tuition money, now he lived with his parents in Salinas. "Thirty-three and back with my parents," he said. "Fucking bullshit." That was why he drove an hour and a half through the Coast Range to play drums in this empty lot.

When I said it was nice of them to let him stay there while all this blew over, he twirled an unlit cigarette between his fingers like Mötley Crüe's drummer Tommy Lee and shook his head. "They treat me like a kid. They're hardcore Asian and want that respect thing, old-world-tradition style, like 'Yes sir,' 'No sir.'" He spit when a fly landed on his lower lip. "I'm supposed to bow and be like, 'Hi mother,' 'Hi father,' but if I do, they'll treat me even more like a kid."

With his third cigarette lit, he bowed and forced a painfully saccharine smile. "And I try to get them to loosen up and be like, 'Hey, how's it going?' and 'What's up?' but they're not having it."

I expected him to jump back on the stool and beat those drums some more. Instead, he stood there beside me in the sun, leaning against the warm van, watching the wind stir whitecaps on the forebay below us as the shrinking levels exposed brown shore. Along the eastern shore was a little cove where a coat of drowned thistle, beer cans, and plastic bags had collected in a layer so thick it actually stopped incoming waves without showing any sway. Canals radiated out from the great earthen-gray wall of San Luis Dam, watering the barren plain that once tormented Brewer and Derby and feeding the masses, whether we knew it or not. Electric lines swooped down over the water and disappeared into the San Joaquin Valley's haze of distance and dust. It was a very industrial landscape to recreate in. Still, the forebay offers a nice seminatural escape, something neither urban nor agricultural, unlike most of the Valley's sixteen thousand square miles. So cars park along gravel pullouts on either side of Route 33 to fish and drink beer and relax by the water. After drumming with Bae, I think of it as the San Luis Creek Rock 'n' Roll Recreation Area.

I left Bae with his double-bass dreams, as he cursed and struggled with his lighter. And as I slid into my rental car, flies swooped inside, and the chaotic, speedy thump rose once again from the van to tear through the silence. That ecstatic hammering. That boom bap boom.

Boom boom boom. Boom.

6

Nocturnal Life

The fog was said to be an old Yokut curse on the white man.
*Take our lake and you will be haunted by its vestige, the
creeping mists, for generations.*

—Mark Arax

Near another small town, on the northbound lane of the interstate, a sedan flipped upside down. The roof was crushed. The car doors hung open, and an ambulance's flashing lights cast the car red. It was 10:20 on Friday night.

"Oh god," the young driver moaned. "Cover my feet—they're fucking cold. Oh my god." His arm was severed above the elbow. He lay on a stretcher, parked half on the grass, half on the shoulder. A dark field stretched behind him. Grass glistened with moisture, and the winter sky seemed poised to smother Stanislaus County with its wet wool. Not four lanes of highway traffic nor the vastness of space could dampen the man's cries.

In winter, California's rural interior gets cold. Farmland increases atmospheric moisture, and moisture condenses into what locals call tule fog. In the San Joaquin Valley, tule fog can cut visibility to as little as a foot in the span of seconds. Cars rear-end each other in massive pileups. On November 3, 2007, on this very highway, over one hundred cars and eighteen big rigs slammed into each other in a fogbank between Fresno and Fowler. The crash killed two people and injured thirty-nine. In February 2002 two more people died in an eighty-car pileup on Highway 99 between Selma and Kingsburg.

Then there were the five people killed and twenty-eight injured in 1997, south of Sacramento on Interstate 5. This night, it wasn't tule fog, but the night was young.

"Oh fuck!" the driver yelled. "It's cold. I'm going to die." Blood soaked his tattered sleeve. The wound was so fresh that paramedics hadn't wrapped it, and the stump was a deep crimson punctuated by a speck of bone that could have been the moon. The rest of his right arm was in the ambulance, on ice.

Two truckers rescued him. They'd seen the overturned car while driving by. "I knew there was somebody there," the trucker told me. He leaned over to his passenger to yell over the engine noise. "For some reason, in my instinct, I had to pull over. I say, 'Let's go, let's go.'"

The two ran down the shoulder, threw open the car doors, and pulled out the driver and his brother. "His arm," the trucker said, "it was . . ." The driver had a bushy silver beard and deeply chiseled features. He spoke excitedly, proud but uneasy. The passenger stared into space. He was young, clean shaven, and shocked. When he lowered his hoodie, his wide eyes locked on the distance, as if scarred by images now etched on his irises.

From the stretcher, the driver said, "Where's my brother? Is he okay?" A kid with blond shoulder-length hair stood at the back of the ambulance, his arms crossed over a black leather jacket, talking to two police officers. The paramedic didn't answer. She was speaking into her colleague's ear.

When a medic raised the stretcher, the young man yelped, and the other paramedic leaned over him. "This is going to hurt 'cause it's bouncy," she said. "Hang on." She nodded, and her partner popped the wheels off the grass and eased the stretcher onto the shoulder. The rutted dirt rattled the metal frame as it rolled toward the ambulance.

The trucker said, "We have to go, amigo," and the passenger nodded and slammed his door. With a hiss, the semi lurched forward, coasting along the shoulder until it got fast enough to merge into traffic.

This winter, on the edge of the Mush, mist hung from the trees at a nearby rest area. Semis' headlights cut white cones of light as they coasted along the off-ramp and eased into parking spots between other semis. The trucks idled. Their engines went silent and headlights, dark. In trucks' dormant mode, generators kept small running lights bright and powered TVs inside the sleepers.

While most of us sleep, rigs with names like Bridge Transport haul onions and shiny tankers full of sloshing milk and rendered cow parts at all hours, day and night. When drivers rest, some park in truck stops. Some park along quiet roads near hotels or dirt lots. Others park in rest areas.

This rest area sits amid fields and straddles both sides of the highway. Each side is divided—half for car parking, half for semis. On this night at 10:30 p.m., seven passenger vehicles were parked in the southbound side, and one long row of semis, eleven trucks deep, stretched across the lot.

Juan was driving ten hours to Calexico, over five hundred miles away. He'd parked in the middle of the lot between two dark trucks. His idling engine filled the perimeter with a deafening noise. To speak, he leaned close and yelled in my ear. His truck had no payload. He was dropping off the tractor. "I take the truck out to the country," he said. "I gotta drive it to the border, and somebody else take over. Take it south." From Calexico, he would take a bus back home to Stockton. "Fourteen hours," he said with a shrug.

He was born in Mexico. He wore a red-and-black flannel and had a wide round face and warm eyes webbed by deep creases. A thick mustache covered his lip. Before driving trucks, he worked at a cannery and picked tomatoes, peaches, oranges, and grapes. "All kinds of fruit," he said. "It was hard work. This is better work." His two kids go to school in Mexico. They don't want to drive trucks. "Okay, amigo. I gotta go." When his truck pulled away, the lot fell silent, and ten semis remained. All had their engines off, and many had visors pulled down over their windshields.

The rest area looks like the edge of a small city park. It has soda machines and bathrooms, picnic tables and a lawn. During the day, feral cats patrol the grounds, darting between tables in search of scraps and retreating into the neighboring orchard, while a troop of young maintenance men in reflective vests stab trash and sweep leaves into dustpans. At night sedans mix with minivans mix with pickup trucks.

In one gray four-door, an older, silver-haired man sat in the dark in the driver's seat. Every so often, he put his hands to his head and gripped his temples, as if trying to calm an ache or silence unsettling thoughts in his mind. No other cars contained visible passengers; people were sleeping in their back seats or campers. Minivans and pickups are ideal for rest. Rest areas are not. Unless you're encased in the protective metal of a big rig's sleeper, you're exposed. When thieves shot Michael Jordan's dad in a North Carolina rest area in 1993, he was sleeping in the front seat of his car.

On the rest area's northbound side, fourteen dark semis parked in a row. No drivers smoked outside them. No one paced around. In the narrow blank space between sleeping semis, a chilling noise arose. A deep guttural squeal. Something snarling.

Inside two darkened trailers, pigs fussed like captive demons, snorting and charging and clacking their teeth in internal disputes. The sounds escaped through the cars' ventilation holes, and the barnyard stench of animal hide filled the air. Some pigs leaned their fat backs against the metal, filling the holes with tan tufts of hair.

In the Bible, demons came out of men and entered swine. Although I'm not religious, the way the Gospels describe it always stayed with me. Two men possessed by unclean spirits met Jesus as he arrived on the shore of Lake Gennesaret. The men lived in a cemetery, and their violent temperaments kept people from traversing the area. When they saw Jesus, they started screaming, "Why are you interfering with us, Son of God? Have you come here to torture us before God's appointed time?" A herd of pigs was feeding in the distance. The demons begged Jesus, "If you drive us out, send us into the swine." And Jesus commanded, "All right, go!" So the demons exited the men and entered the pigs, and the whole herd, some two thousand of them, plunged down the steep hillside into the lake and drowned in the water. The men tending the pigs ran to the city and reported what happened to the demon-possessed men. Then the whole town came to meet Jesus, and when they saw him, they begged him to leave them alone.

At 11:13 p.m. a truck pulled in, and a woman emerged from the mist. She'd stationed herself somewhere in the grass, maybe by the building, maybe by a tree. I didn't see. When the semi came to a halt, she approached the driver's side. The driver declined, and she walked back around.

I unrolled my window and rested my arm on the sill. "How you doing?" she said. Fine, I replied, and you? "You looking for company?" Hers was the sweet, strained voice of a smoker who understood how to make a stranger feel special. She came over and stood by my window. Her name is Terry.

People call truck stop sex workers "lot lizards," but Terry rejects the moniker. "I call it work," she said. "I'm at work." She works this rest area almost every night.

Born in Modesto in 1960, she's lived in a farm town most of her life. Short, with long stringy silver hair and roomy jeans, she clutched a brown purse against her side. She's been selling sex since 1990.

"I had a real bad drug habit for about ten years," she said. "I been clean for about six years, but that's how I got into it in the first place. Now I'm still in it 'cause I need the money. I live with other people. I'm off the streets, but I lived in a tent for *years*, off and on for a long time. 'That which does not kill us will only make us stronger,' my grandma always said. I believe in it now. I always believed in it."

Terry spoke quickly, running her thoughts together in brisk anxious sentences, as if a cop or new customer might interrupt before she had a chance to express them. When she laughed, she laughed a brief hesitant chuckle to which she only partially committed.

"I used to panhandle. I'd come out there, and I'd tell people, 'I broke down; I need gas.' Honestly, the guilt got to me. I'd lay in bed at night and think, *Oh my god, how can you sit there and look these people in the eye and lie to them like that?* Some people would dig in and give you the last five bucks they have believing your story, and I felt like a piece of shit doin' it. I didn't even want to face myself in the mirror, you know? Now, this might not be, as far as some people are concerned, a 'better thing,' but I can look myself in the mirror. I don't feel guilty. I don't feel like I'm lying or hurtin' anybody. That's just my thing. The guilt got to me. I couldn't do it. I felt really—just dirty. You know what I mean? I just felt like a piece of crap. I see people out here doing it all the time, saying the same story. You're not broke down in the same place that many times. I can tell by lookin' at 'em."

She got arrested for drug possession in her early thirties. While on parole, she worked the streets in Modesto. "I didn't really care for it," she said. The standard image of the American sex worker is a woman walking downtown, fishing for johns while keeping an eye out for police. But on city streets, Terry explained, menacing pimps demand big cuts. Territorial disputes flare up with other women. Crime is common, people are unpredictable, and everything gets done in the gaps between police patrols. Without her own car, Terry needed to stay in Modesto after her arrest so that she could ride the bus to the probation office. When probation ended, she moved back home and started working rest areas.

"There's a lot of crazy stuff out there," Terry said through a grin. "I've seen a lot of crazy stuff. Working out here, it's a lot different than working on the streets, 'cause out here it's just truck drivers. They just want something till they get home." Besides crime and pimps, she encountered men in town so desperate and perverted that the only way they could have sex was to pay for it. "They're usually so butt-ass ugly or got weird fetishes or something," she said. "You just don't know. I feel safer out here anyway."

Back in the early 1990s, local rest areas were also lucrative. Five or six women would work this one, and they'd all make money. "Now I'm out here by myself," she said, "barely making enough. It's hard."

Terry makes an average of $20 to $40 a night. She doesn't work set hours. She stays until she makes enough. Often that means arriving after sundown and going home as late as 4:00 a.m. Tonight she caught a ride with a friend around 9:00 p.m. It was nearing 11:30, and she hadn't made a thing.

"I have some dates that I'll still make a hundred dollars off of," she said, "or make fifty off of, but not for the most part." Nowadays, she does about one or two dates a night. She stays, in her words, "however long it takes."

Early Valley towns like Visalia and Hill's Ferry had brothels, where women sold sex to miners, ranchers, and cowboys. Now the sex industry has moved online and to big-city streets, and in some cases, it endures in the margins of the wheeled-freight industry, hidden here in the shade of rest areas and truck stops, where drivers have taken over the work of hauling food and materials that steamships used to haul on the rivers.

New state regulations have cut into truckers' profits. "They have to have all this catalytic converter and everything," Terry said, "put fourteen thousand dollars into their truck to get it up to spec to even come in to California, with emissions and everything. It's outrageous." Changes in trucking have affected her income.

Truckers used to park here for two or three hours and leave. California law now requires that they park their vehicles for ten-hour blocks of time. The hope is that if trucks remain idle, drivers will sleep. Left to their own devices, many long-haul truckers drive as long as they can, trying to reach their destinations more quickly in order to get maximum pay and add additional jobs to their schedule. To do this, some avoid scales. Some forge logbooks or run two separate books. They push themselves to stay awake longer to drive farther, and when they do, they fight fatigue with coffee and cigarettes and sometimes amphetamines. The state law is designed to reduce risk.

With trucks parked for ten hours, there are fewer available parking spaces, and Terry sees fewer customers. At $10 to $30 a date, she needs a high turnover. Volume is one problem.

The way truckers find sex has changed too. Drivers search Craigslist personals and use call girls or other online channels. "You don't even get on the CB radio anymore," Terry said. "I used to be on the radio all the time talking to 'em. Half of 'em don't even turn on the radio, and a lot of 'em can't speak English anyway."

She brushed her hair from her shoulders and clutched her purse. "I think who's ever making these rules in Congress needs to get out from behind his desk and get in a truck for about a month and ride around and see what it's really like. I bet he'd change his mind about a lot of the rules."

In 1992 she met a trucker here who became a regular. "He'd come down and see me all the time," she said. "I have a lot of repeat customers. I got some guys I've been dating ten or fifteen years. I'm good to 'em. I don't steal, because that's a big thing too. A lot of guys take me to their house. If they're married, I will *not* go into the bedroom. I will not get into anybody's business. I won't step over that line." She married this guy in 1993, moved with him to Texas for six years, and drove a truck with him for two. Then she came to what she calls her senses and came home. "He was cheatin' on me. It was just all bad. I didn't know I was gonna be wife number five. I didn't know he was still married. Guys can be really dirty, you know what I mean? They can run a game on you, and you don't even know. I didn't realize someone can lie so much. I'm not that stupid normally, but stuff happens. You know?" She laughed her nervous laugh. "I mean, come on."

When she moved to Texas, she was young, using drugs, and had abandoned traditional employment. She thought life could only improve. "But I'm back to doing the same thing again," she said. "It is hard when you're out there to get ready to *get* a job, have the right clothes, have the right everything. Not that it's a cop-out, but a lotta times it's hard to get a job when you're on the streets." Despite her rapid speech, she stood perfectly still when she spoke. "I tell a lot of my friends that are homeless, 'Get a job driving a truck. You have your house with you. You got a place to sleep. You get to drive around the country all this time.'"

Her ex-husband died a few years ago, and she hasn't worked anything like her old bookkeeping jobs since 1998. She mostly sells manual and oral sex, sometimes intercourse. "I've got five rules I don't do no matter what," she said. "I don't do women at all. I don't do black people at all. I won't let you kiss me. I won't let you go down on me. And I won't let you do butt stuff."

Terry smiled when I asked about the rules. "Like I said, I can look myself in the mirror every day. There are certain things I have to save so when I'm not at work, if I'm at home—you know what I mean?— it's not work related, like someone going down on me. I just won't do that, because that's something that means a lot to me." A huge semi's breaks hissed, and she shifted her weight to her other leg. "I'd make a lousy lesbian, huh?"

A lot of men ask her to do anal. "I tell 'em, 'Yeah, sure, you first.' Then they change their mind. You go first and see how you like it!"

Four of those rules made sense to me. I asked about the racist one. "It's just—I don't know," she said. "I think God make 'em black and us white so we can tell the difference so we don't interchange. I've just never been that close with black people." She was wrong about race but right about work. "My brother teases me all the time," she said. "I'll say I gotta go to work, and he'll say, 'Why do you say you're going out to work?' I say, 'What do you want me to say? I'm going to go out and hustle?' I just say I'm going out to work. It's work. It can be a lot of work sometimes."

Prostitution is work. I told her I agreed that prostitution was a legitimate and respectable form of it. She can walk to this location, and when she's done, she walks home.

Along with her rules, Terry has numerous safety techniques. "If I don't know 'em, I'll usually sit and talk to 'em for a few minutes," she said. "Truck drivers *love* to talk, because some of 'em have been on the road so long without talking to *anybody*. You know?"

The length of dates varies. "Could be anywhere between five minutes and an hour, but normally not that long. It just depends on if I know 'em or if they want to talk."

She won't get into a vehicle with anyone who's been drinking alcohol. Their behavior's unpredictable. "And of course," she said, "they have a hard time achieving what they're trying to achieve, and I don't have a whole lotta time to waste. There comes a time where you just pretty much know it's just not going to happen."

"I kinda got to be a good judge of character. I'm not going to put myself in jeopardy. If I don't feel comfortable with 'em, no matter what, I'll leave. There's no amount of money worth my safety. I got a son and a granddaughter out there who I worry about. I don't want to have them worry about something happening to me." Her son lives in Modesto. They stay in touch.

In the average parking lot nowadays, few truckers will say yes to her services. "I don't hit every single truck that comes through here." She laughed when I asked how she chooses. "I don't know," she said. "I just go up to 'em, you know? Usually, I'll catch 'em when they're coming in. If they're sleeping and they turned their light off, I don't bother them, because believe me, if you wake 'em up, they don't want no part of anything but yelling at you."

As we spoke, I tried to imagine Latta speaking to her but couldn't picture him listening without moralizing her profession the way so many people still do. How would he have navigated this sensitive conversation? Would he have talked nervously over her mention of anal sex? Or would she, back in his day, have never uttered the term?

Light rain fell on the parking lot, and mist had collected on her hair and face. "A lot of people tell me, 'You gotta find a guy and settle down,' but I don't want a man to support me."

She shook her head about how much longer she thinks she'll work this job. "Not forever. I won't last that long." She wants different work but doesn't feel marketable enough to feel hopeful. "I keep my ear out for it, but . . . I mean, I have an education. I went to college and everything. I was going be a bookkeeper and an accountant and all that. My grandfather worked for the city while I was growin' up. But no one's going to hire me at fifty-four years old. I haven't worked since 1998." She shook her head and didn't let a second pass between sentences. "That's one thing that's sad about women, you know? We live with our husbands for twenty-five, thirty years when they pass away or leave us or whatever, and we have no work history. A lot of us don't."

A woman walked by with a small dog on a leash. The woman had been collecting cans from trash bins around the property and stuffing them in a bag in the trunk of a maroon sedan. Terry turned to her. "How's the puppy doin'?'"

"Fine," the woman said.

"How are you doin'?"

"Not too good," the woman said. "My grandma died. She was sick."

Terry's voice raised to a sympathetic pitch. "Oh, I'm sorry. I am sorry." The woman thanked her and kept walking. "You have a good night."

The woman and her boyfriend came here every day to collect cans. "I talk to everybody who wants to talk," Terry said. "I don't have a problem with people. You meet a lot of people. A lot of people travelin', going here or there or wherever they're going. A lot of guys going from LA up here to work, or vice versa. I stay on this side most of the time, because I go home from this side. I don't like crossing the street." By "street," she means the six-lane highway. "I mean, I will. I have before. I walk across; I don't run. Obviously, when there's no cars." She laughed her first hearty laugh. "I learned to cross the street a long time ago! Look both ways! I'll tell you what, on those super-duper foggy nights around here, I can't see the headlights or anything."

This mist hadn't condensed into fog, but the parking lot glistened with rain, and a low gray ceiling hung overhead, blocking the stars with its own moist twinkling.

A truck's brakes hissed as it pulled into the lot, and Terry turned to eye it. She clutched her purse and ran her hand over her head. "Well, good luck with your marriage," she said. I wished her luck, too, and told her that the next time I was in the area, I'd say hi.

The semi eased into a vacant spot. Its running lights stayed on, and instead of approaching it, Terry shuffled toward the building, moving somewhere onto the lawn, maybe by the trees, maybe by the vending machines, before disappearing from view.

Denny was driving a load of diatomaceous earth to Madera. He left Sparks, Nevada, at 7:00 that morning and was parked for the night at this rest area, fifty-three miles from his destination, because of the federal regulations that require truckers to log out for ten hours. Like many drivers, Denny would rather keep driving.

I found him wandering around the lot. He got cooped up if he stayed in his cabin too long.

"You work thirteen and a half," he said, "eleven hours of driving, thirteen and a half total." Many truckers run two books, because when they don't use an electronic log, they can hide their long drives behind an alternate itinerary. Time is money, and truckers want to get where they're going quickly to fetch the next load and get home.

Denny had plenty of time to complete his 438 miles. He just preferred to use less of it tomorrow fighting Monday morning traffic. He'd dealt with traffic all day today outside Sacramento. He said it took him fourteen hours to go eighty miles—five miles an hour for hours. He was exaggerating. I let him have his frustration. As he drove south, he wondered, *Where in the hell are all these people going? Why aren't they home?* Sometimes he came over Donner Pass. Sometimes he came over a pass by Bakersfield. It didn't matter. He hated this route. "It's a hole."

His tense eyes peered down at me from under the bill of his mesh cap, and he leaned back when he spoke, tucking his fingers into his back jean pockets and pausing to gauge his comments' impact. Behind him the pigs snorted in the darkness.

"Well," he said, holding up his hands, "nothing you can do about it, because the minute you start, whatever time you start in the a.m., you got fourteen hours after that. Then you're done, no matter if you go there across the street. Fourteen hours, you're done whether you cover one mile or five hundred. You're done." So over the years, he had developed this routine, where he parked as close to his destination as possible.

The diatomaceous earth he was hauling was similar to the stuff that lay under Tulare Lake. "It's real porous, like a sponge," he said.

Wine producers use it to filter out little bugs and plant parts, and manufacturers use it in swimming pool filters. "It's just white fluffy dirt." Once he dropped it in Madera, he'd pick up transformers in Fresno to take back to Nevada. When he was lucky, he crossed the Valley at night, when traffic was light and he didn't have to look at the place. "Today was ugly," he said. "I go through this fast as I can and avoid it if possible." If he were headed to Bakersfield or LA, he'd take I-5, not Highway 99, since fewer drivers use the 5 and it has truck stops everywhere. "This way here," he said, "nothing."

He was born in Covina in Los Angeles, and his family bought a resort up in Clear Lake, which was nice most of the year. In the summer, he said, the water filled with brown, pink, and purple algae. "Yeah, it's all right, until the algae comes up and the thing stinks like a cesspool," he said, "but it's all right." He left Clear Lake to do construction in LA. When he found himself out of work, friends in Vallejo invited him to work at their glass company, which he did until Vallejo's construction market slowed.

Denny's father-in-law had worked as a welder and ironworker, which earned good money until the work tapered off, so he bought two trucks and started driving all forty-eight states. Since he figured Denny needed to be making money if he planned to be with his daughter, he invited Denny to join. "When I got to Vallejo," he said, "that's when I met the truck. It's been go, go, go ever since."

The company Denny worked for could travel all seven western states, but the owner kept him hauling raw material and wire panels between Nevada mines and California farms. Mines brace their walls with wire to keep rocks from falling when they're blasting. Then they recycle it. Denny would be happier driving a wider route instead of this Groundhog's Day circle. "This is a treadmill," he said. "Same stuff over and over. Just gets old."

If Denny had a refrigerated truck like some of the ones parked ones nearby, he'd haul produce and perishables. If he owned his own truck, a hay broker he knew in Tulare would have him hauling out-of-state hay to local dairies all year long. He'd considered buying one, but rates were down and fuel was up. And he needed loads both ways to make it work.

Owning your own truck is profitable if you work for a company that pays a high rate and has reliable, regular contracts with industries like electronics and the government. Otherwise, truckers have to find their own business through brokers and online databases where people post what they need hauled. You could live off it, he said, but you weren't going to get rich. He guessed that his employer bought this $130,000 truck two years ago and already paid it off. "He's got to buy two more because of the emission standards in California," Denny said. "The rest of the fleet can't come to California no more. They can go anywhere else in the world. They just can't come to this place." The state wanted them to buy some fancy mufflers that were supposed to do something with the diesel exhaust to reduce pollution.

"Well," I said, "the air pollution in this area is some of the worst in the world."

Denny stared at me. "Wow."

That wasn't his problem. It will be if he lives long enough to experience climate change's effects on agriculture and commerce. For now, his job was to get the load to the destination in the time the law allotted and still turn a profit.

He admitted that those mufflers must do something, because he didn't have black soot on his exhaust pipes, but for him, additional filters and fuel tanks were just more expensive things to buy in an industry whose regulations already hung a black cloud over drivers' heads. "It's all it is, one more freaking thing," he said. "Always adding something. You can't do this anymore. You can't do that anymore. It's always something. It just don't let up."

With trucks having to park for ten hours, pullouts like this fill quickly, forcing trucks to line up along the highway. "There are just not enough places for us." With a nod, he pulled his hands from his back pockets and said, "See you later," and climbed into his truck.

Like these truckers, I kept driving. I welcomed the movement, but I understand how the distances could wear on you.

Sometimes in those massive green gaps between towns along the highway, grain silos on train tracks are the only signs of life. Then you pass a motel where you can't imagine people staying. Not because it's unsafe. Because it isn't near anything, and it stands in the middle of the road, spread along a narrow median between north- and south-bound lanes. The sign says Vacancies, and rooms are cheap. But you can't even tell how to reach it. Was there an exit you missed? A small turn off from the fast lane? There's no frontage road. The sight sets your head spinning, and before you can take a closer look, the motel rushes past and shrinks in the rearview.

In these parts of the Valley, semis rumble by all night, and the darkness runs deeper than black. Alfalfa stretches for miles. Crops leave a band of exhaled moisture above the fields, blurring distant lights to ghostly suggestions. To the west: blackness. To the north: blackness. The air smells of hay and manure, animally but good. A big processing plant looms off the highway, its corrugated surface lit by hidden bulbs. It looks like a rutted face half in shadow under the bill of a hat, except the bill of the hat reaches across the entire world.

A sign for the Family Tree Farms Research Center passes; then the three-lane highway narrows to one. Cars file into place. You creep through the darkness at ten miles per hour. At that slow speed, you can see the expressions of the men in orange vests laying orange cones on the opposite side of the highway. They drop them from the back of a white pickup truck. One man has a scar on his cheek. One has a mustache. You were just moving fast enough to kill somebody; now you move slowly enough to touch the divider. You roll down the window, hang your arm out. The road made you sleepy. The cool air will rouse you. Construction crews' floodlights combat the darkness that crowds everything else. They're widening the highway, widening it again. Three lanes are no longer enough. Four won't be either. Working at night reduces the impact on traffic and commerce, and it spares workers the daytime heat. A highway patrol car sits on the shoulder with its lights flashing. Through the wind, you hear a dog bark in what must be the only house here, which you can't see. A sign lists the construction project's end date, as another huge silver silo appears up ahead, a billboard attached to the side of one tank. "Real California Milk," it says. "Look for the Seal." Then the cones end, and the other lanes open. And all those drivers behind you, all those people you shared this quiet moment in the night with, dart into the neighboring lane as soon as they can so that they can race around you and speed into the distance, never to be seen again.

After arriving in San Francisco by boat in 1868, John Muir immediately started walking to Yosemite. Even back east where the thirty-three-year-old naturalist grew up, a lot of people were talking about the Yosemite Valley's grandeur. A few Yosemite homesteaders had built primitive hotels to accommodate visitors, and President Lincoln had just set part of it aside as a nature reserve, a precursor to our National Park System. Muir wanted to see it, so he walked across the San Joaquin Valley to reach it.

Muir was a walker. He walked one thousand miles from Kentucky to Florida just to see what he could see. He climbed Mt. Shasta, Mt. Whitney, and Mt. Rainier with simple equipment. For two years in his twenties, he'd subsisted on wild foods while botanizing Canadian forests. Now he walked for six weeks to Yosemite. When he reached the San Joaquin River, he did what so many gold rush miners with equally long beards did and crossed at Hill's Ferry.

"Never were mortal eyes more thronged with beauty," Muir wrote in his journal outside Pacheco Pass. "When I walked, more than a hundred flowers touched my feet at every step closing above them, as if wading in water." The sight of Yosemite instantly enchanted him, and he got a job herding sheep so that he could spend the next few years exploring the area. He filled journals that became his most popular books. Later he formed the Sierra Club and advocated for responsible natural resource management. His first contact with the Sierra Nevada determined the course of his life, just as his writings about the San Joaquin Valley, his "bed of honey-bloom," changed the course of mine. Muir crossed into his new life at Hill's Ferry.

Founded in 1850, the Hill's Ferry crossing grew into a 250-person town set amid fields of waving grain. It had seven saloons, a thirty-room hotel, multiple grocers, and a popular brothel. During floods, steamships floated beside the hotel to fetch people trapped on the second floor. One ship rammed the hotel and broke the wall. Most days, people shipped wheat and cattle from the two dockside warehouses, and they got drunk, robbed, and rich. "Mexican horse thieves and white outlaws," the *San Francisco Morning Call* wrote in 1883, "always used it after their raids among the settlers of the valley and always tarried long enough in the place to clean out Mr. Hill's barroom at the point of their pistols and clean out his bottles and jugs with their mouths." It's hard to picture a serene, doe-eyed Muir in a place like this, but like most commuters, he was just passing through.

When William Brewer visited Hill's Ferry a few years before Muir, he found "a dirty place, where a drunk 'Secesh' made an uproar the whole night," where thieves stole four horses, authorities arrested a murderer, and some vaqueros herded a group of wild Spanish cattle onto the ferry with some impressive lassoing. When the railroad laid more tracks and drew the freight industry to it, Hill's population migrated west to the town of Newman, and it quieted down for good. Latta's elementary school was near Newman; it was the school where, in 1906, his teacher convinced him to interview settlers for the school project that became his life's work.

In this part of the Valley, a more experienced Latta interviewed a few settlers for his "Pioneers of the San Joaquin" newspaper column. He spoke with Henry Mills in Newman, who helped plant the first grain on the west side of Stanislaus County before there was a single well. He spoke with Newman police officer William G. Newsom, whose father saved the family house in a flood by chaining it to a tree and who described the six cattle thieves authorities hung from a big oak tree. And he spoke with Rudolph Bambauer in Gustine, whom Latta first met as a boy of eight and who built an important canal through there and watched a Spanish vaquero catch a wild stallion and race him near Firebaugh. Latta lived to save stories like these from oblivion. Now he was making history himself.

On Friday morning in 1938, Latta made a phone call from Fire-baugh, telling the *Bakersfield Californian* "all's well." It wasn't, but he put on a good face. He planned to reach San Francisco by Tuesday. When the *Alta*'s motor broke outside Hill's Ferry on Saturday afternoon, the crew dragged the skiff to shore and tied it to a tree. They had a backup motor, but since it wasn't strong enough to get them to a big enough city before nightfall, they camped in the shade to fix their motor the next day. This was their seventh day, and on the seventh day, they rested.

The Hill's Ferry that Latta found was a rotting boat landing amid bushy trees. The Merced River flowed into the San Joaquin here, creating a dark line of silt where their waters met. Sunday morning, Latta walked down a rural road to the closest farm and called for help. His crew spent all day on the river waiting for parts for their carburetor to arrive from god knows where. As word got out about the *Alta*'s predicament, locals showed up from surrounding farms. People brought food and water, talked about their journey, detailed their own experience with the flooding, and helped Latta tinker with the broken motor, to no avail. They probably lit a campfire, made some coffee, listened to the water lap against the *Alta*'s hull. Hunters had long ago eliminated grizzly bears in the Valley, but cougars still came down from the mountains to prowl what riverside woods were left and to drink from the cold streams. When the sun set, the crew spent another night under the trees, listening to an owl hoot and hoping the sounds in the dark were just raccoons pawing the dry leaf litter, searching for crawfish and grubs.

When the carburetor parts arrived Monday morning, the *Alta*'s crew fired up their engine and motored toward Stockton, their second-to-last stop. At this rate, there was no way they'd reach San Francisco the following day, or even Stockton. By now, they understood that delays were part of the program.

Sometime on Monday night, June 27, Latta called the Stockton Chamber of Commerce to say the *Alta* was headed their way. They'd stopped to use the phone in San Joaquin City, a small, now extinct settlement near where the San Joaquin and Stanislaus Rivers meet, not far from my beloved Caswell Memorial State Park. San Joaquin City was meant to be a shipping center as big as Stockton, but only a plaque on County Road J-3 remains. Stockton was the *Alta*'s last stop before leaving the Valley.

7

The End of the Road, San Francisco

California is about the good life. So a bad life there seems
so much worse than a bad life anywhere else.

—Sarah Vowell

On Thursday, June 30, the thirteenth day of the *Alta's* trip, a small
group of boats led Latta's crew from Stockton through the estuary
where the Sacramento and San Joaquin Rivers meet. This is the California Delta. Every creek, stream, and river that flows into the Central
Valley eventually empties into this sprawling 1,100-square-mile tidal
marsh of reedy channels and peat islands—nearly half the state's
surface water. If California's coast and interior meet in one place, it's
here, where fresh water mixes with the salty Pacific. Because of the
volume of water passing through this central location, the state and
federal governments built a complex system of pumps and canals to
redistribute its water throughout the state.

The delta gives California 40 percent of its drinking water and
45 percent of its irrigation—not wells, not the dams built on Sierra
Nevada rivers or the canals they feed, the delta. Yet incredibly, the
delta only covers 1 percent of California's total area. Pumps extract 7.5
million acre-feet of delta water each year. Of that, 5 million acre-feet
are used to water farms and cities in the San Joaquin Valley and the
southern and central coast. Delta farms are irrigated by 1.7 million
acre-feet, and about 100,000 acre-feet go to the Bay Area. Then 21
million acre-feet flow unobstructed through the San Francisco Bay
and, as Allen in Hanford put it, "just goes out to the ocean." For all

that natural flow, the state still puts 25 percent of delta water to use, and that supports 23 million Southern Californians. Was that not enough? Did Allen not see the empire California built from that 25 percent? If small-town folks fear that their towns are filling with people and becoming Fresno, they should think of that 25 percent as a protective cap, not a governmental deprivation serving some endangered fish, because more delta pumping will only support larger crowds. California's growth has to peak somewhere. Maybe it's here.

One critical limitation to the state's continued growth is that the delta doesn't contain enough water to support much more population and agricultural acreage. It can only give so much, and by some estimates it already suffers a 1.5-million-acre-foot deficit. What's important to recognize is that that 25 percent is 25 percent of what reaches the delta. Dams and canals siphon so much water from Valley rivers before it even makes it to the delta's pumps. Some estimates say that in drought, 75 percent of the water that used to flow into the bay never arrives. In average years, it's 50 percent. John Wesley Powell believed that only 2 percent of the western Untied States' arid lands were fit for farming, and he advocated for drawing state lines based on watersheds and keeping most of the land for grazing, not irrigated agriculture. As he said in 1883 about irrigating the West, "Gentlemen, you are piling up a heritage of conflict and litigation over water rights, for there is not sufficient water to supply the land."

In addition to water, the delta supplies huge amounts of food. Tides from the west and floods from the east shape this sea level landscape; four to five hours after the tide arrives in San Francisco, it reaches Stockton seventy-eight nautical miles inland. To keep these lands dry enough to farm—a process Americans call "reclaiming"—people have built one thousand miles of levees. Now these 625 square miles of farmed sod and compacted reeds grow everything from asparagus to tomatoes to grain. Levees have caused compaction, and at least 50 percent of delta farmland has sunk below sea level, sometimes twenty feet below, conjuring comparisons to Holland for its richness and subsistence. When you drive the delta's winding roads, you might be startled to see an enormous tanker float past you, its shining hull perched atop a neighboring levee whose waterline somehow sits above the road.

As the farmland sinks, the pressure that water exerts on the levees increases, as does the risk of breaches. Half of these levees fail to meet federal safety standards, and breaches have flooded thousands of acres over the last century. A local industry of dredging and structural reinforcement has grown up around levee maintenance, but no one knows how much longer this whole system will work. Many of the old islands of farmland that once stood above the waterline are now bowls—their fertile soils, surrounded by rising walls of water pushing to get back in. Even the head of the Bureau of Reclamation's California office once suggested retiring all the leveed farmland to turn it into a recreation area. But what happens in the delta affects people on either side.

The Valley needs the San Francisco Bay as much as the San Francisco Bay needs the Valley. Here's how it works. The fresh water flowing out of the Valley used to push the ocean water back and keep it, literally, *at bay*. As fresh water gets pumped out and the drought further strangles supplies, the salty ocean faces less resistance and pushes deeper into delta farmland, threatening industry.

The entire 435-square-mile San Francisco Bay ecosystem needs to receive regular fresh water to flush out pollutants. Tides aren't enough to draw out all the waste and agricultural chemicals. It needs new fresh water flowing in, and there's less and less of it arriving from the delta. In 2014 the flow of fresh water into to the San Francisco Bay dropped by half.

The delta doesn't just clean the bay. It delivers huge amounts of nutrients, soil, and decomposing vegetation from the Valley and Sierra Nevada, which support a thriving marine ecosystem and its related fishing industry. Half the reason the San Francisco Bay teems with the sea life that it does is because the delta, not just the ocean, built it up. A bay is more than water. The bay's ecosystem includes the water's chemistry and temperature, suspended solids, and a host of invisible elements. Bays have their own form of top soil. It's suspended in liquid, measured by sediment load, temperature, and chemistry, but estuarine fertility is ultimately no different than terrestrial soil. Farmers protect their soil. They use manure, fertilizers, and compost to build it up. The San Francisco Bay ecosystem is a farm, too, and the delta provides that fertilizer to replenish it. What so many people like Allen fail to understand is that ecosystems are not just for plants and animals. They're made of people and serve people. We live in an ecosystem. We are an ecosystem, and everything we harvest depends on the health of those living systems. What this means here is that the bay and the Valley have a deeply intimate relationship. Mountains, Valley, and bay are one, not separate entities, and the delta is the intermediary that links them. It's the handshake that connects California's embattled worlds, the elbow joint in the state's giant pipe, so the fates of the bay and the Valley are intertwined, just as the fate of the coast and interior are intertwined.

Millions of people think that they would be helping farmers by pumping more water out of the delta. But the more water that gets pumped, the less water there is to dilute the salty, chemical-laden runoff that the farms and cities of the Valley send into San Francisco, and the less fresh water there is delivering nutrients. That agricultural runoff kills salmon, Dungeness crab, and other marine life, and that affects the fishing industry that relies on the bay. Jobs are at stake on the other side of the mountains too. As the Valley's farmers struggle with salinization and drought, farmers in the California Delta deal with the salinization caused by reduced water flow, rather than percolation, and salmon fisherman deal with declining stocks. Delta water management isn't just about protecting some endangered smelt for the smelt's sake or about environmentalists versus industrialists. It's about recognizing how sharing water unites, rather than divides, nearly all Californians. Farmers using water in one location hurt farmers who need water in another. When pumping more delta water for the Valley's farmers means less fresh water for the coastal fishing industry, the question becomes, Whose jobs do you value more? If all the people connected to agriculture in the Valley truly value the hardworking blue-collar people who "feed the nation," then they should also want some fresh water flowing through the delta to protect fisherman. But folks in the Valley can't blame San Francisco and Silicon Valley for ruining their land any more than those in the Bay Area can blame the Valley for salinizing its soil and wasting its water. Supply and demand and government subsidies shape both worlds, and as alien as Alpaugh farmers in pickups seem to diners in Berkeley vegan restaurants, what people do in Modesto affects life in Oakland. John Muir put it this way: "When we try to pick out anything by itself, we find it hitched to everything else in the Universe." Or as the old country saying goes, what goes into the well comes up in the bucket. The bucket is now the entire state of California.

Calling the delta complicated is an accurate simplification of its ecology and hydrology and the conflicting demands and legal claims on its water. It looks simpler from the road. It looks daunting from a boat.

Miles of channels make the delta both a recreational boater's playground and an important shipping corridor for agricultural products. Most of California's exported wine and grain goes out from Stockton on huge tankers and freighters.

A fifteen-foot skiff is a twig on these waters, so the Vallejo Yacht Club escorted the tiny *Alta* from the delta through the Carquinez Straits. The Carquinez Straits are the narrow break in the Coast Range where the delta waters flow. Before the Southern Pacific Railroad built its railroad bridge in 1930, a ferry long enough to haul whole freight trains used to operate here. The *Alta* passed beneath that bridge. It was the second-longest rail bridge in America, and it still spans the water, nestled between the modern Benicia-Carquinez Bridge's lanes of commuter traffic. The *Alta* motored past Suisun Marsh, the largest marsh in America, past the site where a clutch of retired World War II warships would one day float as part of a national defense reserve fleet, their peeling paint chips drifting into the water, and motored to the wharf on the south side of Treasure Island in San Francisco Bay.

"Acclaimed by thousands of San Franciscans and by a group from their own home county," the *Californian* reported, "crew members nosed their 15-foot skiff into the pier last night at night at Treasure Island after a 455-mile trip by water from Bakersfield to San Francisco." I didn't see the thousands. The photo showed one man in a tan hat helping guide the boat to shore with a cord. Miss 1939 Golden Gate International Exposition, who was supposed to "greet the adventurous crew," never showed.

No matter. The *Alta* landed safely, and members of the San Francisco and Bakersfield chambers of commerce helped the exhausted crew onto dry land, completing a journey that had never been taken before and would never be taken again.

With all the delays and layovers, the boat trip lasted ten days. Latta's crew floated between 450 and 455 miles. According to my odometer, I'd driven 703.4 miles loosely over the *Alta*'s course.

On the twelfth day of my trip, I headed west from Manteca. Valley residents consider Stockton the boundary between the delta and the Valley, so I skipped it. The 580 Freeway channeled me past the Valley's first ferry crossing, lifted me through a sunny notch in the mountains, out of the interior, and through the gap between California's two frontal lobes, where the dry golden grass gave way to coastal hills covered with houses. Fighting Oakland's bumper-to-bumper traffic, I drove over the San Francisco–Oakland Bridge, high above Treasure Island, which I could see from my open car window while enjoying the cool bay breezes in traffic. Descending into the Mid-Market district, I landed my craft not on an island but at Mint Plaza. Crime novelist Dashiell Hammett set a scene in his famous 1929 novel *The Maltese Falcon* here when it was called the Remedial Building. Now the Blue Bottle Coffee Company had a shop in it.

I got in line beside a blue-gray wall of merchandise. Light flooded the high-ceilinged room. Communal tables and lack of wi-fi created a conversational atmosphere free of the teeth-grinding remote workers who populated other shops. Instead of staring at laptops, people sat reading and sipping their drinks.

I took my green tea and tiny lunch outside. I had just lived off ham and eggs and tacos for two weeks; now here I was, overpaying for a cranberry bean salad that came in a jelly jar with a compostable spoon.

The sunny setting was worth it. Just sitting in the California sun, you feel like you're posing. I mean, I was posing. As much as I loved the Valley, it felt great to be back in a big city, and I shamelessly wanted people to wonder what interesting things I did in life when I wasn't hanging around here, to see me in my dark stylish sunglasses and receive the subtle suggestion that I was the kind of person who would drive seven hundred miles and sleep in my car to write a book.

San Francisco is a bundle of contradictions. Before the last tech boom, many outsiders viewed it as a dreamy paradise of food and culture at the end of the rainbow, where plants flower year-round in front of colorful Victorians. Many small-town Californians dismiss it as a dirty, polluted mess of a place colored by spent syringes and public urination. It's both, but for the first time in two weeks, my tea tasted green again. For a city this size, the water is good. That's because it's been pumped across the San Joaquin Valley from the Hetch Hetchy Reservoir in Yosemite National Park since the 1930s. Even though recent water-conservation measures were going to start adding local groundwater to the mix, the municipal supply would surely still taste clean enough not to ruin every tea leaf people steeped in it. Hanford and Bakersfield could brag about their ample parking, but they couldn't say that.

As troubled as it is, San Francisco is one of the best places to eat in America. Alice Waters helped start the slow-food movement and California cuisine here in the 1970s, and the concentration of wealth creates a demand that the abundance of fresh seafood, dairy, and inland produce readily supports. In a sense, the Valley has always been supplying San Francisco, dating back to Tulare Lake's turtles and Henry Miller's cattle in the late 1800s.

I assumed that anyone discerning enough to drop big money at high-end coffee shops might have strong opinions about California's food system. What would they know about the San Joaquin? The fact that the first people I talked to were both connected to agriculture was evidence of how intricately the Valley was integrated into Bay Area life or that I at least visited the right place.

Mark Benedetto and Roxanne Kessler stood in the sun by their bikes, facing west. She was thirty-five and grew up in Stockton. He was thirty, lived in San Francisco's Sunset District next to Golden Gate Park, and grew up in the East Bay. "Not as east as Stockton," he said; His childhood home was in Castro Valley, which he called a place to sleep, not live. I'd driven through it to get here.

Wearing T-shirts and cutoff jean shorts, they sipped their coffees and laughed a lot. Roxanne was here visiting Mark and biking around the city.

Mark graduated from culinary school in the Tenderloin District. He used to manage a café. He'd cooked at a North Beach vegetarian restaurant, making his own seitan for vegan shwarma and filling taquitos with cashew cheese. He left the kitchen to work in coffee when the technology company Dropbox hired him to create a beverage program and café to serve its 1,500 employees. He loved it. "But yeah," he said of his career, "food, big time."

Roxanne earned her bachelor of science degree in wildlife management at Humboldt State University ten years earlier. She now worked seasonally at different parks around the Sierra Nevada and was trying to secure permanent work in fisheries biology. This itinerant arrangement had her living part-time in Stockton between jobs since 2009. In fact, she'd been in Stockton the previous night, engulfed in the same tule fog that had engulfed me in Modesto. She'd even called Mark to tell him, "This fog is incredible!"

San Francisco's fog had always charged the city with a romantic, noir mystery. The Valley's fog was mostly dangerous. Growing up in it, Roxanne could never figure out how so many people drove so fast with zero visibility and trusted "the nothingness." Her technique for safely navigating it was more conservative. She pulled slowly up to intersections and rolled down her window to listen for traffic before crossing; she never worsened the visibility by turning on her brights. Other people she knew had elaborate fog-navigation techniques where they'd drive certain roads lined with trees that could guide them home, or they'd tail semis to follow their lights.

In tule fog every inch looks the same, but even in daylight one Valley town looked like the next to Roxanne. "You're like, oh, Fresno is kind of like Sacramento, kind of like Stockton, or Lodi is kind of like Visalia," she said. "That is the Central Valley style." And that was why so many people saw the Valley as a flat, ugly place.

Snickering, Mark said he could name places in San Francisco that fit that description. Unlike the Valley's ag smells, San Francisco's smell came from human manure. "Hu-manure," he said. In fact, he just saw a disturbing map showing all the reported fecal matter sightings in the city.

Amid the feces and flowers, the city has vegetarian restaurants that serve organic ketchup sweetened with agave nectar and where diners carve the word *vegan* in the top of the toilet bowl; yet thousands of San Franciscans go hungry each year, suffering from poverty and malnutrition just blocks from the city's fancy restaurants and grocers.

Mark's career in food connected him directly to California agriculture the way Roxanne's life in Stockton connected her by proxy. Growing up between the Bay Area and the Valley, he knew that the land to the east produced a lot of food. "I could point on a map exactly," he said, "but I'd only been there a couple of times." His culinary career put him directly in contact with the people who farmed there.

He used to work at Frog Hollow Farm's storefront café in the famous San Francisco Ferry Building. It was a true farm-to-table operation, with owners Becky and "Farmer Al" Courchesne growing certified-organic stone fruit, pears, apples, olives, and barley on 143 acres in the town of Brentwood. "Not the O.J. Brentwood," Mark said; he worked at the far East Bay one, past the last BART stop, on the edge of the California Delta. Frog Hollow served their own seasonal produce, used local asparagus and garlic, and sold their own jams. The Ferry Building was an ideal location to showcase their crops and land stewardship. Built in 1898, it was redesigned in 2003 as a public food market, with a mix of permanent stalls and seasonal vendors. Becky Courchesne used to work as a pastry chef at Alice Waters's Café Fanny, and she knew the power of local sourcing and good branding. This is no different than Henry Miller's approach, making a killing by selling Valley products to the wealthy San Francisco market. As if to represent this, a beautiful aerial photo of the farm hung beside the café's register. The lens faced east toward Mount Diablo and the Bay Area's money.

Many older people dismiss millennials as unaware and self-absorbed, but Mark knew more about soil chemistry, economic systems, and environmental perception than most of my fellow Gen Xers, and his location fed his interest. "At least in San Francisco, there's a great deal of importance placed on where something's from," he said. "But still it's only top level; it's not a really, really deep understanding of where that place is and exactly what their dirt is all about and why, and the seasons."

From his experience, some of the more dedicated chefs know about their farmers' techniques, water requirements, plant varietals, and soil chemistry, but cooks were far more cooks interested in that than consumers. Of the Bay Area's upscale diners and coffee drinkers whom Mark had encountered, 90 percent would hear, "Oh, this lettuce was handpicked by Suzanne in Marin County," and they'd think, *Cool, I know the name of the farm, so I can feel good about myself—that's enough for me.* Customers can connect with that, because a person's name humanizes and simplifies the massive, faceless food system. They can point to Marin on a map and feel empowered, as if they're supporting somebody, not some corporate entity, even though most of the eight hundred thousand farmworkers who harvest California crops are exploited, underpaid Latinos, not a white girl named Suzanne in Marin County. Mark said, "Nine percent will be more interested in asking a question like, 'Oh, where in Marin is that farm?' And servers will tell them, 'It's coastal something and something.'" These are the people who might go to a restaurant's event where they pick ingredients at a farm and bring them back for the chef to make dinner out of them. And then 1 percent will really nerd out and go visit the farm on their own.

At one point, a tan man walked by carrying a forty-ounce bottle of Olde English malt liquor, and two customers in sunglasses parted to make room for him.

"You know how they call California the Golden State?" Roxanne said. "I don't know if it has roots in the gold rush."

"Maybe," Mark said. "Or because of the sunset, like there's this golden hue, but I also feel like part of that even comes from it being so dry. It is this dry environment during certain times of the year, and everything turns yellow or gold—golden, so the Golden State."

Roxanne turned the interview around and asked why these subjects interested me. I explained how after reading John Muir's descriptions of the Valley nearly twenty years ago, I thought, *There's something else going on here*, and I started exploring it. "I feel like part of the Valley's story is about perception, you know? It's not just about agriculture. It's not just about being sort of unappreciated. It's about how people look at it and how sometimes they're right about it and sometimes they're wrong."

Roxanne understood. As much as she liked Stockton, she described it as a place where she didn't thrive. "I liken it to a redwood," she said. "Redwoods grow there, but that's not its environment, and they always look kind of brown and dusty." She paused. "We have a port in Stockton too." Stockton also provided the setting for one of America's best modern novels, Leonard Gardner's *Fat City*. She hadn't read it yet, but she wanted to.

In protected areas like Kings Canyon National Park, Roxanne said, visitors treated waterways with reverence. But in the Valley, she noticed how disconnected many people were from their landscape and that they didn't connect their health with the quality of its water and food. To educate the public and let locals know that the rivers flowing through town were not garbage dumps, a group called the Friends of the Lower Calaveras River put up signs with messages like

"This is the Calaveras River." People drive over little bridges and walk across muddy sloughs every day during their daily life, and too few saw those waterways as places that support salmon runs and provide their drinking water. "It looks like a ditch to most people," she said. "That water did come from the sierra at some point and then flowed through Stockton and eventually out through the Golden Gate, and I don't feel like a lot of us in the Central Valley really comprehend that." She liked the signs because their messages said, "This is your river. This is something that should be cherished."

When she says where she's from, many people nod solemnly, almost apologetically, and say, "Oh, Stockton." She tells them, "Dude, the Central Valley is beautiful." She likes how its flatness lets her see both the Coast Range and the Sierra Nevada, instead of just the sides of surrounding buildings—at least on clear days.

Mark had lived in the Tenderloin for a year. "It is a dump, and you're connected to everything," he said. He compared it to Stockton—as rough and unappealing as it seems, it's a nexus, close to many things, like Yosemite, the coast, Lake Tahoe. "There are gems everywhere. Stockton is not just a murder capital. Tenderloin is not just drug addicts or whatever's going on. So there's value there too."

She agreed. She still didn't plan to stay in Stockton.

Roxanne believed that many Stockton residents tolerated it because they could escape to nearby places like San Francisco on the weekends. It wasn't a place often loved on its own merits, but she wanted to see more residents recognizing the cultural diversity, the rivers, and the agricultural productivity that they had. She just wasn't one of them.

Mark didn't think it was ideal to live somewhere that only gave you access to other, better places. "What about what you got in front of you?" he said. "Is it just you just make it through the week and try to dream for the weekend so you can get the hell out of town?" As a Bay Area native, he'd only had to deal with that issue for part of his life.

They had to leave. They had many miles to bike and only so many hours for her visit. We all admitted feeling guilty for enjoying the weather. If this is global warming, we said, it felt great so far.

From Blue Bottle, I drove west to Alamo Square. Surrounded by historic apartment buildings and Victorian houses, this beautiful four-block park afforded famous views of the downtown skyline to the east and views of the ocean four miles to the west, past Golden Gate Park.

When I arrived in late afternoon, people were walking their dogs and relaxing on park benches. Groups of young people lay on blankets on the slopes, drinking wine before sunset. *Alamo* means "cottonwood" in Spanish, but here native cypress spread their thick limbs over lush lawns. The mix of garden and leisure was quintessential San Francisco, the kind of scene that resembled a painting and always made me want to move here during every visit. The first person I talked to dampened my enthusiasm.

Victor was a forty-nine-year-old retired graphic designer who regularly walked his dog, Catfish, in the park. One day, a local homeless youth handed Victor the dog's leash and said, "I'll be back." She never returned. He was grateful for Catfish, but he couldn't stop complaining about the two twenty-something tech workers he shared a nearby apartment with.

"They're young, and so they don't have any perspective of history," Victor said, "and I really do think—whatever. They're just sort of removed, and I don't know. It's the first of like, not generations, but ten-year groups, and they're really just seeing."

He had so much to say that he seemed overwhelmed trying to get it all out. All he saw in these kids was a generation of greedy, smartass materialists who ignored the larger social and environmental issues of our time, like population growth and drought; who didn't read or even come to the park; and who thought they were awesome even though they hadn't done anything except stare at their phones and design lucrative apps for giant corporations. He admitted he was cynical, but he didn't feel much hope. He'd grown up in San Francisco. "I mean, don't get me started on how changed it is decade over decade," he said. He remembered what it was like to be young and clueless. He'd been naively ambitious at their age, but he thought this tech generation created more problems than they solved. I imagined that his roommates worked for companies who stocked Blue Bottle in their offices, along with having napping stations and giant plastic exercise balls for chairs. "It's like, wow," Victor said, "I spend a lot of energy for their future, and they don't give a fuck, and I am honestly just like, okay." He shrugged. "I haven't really pursued it." In a sense, maybe he saw in them a younger version of himself.

A visual artist, he'd gone to art school and ended up in advertising, because one ad could earn him a lot of money. The more he worked, the more he learned how images influence us to buy and behave the way we do, and he started thinking about how he could use graphic design to help shape society. That's what advertising is, he explained: manipulating human psychology. By studying human behavior, he would "know how to fight the man." Silicon Valley's second tech boom was charged with the same youthful naiveté and a similarly ambitious sense of revolutionary possibility, the idea that technology and innovative thinking could disrupt existing systems and improve anything about the world, from shipping to medicine, and of course subvert the existing hotel industries by convincing civilians to offer their own houses for part of the profits, all under the guise of a social movement. Airbnb wasn't building a system of motels, they now said; it was a global community.

Drawing for a living was fun at first. Two decades of logos, rebrands, and ad campaigns took the joy out of it, and as his subversive impulse got subverted by supply and demand, the industry left little energy to be part of America's environmental solution the way he'd envisioned. When a computer crash destroyed all his files, he welcomed the opportunity to build a less soul-sucking profession atop the scorched earth.

"I'm headed in some other direction now," he said, "and I'm not quite sure, you know?" He needed something soon. San Francisco rent was expensive, and he turned fifty in five months.

We stood under a native cypress tree and an imported palm. Dressed in blue jeans, clean brown Converse All Stars, and a brown sweater under a gray wool vest, Victor kept his long gray-streaked hair under a straw hat. He bounced on his toes as he spoke, and he spoke with the textbook, super-slow stoner affect, where he paused to make you wait for his observations but mostly gave you sentence fragments. Victor would have tested Latta's patience as an interviewer. Latta might not have interviewed him at all, but I was fascinated.

As we talked, he took bites of a coconut-almond trail mix bar covered in dark chocolate. It had a low glycemic index, and he watched his blood sugar.

As a voter, he voted green. As a consumer, he allowed his environmental concerns to be directed by his purchasing habits. He also had allergies, so he ate a diet of mainly nuts, fruits, and vegetables. He admitted that he ate too many trail mix bars, but six of his weekly meals were specially blended drinks composed of fruit, raw oatmeal, raw almonds, and eggs. Growing up, he'd frequently driven the Valley's I-5 corridor with his parents. Even though his healthy diet relied on so many thirsty crops from the Valley, he knew little about it. "It's dry," he said. "Lots of the water comes from other places, the Colorado River, etcetera. You know. Whatever."

The Colorado River ran 260 miles east of Bakersfield along the Arizona-California border. It fed Phoenix, Los Angeles, and farmland in between. It didn't water the Valley.

He took another bite of his bar.

From his drives, he'd only come to know towns like Fresno and Visalia as points that marked his north-south progress along the highway, and he perceived the land on either side only vaguely as "Little feeder roads and whatnot." Because of his allergies and all the pesticides, he avoided spending time there.

Victor scratched his elbow. And his head. His ticks were part of his shtick. "It just seems like farmers. I know it's very conservative, so I'm just not drawn to it. I'm drawn *through* it, to get other places. It's built up. It's already such a fixture. It seems like less fields from driving up and down when I was a kid, but that might just be my imagination. Seems like there's more dry spots. But yeah. The idea that they pumped the water in always, even as kids, seemed kind of weird. Certainly does more now. But you know. Alotta stuff. New ideas. Some of them pan out; some of them don't." New ideas like what, I asked, groundwater pumping? "Yeah, that. Little things like that. Just thinking about when my mom was pregnant with me and I was young, even just stuff like DDT. It was just so much, like, postwar enthusiasm and all sort of things, you know? Even—" He bounced on his toes. "Anyway, they got the infrastructure, but we got less and less water."

In a sense, water limitations were one reason San Francisco was going to mix groundwater with its imported water, but they weren't in a crisis. According to one statistic, all the houses and businesses in San Francisco used 0.11 billion cubic meters of water combined. California almonds used 3.4 billion cubic meters of water. And that was just one of nearly three hundred crops in the Valley. If anyone was getting less water, it was farmers who were depriving their own industry of it. What Victor failed to acknowledge was how difficult it was to live in a city like San Francisco and not contribute to the things you hate. Food, water, crowding, capitalism—we fight, yet we end up complicit.

I pointed out how many almonds were in his MOJO bar.

He studied the package. Victor didn't have diabetes. "Trying to just keep myself . . . level," he said. Almond protein was part of why producers marketed almonds as miracle food—all that protein and good fat in that little portable nut! It was also why some critics claimed its protein took too much water to create. I was now convinced that almonds grown with drip systems were better for California than any milk protein.

With all the bad press about California almonds using too much water, he didn't feel bad about eating the nuts. "I love almonds," he said. "I do feel like it's part of my heritage, actually."

So he felt that farmers were depriving his city of water during the drought, but he believed that the almonds that used that water were part of his identity as a Californian?

"Frankly, I think we're fucked," he said. After his career creating images to manipulate consumer behavior, he believed that the average American needed something visual and catastrophic to wake them from their capitalist phone-zombie slumber. Farms' slow death by dehydration wasn't photogenic enough to convince most people to change their lifestyles. They needed to "feel pain," he said, to feel the heat of global warming, in order to act. "Anyway, I just don't think enough people care in the big picture and fast enough, you know, that pain thing. People got to hurt before they really move."

Pain hadn't moved him toward ecological awareness. He just found it impossible not to look around at the growing human population intersecting with the loss of farmland and water and not see the sum of these parts.

"There is a point where you just kind of go, 'Fuck it. Yeah, I love almonds. I don't give a shit anymore.' You know? All it does is make me feel anxious and stressed out."

That was the rub. He *did* give a fuck. Caring is exhausting, especially when you're approaching age fifty and feel that the world is determined to undermine your efforts. Living with those twenty-somethings made the West Coast's post–Summer of Love progress seem wasted. But he didn't acknowledge all the people who *were* doing something to improve social, ecological, and agricultural conditions in California, all the people like Michael Pollan and Alice Waters, and the thousands of unfamous people like Jihadda Govan laboring behind the scenes at government agencies and nonprofits like the Center for Biological Diversity. The list went on. He felt like nobody did anything, so it was easier to eat his destructive death almonds and wait for the shriveled West to blow away. The sun would eventually swallow the whole solar system anyway. Why bother?

I couldn't help but feel that it was all worth it. No matter how wasteful the state's water-distribution system was and how mindless parts of this conversation, the Valley afforded us moments of beauty like this. All around us in the grass, people faced west. They faced the pastel light as it accumulated over the ocean, here where centuries of European settlers had searched for new beginnings at the end of the continent and created the mythic ritual of the California dream. These San Franciscans had commandeered a piece of the good life, and as much as the Valley enchanted me, the mountains blocked my ocean view. And I missed the ocean.

It was Sunday. Tomorrow, Govan's water will not have come, and the pollution will keep funneling through the East Bay to clog Bakersfield's air. Maybe California would get a reprieve this winter. Maybe snow would fall in the sierras and end the drought. Climatologists didn't seem confident. In the Valley, many big growers' almonds would fatten either way; corporate growers had well water and mist systems, as well as the money to keep pushing wells deeper into the shrinking aquifers.

Victor stumbled down the hill toward the street, and I headed to the crest to watch the sunset. As the light waned, a cold wind blew up to the top of the hill.

The cold made me want to leave, too, but the show was about to begin. And I hadn't seen a Bay Area sunset for ten years.

On the crest, two men stood with their dog, Luna. Adam, twenty-eight, was born in San Francisco, raised in Palo Alto, and now worked for a startup that built software for social good, including literacy, food production, and the environment. As a Bay Area native, he'd driven the 5 to LA countless times, but he only stopped for In-N-Out Burger.

His thirty-two-year-old friend Aaron, also born in San Francisco, worked for a company that developed tech and policy systems to help make residential solar easier for homeowners to install. These kinds of job descriptions confused me. He clarified: "People who want to join the revolution."

Aaron avoided the Valley at all costs, though he had a succinct impression from the air. "It's just a giant grid," he said. "Farms forever." Aaron's description resembled the opening paragraph of Gerald Haslam's book *The Other California*. It begins, "Glimpsed from an airplane during summer, California's Great Central Valley is a grid of sharply defined, multicolored fields sliding below." But the distance these men put between themselves and the land only created room for inaccuracies.

"I've had this conversation recently with several people," said Adam, "about what the future of food production looks like. A lot of people are starting companies now to, like, grow food on rooftops and make it way more efficient and that kind of stuff." He shrugged. "That's a very, I guess, Silicon Valley–centric way of looking at things—that, like, technology can solve this problem, maybe. There are definitely some people working on that, so." Not everyone would feel relieved to know that the people whose main contact with the Valley was at a burger chain were the people trying to shape the future of agriculture.

Adam's company was designing software solutions for an area he called sustainable food production. "So that's definitely starting to be on the radar," he said. "Like, dairy farming in the Midwest uses a ridiculous amount of water, and how can we use software, for example, to manage that. Because a lot of customers of big dairies are starting to demand more sustainable farming practices, so. That doesn't actually quite exist yet." Did he think the Valley could use their help? "It really is dangerous to have a monoculture like that. Like, 80 percent of our almonds are coming from there. If they have a bad year, then we don't have almonds. Just like in, wherever, Iowa, where they produce all the corn, and they produce high-fructose corn syrup so they can stick it in all of our food for no reason. And also if there's, like, a disease or something."

But the Valley wasn't a monoculture. It grew nearly three hundred crops, more than most regions in the world.

Aaron shifted his weight from one boot to the other. "Also, clearly the way we do agriculture can't work in the very long term," he said. What did he consider were the problems threatening modern agriculture's longevity? "I think the runoff of chemicals is deeply problematic, but also the vulnerabilities associated with monoculture."

"People are saying the solution is, like, you know, urban agriculture," said Adam, "and everyone's raising food, and it's all local and shit. And I just, like, it's not efficient or sustainable. It can produce some stuff, but you have to have this other large system, because there's a lot of . . ."

Aaron picked up where Adam stopped: "You hear about these Japanese researchers who came up with this football field–sized indoor hydroponic model with, like, perfectly tuned LEDs that only gave the perfect band of light. So it's the size of a football field, maybe twenty foot tall, and it produces ten thousand head of lettuce a week. So I think there is room for some distributive model."

"I'm sure there's also something in there with labor practices," Adam said of big ag's problems.

We agreed about the necessity of urban agriculture and the threat of chemical runoff. But the idea of Silicon Valley "solving" agricultural problems had me thinking that these people spent too much time with people just like themselves, reinforcing their insular knowledge of the way they think the world works, rather than spending time with farmers and integrating knowledge from people who don't work in tech or live in the city. If California was going to solve its agricultural problems, the coast and interior needed to collaborate.

The sky turned orange, and dogs raced across the grassy knoll as if the cold wind had blown them. Once the sunset dipped below the horizon, my trip would be over, and I would technically be on vacation. The time had come to have some fun.

Both Adam and Aaron were really into food, so I asked for dinner recommendations. They raved about a nearby upscale soul food restaurant where they'd eaten the previous night and had paid around $14 per entrée. That cost too much for me. "But it's *really good*," Adam said. "We kind of went all out." When I asked for lower-priced suggestions, they asked what kind of food I like, and I told them Vietnamese, Japanese, Korean. Aaron suggested a Thai restaurant on Divisidero, but Adam wasn't crazy about that one.

"It's *pretty* good," Aaron said, defending his suggestion with a smile.

Adam shook his head emphatically at me. It wasn't.

"Okay," said Aaron, getting snappy, "you want to get picky?" I do,

I said. I was in San Francisco. After driving seven hundred miles and taking in this dizzying mixture of worldviews and perspectives, I needed to treat myself to something above average, or to at least try something new, and I wanted to enjoy a silent moment by myself with a plate of food, to gorge on an uncool, unphotogenic salt-of-the-earth dish free of opinions or political attachments. Out west, there was no such food.

Then Adam suggested I drive two miles to try either a popular Burmese restaurant or another called Mandalay if I couldn't get in there. Aaron nodded in agreement.

I'd never had Burmese food. They gave me directions.

The park lit a blazing peach and blue, and I buried my head under my insulated hood.

As the sun dipped behind the horizon, Adam told me about the land east of the Bay Area. "We make fun of the fact that there's, like, swastikas and people with guns and stuff and crosses," he said. I asked where in the Valley he saw crosses and swastikas. "On the way down through who-the-fuck-knows," he said. "The Salinas Valley is more the Steinbeck, like, utopian vision of agriculture in California. I don't know much about the San Joaquin."

On the Friday after arriving in San Francisco, Latta woke up with what he called "a bath, a shave and a good night's rest," before returning to Treasure Island to check on the boat. Freshly showered for the first time in nearly two weeks, he and the boys left their comfortable hotel beds to spend the day like tourists. They gawked at skyscrapers, visited the newly constructed Golden Gate Bridge, and fed some sea lions; then they did an 8:00 spot on the popular KGO AM radio station in Oakland, to describe their epic trip. After that, Latta said, they planned to "spend a few days in relaxation before returning home."

Tensions between San Francisco and the Valley now run so high that I had to wonder what Latta thought of San Francisco in his day. Like many people in small Valley towns like Hanford and Kingsburg, did he try to avoid it? In the 1930s there were reasons to both love and loath the Bay Area. Trains, horses, and trolleys congested cities before cars did. Before modern drug crime and grime descended, it had opium dens, the illegal liquor trade, the mob, and sanitation issues. And yet San Francisco still had patches of woods filled with rare native butterflies and wild space. I imagine the crew felt elated to have survived their trip, only to have been rewarded with time to recuperate where the air was cool and flowers bloomed on green hills, and out of the punishing sun, they could sit down to a steak and bowl of clam chowder.

At the end of my trip, it became clear that Latta wasn't the sit-down kind of guy. You grow intimate when you spend two weeks traveling with someone, even someone whom time keeps at arm's length, rather than chatting in your passenger seat. Latta didn't write intimately about himself. He didn't process in public the way we modern-day memoirists do, or certain travel writers for whom the content of their own mind is as interesting as the place they're exploring. Latta mostly kept his interior life interior. His gaze aimed outward. For that, he will forever remain unknowable, leaving me to guess about him more than I'd like. Another part of me appreciated the mystery, the sense that he, like the unplowed Valley under the Yokuts' care, would always stay somewhat out of reach, visible but hazy. On the back roads, between his book covers, on dry Tulare Lake, I constantly wondered, Who was this obsessed documentarian I'm following? He said he gathered stories because he "couldn't help it," but did he believe that his compulsion accomplished something in life? Was he satisfied with his contributions? For Latta, the point was always the people he interviewed—"the source," not the author. For me, it was about him, too, but he wouldn't play along.

Brought together by mutual interests, Latta and I engaged in a kind of conversation, whispering to each other across generations, and we have both spent too many days listening to the echoes of the past. As someone who understands obsession, I understand that part of him. But in his silence, we learn about him too. Uninterested in explaining his particular attraction to the Valley or in reflecting on his dual career, he let his work show how certain he was of the Valley's importance. Although I couldn't entirely understand my own fascination with the Valley any more than I could understand his, there in San Francisco watching the sunset, I did feel that I knew him better than I had when I first photocopied those *Bakersfield Californian* articles years ago.

Latta was a worker bee. He appreciated ephemerality and the fragility of human life, and he let nothing slow his quest to rescue this unique region from time. It's a lonely place to live, out there on the frontier's margins, your interests barely registering on the margins of society's interests. Like his subjects, he was a person both of his time and out of step with it; thriving in a brief window between epochs, forever in danger of disappearing, his work was quickly buried by the work of more prominent historians, as the Valley got buried in concrete. He probably knew this would happen. I imagine his work's disappearance, like the loss of the Yokuts' languages and the death of the Chunut, weighed on him. How could it not? The hope that some future historian would rescue it from obscurity was too thin a hope to cling to. Working felt better than standing around thinking about it.

As nice as San Francisco was, a few days sightseeing and recuperating were enough, and Latta rushed back home to his Valley, his family, his work. He always worked. Research gave his life shape. With this boat project completed, he could get back to his other projects, because as the title of an article later put it, his life was a "History Project That Never Stops."

With four books to his name, Latta served as president of the League of Western Writers in 1938. The following year, the Kern County Historical Society published his fifth book, *Alexis Godey in Kern County*, detailing one of the lesser known trappers in John C. Fremont's 1840s California expeditions. It was thirty-two pages and part of the society's annual bulletin series, and he assembled it while interviewing aging pioneers who knew the Dalton gang, Joaquin Murrieta, and Tulare Lake, to complete what he imagined were his next books.

Throughout the 1940s, Latta stayed particularly active, publishing syndicated columns in the Valley's many regional papers, including the *Tulare Times, Lemoore Leader*, and *Livingston Chronicle*. His San Joaquin Primeval series was popular. It included two thousand columns and his usual mix of oral history, archaeology, and natural history.

In 1942 Latta transferred from Shafter High School to a school in Bakersfield and hammered away at more books. Even though his popularity grew, he stayed regional. No mainstream magazines like the *Saturday Evening Post* or *Harper's* sent reporters to write in-depth profiles of interior California's version of the tireless John P. Harrington, but local museums, historical societies, and men's clubs hired him as a speaker. At luncheons and in small town halls, he regaled audiences with stories of the boat trip and flood and of all the bumpy roads he traveled to record people. In a sense, he had fashioned himself into the very pioneers he'd spent decades interviewing, a source of rare experience who'd witnessed what was left of the Valley's shrinking frontier and returned to tell the tale. He lived history through his scholarly work; now his life as the child of pioneers made him the object of other peoples' interest. Audiences ate it up.

When Latta was teaching in Bakersfield in 1944, the president of the Kern County Historical Society asked Latta to help them develop a museum to preserve the artifacts and history of Kern County. They wanted him to serve as its first director. It was the ideal job for him—a mix of public outreach, cataloging, and curation and the chance to finally teach history instead of drafting and carpentry. Latta was trying to save money for retirement, though, so initially, he worked part-time and kept his teaching job. As the *Bakersfield Californian* reported, he liked the Kern Country Museum so much that "the 'half-time' turned out to be ten to 16 hours a day." Of course he couldn't keep away.

Latta put together exhibits. He got Yokuts friends to re-create a village on the Kern River for a video documentary, showing the world before Bakersfield: people bowhunting, people drying venison, people cooking with hot rocks, his usual ethnographic interests, which at this point start to resemble fixations. The museum gift shop sold his books, and they sold well. In 1946 he retired from teaching to work full-time as museum director, and he made sure to hire people with deep local knowledge. Initially, three of his four staff were Yokuts tribes members, including John Garcia, his brother Joe Garcia, and Henry Lawrence, who was the last full member of Bakersfield's Yowlumne Tribe. Latta later hired Pete Barrios, of the Tachi Tribe. The arrangement certainly benefited Latta too; this way, he got to spend his last years in the Valley with the people he loved the most, sharing stories with the public as he always had.

With all his knowledge and anecdotes, I imagine Latta told a lot of colorful stories in his high school classes about people he'd met and things he'd seen. Not the kind of stories that made kids roll their eyes—*Ugh, teach is talking about pioneers again*—but the kind that helped students understand the big picture in place of rote memorization, the kind that used early settlers' challenges to show frustrated students that anything was possible if they kept trying. Rather than a showy, overly talkative teacher, I picture Latta as a helpful, encouraging, approachable one, someone students could talk to about any classroom subject and who rewarded their curiosity with discussion.

Not everyone found him agreeable. His relationship with the Kern County Museum soured. "Frank Latta Fired by Supervisors" ran the headline in the *Bakersfield Californian*'s March 31, 1955, edition. "At a special meeting yesterday," the article stated, "the Board charged Latta with incompetence, inefficiency, dishonesty, insubordination, disobedience and inexcusable neglect of duty." Those sound more like military crimes than the poor performance of a museum director. After finding evidence of misconduct, the county museum commission recommended that the board discharge Latta. An internal audit found what the paper called "many irregularities in the operation of the museum under Latta's tenure," and they were sending it to the district attorney to lay formal charges. Of course, Latta denied wrongdoing and defended himself. In the end, the evidence was insufficient, and the grand jury absolved him. "Latta 'Triumphant' on Tour of Museum" read one July 19, 1955, *Bakersfield Californian* headline. When the charges were dropped, it was too late. Latta resigned as museum director, and he and Jean left the Valley entirely, taking their voluminous research and artifacts with them. Although the controversy faded with time, the story left a big enough impression in the Bakersfield area that, in 2016, the Historic Bakersfield Facebook page wrote, "Quite a number of people have a bad viewpoint of Latta, having heard rumors of what happened to him with the Kern County Museum. But the facts show that not only was Latta exonerated of the charges that were filed against him, he was praised by the Grand Jury for his work." I doubt that he was, as the board claimed, inept, but I can't help but wonder about his reliability as a historian. Did these charges bring the veracity of his oral history work into question? Draw its contents and reliability into question? Having viewed his detailed notes on interview sources—whom he spoke to, on what date and where—I find him too meticulous to be called inept, but I do wonder if maybe he had invented the provenance of his more storied artifacts or if he was too willing to believe the people he got these artifacts from. Spanish daggers? Anchors? Maybe I was the one who was too willing to believe Latta.

After recording Uncle Jeff's story, Latta kept interviewing Yokuts to expand on what Jeff taught him. In 1949 he finally combined thirty years' worth of this ethnographic material and hundreds of photographs into the 176-page *Handbook of Yokuts Indians*, a book five times longer than his last one. This comprehensive, nutrient-dense, proudly obsessive volume includes ethnographic details found nowhere else, and it's many people's only encounter with Latta. The university-educated ethnologist Alfred L. Kroeber wrote a whole book about the Yokuts, yet outside of the tribes themselves, Latta's stands as the ultimate authority on Yokuts culture. Kroeber encouraged Latta during his years of labor, and in the foreword he wrote for *Handbook of Yokuts Indians*, Kroeber said that Latta's careful, patient research made Kroeber "aware of how much I missed that I might have recorded." *Handbook of Yokuts Indians* received accolades in the anthropology community, but it was not a commercial book. Latta wrote it to endure. Time has proven its value, and nothing like it has been written since, because everyone whom subsequent ethnographers would need to interview to write a book like it has died.

Despite Latta's achievement, he didn't rest. He kept finding stories before people took them to their graves. That same year, he published *Black Gold in the Joaquin*, about the first phase in the region's multibillion-dollar petroleum industry, which dates back to when tar seeped from holes in the soil and settlers used it to seal their roofs and boats. Latta focused on the early industry's characters, like successful Coalinga oilman Milton McWhorter, who tapped wells in the dry western hills, and he let these people tell their own stories with little interruption from him. Caxton Printers, a small Idaho publishing company that specialized in the American West, published it in 1949. It would be his last book with an outside publisher. After that, the Latta family formed their own publishing house, Bear State Books, to print the projects other publishers would not.

Time isn't kind to historians. Each year steals more sources and erases the world they document. As time passed, Latta struggled to find old-timers to interview, so he worked the voluminous material he had. The federal government was building dams on the rivers he once floated. As the Valley's highways got busier, towns grew, and farmland filled with the roadside restaurants that forecast the McDonald's of the future. Latta shaved his mustache and wore thin, circular, wire-frame glasses that fit his life of scholarship, though the deepening wrinkles on his sun-chapped skin suggested his other life on rugged back roads. His shirt collars grew with the times, and heavy American gas-guzzlers replaced his old Model T.

On October 14, 1949, he spoke at the dedication ceremony for a historical marker on the Tule River Indian Reservation, east of Porterville. On March 3, 1952, Latta spoke to a meeting of the Tulare County Historical Society at Ducor about the Valley's early petroleum development. But this chapter in his life had closed. He stayed at the museum until he retired in 1955 at age sixty-three, and the Lattas left Kern County for the coast the following year. Frank and Jeanette bought the 725-acre Gazos Ranch near Pescadero. It must have been strange to leave the Valley after sixty-four years there, but maybe in old age he had tired of the heat, the familiar horizon, watching the rapid pace of urbanization. Naturally, the Lattas found a property that looked like old California.

Located on costal Highway 1 north of Santa Cruz, eighteenth-century Spanish explorers Gaspar de Portolà and José Francisco Ortega camped on the Lattas' property in 1769, as the men traveled north on what became the first Spanish visit to San Francisco Bay. The land later became part of a Mexican land grant, and then the Steele family turned it into the massive Steele Ranch dairy ranch. According to a historical marker, the Steele family called their ranch "cow heaven." "Effie Steele and her husband, Edwin Dickerman," the marker says, "built their farm house and outbuildings here in the 1880s. They constructed the cow barn with timber salvaged from a storm wrecked local wharf." The Lattas did the same; they took a window pane and wooden boards from the hull of the *Columbia*, which hit rocks near Pigeon Point in 1869, and added them to their house in a small canyon facing the ocean. For most people, this would sound too wild to be believable. But the Lattas sought out history, and he was a storyteller. He created his own biography. As Latta's life's work shows, in a land this old, history is everywhere.

He and Jeanette decided to bring that history back to life.

Using their collected artifacts that had once filled the Kern County Museum, the Lattas planned to build a family theme park called Pioneer Village. They envisioned a place where kids and adults could experience the look and feel of early California, wandering through a pioneer drugstore, tack and saddle maker, blacksmith, firehouse, Chinatown, and Yokuts houses. Their ranch had eleven original wooden buildings. One already contained an exhibit of their Yokuts artifacts, which the YMCA used as part of its outdoor education program for local school kids. The barn contained what Latta estimated was 350 tons of historic objects and archived newspapers, which they would use to authentically decorate their replica Pioneer Village. "To many people this material would look like junk," Frank told an East Bay newspaper in 1968, "but it represents a cross-section of California life as it was lived many years ago." He envisioned this as a historical version of Southern California's famous Knott's Berry Farm, except, in his words, "without the commercial atmosphere." A living museum would have been a practical use of all their Spanish daggers, pistols, and tack. They planned to eventually add an eighty-acre picnic and campsite area stretching a mile down the coastline.

San Mateo County and the California Coastal Commission, though, didn't want the park or the car traffic associated with it, especially right along the highway. The county stonewalled the Lattas' efforts. Latta kept trying, kept building displays. After years of labor and frustration, Frank and Jeanette sold the ranch to Del Monte and moved into Santa Cruz proper. At their age, it made sense to be closer to hospitals and amenities. The failed plans might have been disappointing for him but probably not for Californians. Did people really want a history-themed Knott's Berry Farm? Latta was more obsessed with history than his contemporaries. In the 1960s the country was looking forward, at space exploration, nuclear power, the inner workings of the molecule. He preferred looking back. In retirement, his writing never slowed.

A life of research had left the family with an enormous library containing not just books but reams of newspaper clippings, letters, maps, and obscure historical documents, filling file cabinets, bookshelves, even locked safes. When one writer visited the ranch in 1970, he found shelves containing "a complete set of Bancroft's works, copies of all San Joaquin Valley County Histories, originals of Fremont's narratives, Prescott's histories of Mexico and Peru, basic Cherokee and other Indian works, and dozens of Smithsonian and Bureau of Ethnology volumes, only to give the reader a sample." And he found Frank "assembling, checking, re-checking, and organizing the raw data which has taken him a life to gather, into publishable manuscripts." As *Madera Tribune* columnist Ira Landerman said of Latta, he "just keeps on going like an old oak."

Instead of relaxing, Latta funneled his energy into new books. As time progressed, he seemed to have scoured every corner of the Valley, and as the Valley changed, he extended his research farther out. He went south of Bakersfield to research Tejon Ranch. He went as far east as Kansas to interview surviving members of the Dalton family for his book *Dalton Gang Days*. He went over the Sierra Nevada to write about the epic struggles of Utah miners who traveled through the Mojave Desert to reach California. He spent ten years assembling the story from obscure newspaper clippings and letters, only to have to wait to publish it himself as *Death Valley '49ers* in 1979. Although he was still doing exhaustive research on Joaquin Murrieta, who remained one of California's most popular folk stories, no single story could top Uncle Jeff's for depth, length, and novelty. So Latta kept coming back to it, expanding, rearranging, and reworking the text. After failing to get *Uncle Jeff's Story* republished by Stanford University Press in the 1930s, he spared himself more disappointment and published a new version himself, seizing the means of production and sticking to his vision. He'd always been a person who did things his way, which shared a lot with John Harrington's way, which was all or nothing and possibly problematic at the Kern County Museum. But in publishing, maybe the commercial marketplace just didn't have a place for Latta's oral history, regionality, and so-called Californiana.

Latta saw his years waning. He labored to get more done. He didn't imagine *Joaquin Murrieta and His Horse Gangs* as his last book. At age seventy-six, he told a small newspaper, "We figured out the other day that we have enough work laid out right now to keep us busy another fifty years. After that, we can begin to worry about what to do with our time."

"In the end," writes James B. Snyder in the introduction to Latta's ethnographic papers in the Yosemite Research Library, "perhaps, Latta's interest did consume him, for he tried to cover too much for too long, extending himself beyond any human capacity to produce what he hoped to for his world." Snyder felt Latta's later work was noticeably rougher, or more rushed, than his early books, but he respected his efforts. "He promised more than he could deliver in the end," wrote Snyder, "yet he still gave more than most can in a lifetime." Snyder called Latta "the right man at the right place at the right time."

The thing about Latta is that his estimates weren't always consistent. In one article, he said he interviewed eighteen thousand people. In another he said nineteen thousand: seventeen thousand white settlers and two thousand Yokuts. He wrote three thousand articles total, or was it two thousand? Mayfield was five when he moved to California; no, he was six. History involves a lot of names and numbers. Even historians' memories fail. But both seventeen thousand and eighteen thousand seem very high to me. All these interviews went into his books, but were the bulk of them used to fact-check his main sources? They couldn't all be. Part of me wondered about how much he created his own narrative. When people reach the end of their life, some try to create a more glowing account of it. I don't want to think Latta invented facts. I don't want to think he dramatized numbers or massaged quotes. But I do think that at the end of a person's life, they want it to add up to something, for all the hard work and effort to mean more than it did, because it never means as much as we need it to. *How many people did you interview in your life, Mr. Latta? About eighteen thousand.* Seventeen thousand, eighteen thousand—what's the difference? That's eighteen thousand more interviews than most of us will ever do.

In 1970 Latta was still laboring on books he never finished: "Henry Miller and the Cattle King," "Waterways of the San Joaquin," "Sontag and Evans," and something called "Just Damn Lies." If he completed parts of the manuscripts, he published none of them. Another unpublished Latta manuscript called "San Joaquin Valley Bandits" sits in the H. G. Schutt Collection in the library at Cal State University, Fresno, and includes a chapter about Clodovio Chavez, one of Tiburcio Vásquez's sidekicks. Drafts of an unpublished manuscript called "Sky Farmers and Mule Skinners" sit in the famous Huntington Library archive in Los Angeles.

Named after a type of dry-land, nonirrigated farming, "Sky Farmers and Mule Skinners" along with other Latta papers fill 121 boxes. The library characterizes the Latta collection's subjects as "agriculture and farming in the San Joaquin Valley, the development of agricultural machinery (combines, plows, reapers, scrapers, threshing machines, tractors and various types of harvesters), livestock, ranches, cattle, and crops, mostly wheat. Also covered are: early aviation, early automobiles, bears, crime, the Dalton Gang, the Donner Party, earthquakes, education and schools in the San Joaquin Valley, floods, freight and steamships on the San Joaquin River, gold mines, irrigation, canals and water rights in San Joaquin Valley, land grants, livestock, lumber, outlaws, pioneers, the Presbyterian Church in California, ranches, rivers, roads, saddlery, sheepherding in California, overland journeys to California and California politics, government and history. Also talked about are women, African Americans, Chileans, Chinese, Mormons, Native Americans and Jews in California." So basically everything. The list reflects Latta's outsized interests, his curiosity, his life's work.

Before his boat trip, Latta speculated that the Kern River had left 250 square miles of Kern County underwater. After seeing for himself, he increased that to 550. By the end of 1938, official state numbers said that floods had damaged $7.5 million of property and crops in the Valley, which is about $86 million in today's dollars.

He wanted dams and flood control, yet interestingly, he didn't fully trust that they would work. In his 1937 book *Little Journeys* he wrote, "The safe guess is that Tulare Lake will continue to play the phantom role regardless of levees, ditches and dams built by white man." So which was it? Damned by dams or destined to remain unruly and free? Maybe his views were evolving. Maybe as a self-appointed civic leader, he said the popular thing that would get him the most attention, views that would elevate his position as a person who had ideas, views that people listened to. He'd certainly built himself into an expert in history and hydrology whose name locals recognized, and he'd had no formal training in either. But for a man so determined to keep the lake alive through photographs and the written word, he now seemed intent on destroying it. It didn't make sense. Was he just fascinated by the region? Was he as obsessed as Harrington with collecting data before it disappeared? He might have been a person of his time, steeped in the language of expansion, who inherited the idea that nature is worth what it gives civilization, that standing water is wasted water in the battle of man against nature. He valued industry and agriculture and didn't write about ecological preservation. History shows that progress marches on, and it takes great effort for a person to slow it. Maybe he was sad to see Tulare Lake draining, and he was just resigned.

But he was also clearly his own person. Like me, he was driven by curiosity and an appreciation for people's speech. But if he saw the Valley now and mourned it, he would have to blame himself.

As always, the Valley went through drought only to flood again. In 1969 high waters swelled Tulare Lake to seventy square miles. In spring 1983, floodwaters breached another one of Tulare Lake's levees and spread across thirty thousand acres of farmland. Oildale author Gerald Haslam called Tulare "the lake that will not die." In May 1983 Boswell pumped those floodwaters from the lake bed into the San Joaquin River, possibly sending with it noxious, destructive white bass, an invasive fish that biologists had until then been able to keep out of the delta and river system. That year, Latta came back inland, too, this time over the dry brown mountains to Hills Ferry Cemetery in Newman, where he was laid to rest seven miles northeast of where he was born at Orestimba Creek, where Spaniards wearing armor used to ride horses spring to spring on the Camino Viejo, and where the *Alta* spent two nights on the river with a broken motor.

In Latta's obituary, an old Bakersfield neighbor told the *Bakersfield Californian*, "There was just one Frank Latta. . . . He was his own man, so to speak." And by the time Tulare Lake flooded again in 1997,

Latta's children—Monna, Nedra, and Donna—had scattered around the state and to Dallas, Texas; raised their own children; and soon took their memories of the family's weekend research trips with them. When I searched for Frank's son, Don, to ask about his memories of the boat trip, I only found his obituary.

What's comical is that different sources list the year of Frank's death differently. One website says he died in 1981. The introduction to his collected ethnographic papers in the Yosemite Research Library says he died in 1978. The *Bakersfield Californian* correctly lists the year as 1983. Does this mean Latta got news of his own death before he succumbed? What would a historian think of these historical inaccuracies? He could capture pages of people's speech without a recorder, but these reporters couldn't get two numbers right. "The man himself is the source," Latta said, "the ultimate authority." He'd said all he could say.

In 1862 William Brewer talked with a shepherd in the Diablo Range, west of Turlock. This rugged country stayed unmapped and largely unexplored by white settlers for decades, and this shepherd worked in narrow Lone Tree Canyon, named for the one tree that grew where the dry creek flowed into the Valley. He hadn't seen anyone for three weeks. "This man said," wrote Brewer, "during the five years he has been here he has never before seen water in it, summer or winter. Now there is a small stream." Later that year, the drought broke, and Tulare Lake swelled to its largest-recorded size.

During my visit, forecasters feared more dry weather for 2016. That would have been the drought's fifth year, but between October 1, 2016, and January 1, 2017, Northern California received a more concentrated volume of rain than it had since 1922. Four and a half inches fell on Contra Costa County's Mount Diablo in one storm. Enormous amounts of snow fell in the sierra's northern half. By March the snowpack in the sierra reached the seventh-deepest it had since 1950, bringing the entire range's pack to 164 percent of its seasonal average. Frank Gehrke, chief snow surveyor for the Department of

Water Resources, measured a field of snow east of Sacramento at ninety-four inches deep. Two years earlier, that spot was dirt. "The winter weather in California is feast or famine," Gehrke told the *Los Angeles Times*. "We have very dry years followed by extremely wet years." Gehrke understood the state's true nature. After this, hopefully others would as well.

Rain and melting snow refilled California's dry reservoirs in such a dramatic, Lazarus-type way that once a few news outlets ran miraculous before and after photos, others republished them. The contrast between drought and relief was more cinematic than any articles listing water levels and cubic-foot data could be. Look at the shorelines! From brown to blue! This revival lent itself well to our visual era of social media and short attention spans. The pendulum swung so hard that the record lows of previous years now created record highs, once again making California a state of superlatives, breaking its own records.

Lake Shasta, the state's largest reservoir, dropped down to 2.67 million acre-feet of water in February 2016. By February 2017 the reservoir contained 4.21 million acre-feet, and the 602-foot Shasta Dam released excess water from its top flood gate for the first time in twenty years.

In February 2015 Lake McClure, north of Fresno, was down to 7 percent of its 1.02 million-acre-foot capacity, or 63,489 acre-feet—the lowest ever recorded. In March 2017 it filled to 696,279 acre-feet.

In 2016, 74 percent of California was classified as suffering severe drought. By April 2017 only 1 percent was severe. Although some sections of Southern California were recovering more slowly than others, another miracle occurred: some irrigation districts in the Valley started giving farmers surface water to irrigate their fields again. That meant that many growers could stop drilling new wells, could stop wondering if this was their last season in the business. Despite the soggy celebration, the California Water Resources Control Board planned to keep its monitory and water-use restrictions in place, though in May they would discuss whether to relax certain restrictions in the future.

"While the emergency has ended, the need to conserve has not," said Metropolitan Water District general manager Jeffrey Kightlinger. "Southern Californians have learned a lot about water conservation during the latest drought. We cannot afford to forget those lessons." They would. Maybe people learned a lot about conservation, but farming dollars still ruled California. And farmers need water. Also, we tend to forget our predecessors. We see the monthly events, not the larger patterns, thinking like Dell in terms of our children, not millennia. With such bounty in front of us, we forget about past lessons and have the privilege to focus on convenience, business, and low-price products. Life moves so fast, and technology speeds it more each decade, dimming the edges of our field of vision until the people who sought answers for us in the past completely disappear. California is a state of emergency, if not a drought, then a flood, with a small field of flowers in between. When the next catastrophe strikes, it feels like the first.

Driving from San Francisco to Sacramento to catch my plane, I considered stopping in Newman to visit the Lattas' graves. I'd been with them for two weeks and with their research for years. Frank's voice was in my ear, but I hadn't had that type of physical interaction that gives a sense of intimacy. Newman was an hour and a half drive from my location; in California time that was nothing, especially after what I'd just driven. I still decided against it. I liked knowing the Lattas as young parents bouncing their old cars on dirt roads, photographing settlers while their kids played in the back seat. That was how I wanted to remember them, alive and wild, like me.

Before Frank died, he and Jeanette started storing their papers and artifacts around the state. They gave some of their Yokuts baskets and other items to the Tulare County and Kern County museums. They gave small collections to friends in Los Banos and Benicia and sold most of his ethnographic research on the Yokuts to the Yosemite National Park Museum and Research Library. The famous Huntington Library near Pasadena paid six figures for most of Latta's research on Miller and Lux. Other papers landed in the Haggin Museum of

Stockton and the Coyote Hills Regional Park Museum in the southern Bay Area. And floods destroyed some papers that were stored at their Santa Cruz house.

When Jeanette died, their kids inherited many of their artifacts, and the kids sold them off to individual collectors. According to one source, their son, Don, inherited many of the historic firearms, Spanish daggers, knives, and ranch brands, and he sold them piecemeal. Thus was the children's inheritance, a gift and further reward for all those weekends spent with their parents on dirt roads, doing the adults' hobbies instead of their own, while their dad carried around his bundle of pencils. But the material had great historic value that could have been permanently protected in a single museum or library. Now the items the Lattas spent their lives collecting are stored in various living room display cases and basement storage boxes throughout the West, who knows where.

Back home in Oregon after my trip, I started typing my trip notes and gathering more research to try to make sense of what I'd experienced in November and during the last twenty years. A year past. Then another. Pages accrued, and gradually I kept working on this story. Valley librarians emailed me documents. They mentioned books. When they couldn't find an obscure article, they suggested that I contact a man named Chris Brewer. He lived in Exeter in Tulare County and ran the Exeter Historical Museum. The museum exhibited local history inside a renovated, hundred-year-old Edison power substation downtown and sold Latta's books. Brewer was the great-great-grandson of the founder of Bakersfield, Thomas Baker, and Latta had given him the family's Bear State Books publishing company and the legal rights required to keep his books in print. In many cases, it was really the right to get books like *Tailholt Tales* back in print, since the originals now fetched collectible prices on the secondary market. If you needed anything Latta-related, librarians said, talk to Chris. "Last I hear, though," one librarian said, "he had fallen ill. But still worth a shot."

In 2017 I emailed Brewer to tell him how I'd followed Latta and wanted to read the two pages he published about the boat trip in *Westside Progress Review*. Librarians couldn't find a copy. Could he?

When Brewer wrote back, he said, "As for Frank, I knew him well and have the information you seek."

During the summers, Brewer took courses at UC Santa Cruz, he used to visit the Lattas at home. "We spent a lot of time talking about his work and life," he told me. Chris missed the Lattas. In a sense, he was Frank's protégé. They both loved history. They both had pioneer pedigrees. "He was an interesting character," Brewer said, "and I always enjoyed visiting with him and Jean."

As it turned out, whatever papers didn't end up in other institutions, Latta gave to Brewer. He not only had the obscure 1941 *Westside Progress Review* supplement I wanted; he had Latta's diary from 1938 and the journal he kept on the boat, as well as some of Latta's notes for the Joaquin Murrieta book—somewhere. He'd have to dig around to relocate everything. Latta's archive was huge and had fallen into disarray, which required Brewer to go back through it piece by piece for me. "It will take time, something that I do not have a lot of at this point," he said, a hint of morbidity in the air. "I wish it was easier, but it's not."

Latta's 8 mm footage from the boat trip was around there too. Brewer had digitized it to play at the museum. It wasn't exciting footage, he said, but it did show the crew and location, which was interesting.

I was floored. I had found the most direct link to Frank, much better than staring at some sad headstone, and I couldn't wait to see what the old footage looked like, to hear Latta's voice, and to read what Brewer had kept from ending up in some Santa Cruz thrift-store donation bin in 1983, piled atop Frank's old shirts and pocket protectors and whatever else his kids had given to charity.

The discovery also irritated me. I wish I would've found Brewer three years earlier, right after I'd returned from my trip, instead of now, when I'd written most of this book. In a sense, I'd taken the trip in the dark, unaware that Latta's account existed. Though, maybe in the dark a purer portrait accrued.

Brewer loved the idea of weaving the story of Latta's trip with my own, and he wanted to help. Unfortunately, he was slammed. The Brewers owned three stores in Exeter, which, along with running a ranch, publishing books, and managing the museum for the last ten years, left them exhausted. Bear State Books was a small operation. Funds were limited, as was interest in Valley history, so they did limited print runs of many titles, which meant putting rare works like *Tailholt Tales* back into circulation only for them to lapse back to the rare state from which Brewer tried to rescue them. Maybe Rare State Books was a more accurate name. In fact, he was organizing Latta's papers in order to sell them to the right historical archive. Maybe the University of Fresno? Maybe the Bancroft Library at UC Berkeley, where all William Brewer's field notebooks are kept? He didn't say.

"Frank's collection is not the only material I have here," Brewer said. "My own archive matched his in size, and the two of them together are a real problem, size wise. The process of selling off the collection is immense and complicated, but I have to start moving it. Otherwise, I will leave my wife in the same position everyone else has left spouses in, with a lot of stuff they have no interest in nor knowledge of." Brewer was also a writer and researcher, with his own books under his name. "I supposed in some ways my life follows that of Frank, except he accomplished so much more than I have." He'd reached that age where something of this size and complexity would be a burden to his wife if he died, and he wanted to spare her the hassle. "My wife is brilliant and well versed in things," he said, "and I am sure she would be able to handle disposing of this huge collection, but I want to avoid having that happen if possible." I could relate.

My basement was filled with boxes of my diaries and travel journals dating back to middle school, many of them worth nothing even to me. I didn't want to burden my wife, Rebekah, with them either. All my notes about the Valley, the endless mundane records and slips of paper that constantly fall from the pages of my research books—why make her deal with that stuff if I die suddenly? But there were jewels in such collections. One that kept eluding me was the *Alta I*'s anchor. Did Brewer know where that went?

"The anchor remains a mystery," he said, "but my guess is it was simply sold at the estate sale by Monna, with no particular connection to the *Alta*. She also sold my great-great-grandfather's rocking chair and other furniture from the Baker family in Bakersfield, unaware of what it was. I have a lot of *things* still from the collection, but quite a bit got sold off as general collectables. A sad ending to a lifetime of collecting. But a lesson for all of us about collecting and family."

Brewer said, "There is a lot that people do not remember about the trip, including the loss of one of the boys to illness." Loss? None of the newspaper articles mentioned a child's death. One early article mentioned the fourth boy, Ted Collins, as part of the boat crew. By day 5, the papers never mentioned him again. Of course that confused me, but I couldn't find any more information. And since the articles had included other errors, I chalked it up to bad reporting or a cover up, or I assumed he'd only briefly hitched a ride on the boat.

"If I can find the files and his diary from then," Brewer said, "you might have a good story to report." I would have to wait awhile for what I needed, though. He asked for my patience. Patience. All I'd ever been with the Valley was patient. I'd been patiently making trips to different sections of it for two decades. I'd been patiently gathering material in libraries and bookstores and on trips. I'd patiently cobbled together my travel notes and research into a story for the past three years, and now I was patiently waiting for the final ultimate source from a busy, infirmed, generous stranger who appreciated exactly what I was doing but wasn't sure he could provide the keys to the kingdom that he held.

No problem, I said, but the sooner he could send them, the better. My wife and I were having a baby in a few months. I wouldn't have time to read every one of Latta's journals in detail for a few months after that, or even a year, though I would definitely try. "Gotta go now," Brewer said, "but I will continue later . . ." Four months later, he hadn't sent any of it.

Initially, that frustrated me. I wanted to see the primeval Valley that Latta saw from the boat and to rely on something more accurate than flawed newspaper articles to narrate the course of the *Alta*'s journey, so that I could quit guessing about the details of their days. I wanted to know what happened to the fourth boy in the crew. No wonder Latta preferred original sources to newspapers. But even without his journals, I got to know that all enough. I'd heard his voice and the voices he preserved, and by traveling the path he traveled, listening to people's stories, I got as close to the heart of interior California as I could as a visitor. Brewer had his information and his reasons, and that was fine. Maybe seeing the footage would ruin the spell that Latta's story had cast on me. In the end, whatever details I got wrong about the *Alta*'s days were fine with me. A good story is more compelling than absolute facts. And where information fails, imagination fills in. For now, that would have to be enough.

When I miss the open highway and the Valley, I like to reread certain parts of Latta's oral history. Of the thousands of pages that Latta wrote outside *Tailholt Tales*, I keep coming back to the two pages about Yoimut, the last member of the Chunut Tribe. As her people always had, she lived on Tulare Lake. When Latta spoke with her in the 1930s, at age eighty, she'd been forced from the lake and lived in Hanford, where he visited frequently, and her words left a mark on me more lasting than the lake shore.

"You ask me, 'Will Tulare Lake ever fill up again?'" Yoimut said. "I got only one thing to say. Yes. It will fill up full, and everybody living down there will have to go away. I'd like to see that time myself. I am the last full-blood Chunut left. My children are part Spanish. I am the old one who knows the whole language. When I am gone no one will have it." She was the one who lived temporarily near the shrinking carcass of the *Alta I*, collecting wild foods and tending her tule house as settlers picked off the old boat's scrap and burned it for fuel. In her world, that rotting hull represented the failure of the new settlers. In another world, it represented the future of all human endeavor—a long, hard look at the Western impulse to exploit and profit until nothing was left and at the dangers of misjudging a temperamental land. In this world, it signaled the end of hers.

"All my life I want back our good old home on Tulare Lake," Yoimut said. "But I guess I can never have it. I guess I can never see the old days again. Now my daughter and her Mexican husband work in the cotton between Tulare and Waukena. Cotton, cotton, that is all that is left. Indians cannot live on cotton. They cannot sing their songs and tell their old stories where there is nothing but cotton."

Yoimut died soon after talking to Latta.

The Chunut man who told Latta about his family's three nights on Tulare Lake also spent two pages in Latta's *Little Journeys* describing his tribe's bounteous lifestyle toward the end of its existence. In loving detail, he recounts how easily his family caught wild rabbits with nets and ducks in flight, how they relished the flavor of wild Tulare Lake salmon smoked and seasoned with salt grass, and how they'd escaped the reservation to move back into dirt houses on their old village site near Corcoran, even though they lived there alone because Americans had forced the rest of their people onto reservations. And he remembers how cowboys eventually kicked his family out, too, and so they'd moved into the tall reeds at Chaw-lo'-win on Atwell's Island, roasting ducks on their boats and collecting plants, trying to get by. The short trip to Atwell's Island took his family four days when the wind died and stranded them on the water for three nights. "They wanted to come back to their old home and stay," he told Latta. Then one day, a group of white ranchers brought a herd of cattle onto the island.

"The water was low," the man said, "and they drove [the cows] across from the east. There were hogs there already, but they were wild. As soon as the white people found out we were there we began to have trouble. The tules were getting dry and we were afraid they would burn us out. So we all left."

I did too. Unlike Yoimut and this man, I could come back. I always would, because I always had, though one day, as history shows, the land I knew would not be there to greet me.

FURTHER READING

The Valley is too big to fit into a single book, so I've published a number of essays about different aspects of Valley life and the people I've met. Some come from my 2014 trip following Latta. Some come from previous excursions. If you'd like to see other sides of the region, you can find these stories in print and online. Portions of some of these essays have also been incorporated throughout the book.

"Across the Ocean of the Mind: 15 Minutes with Petrus," about a desert traveler whom I met while he was passing through Lost Hills. *Catapult* online, December 8, 2015.

"Antiquing in the Desert." *The Common* online, February 22, 2012.

"Come Here My Song," about Trout's, the Valley's last historic honky-tonk, and the role Okies and country music played in the region. *Longreads* online, June 11, 2015.

"Driving the San Joaquin Valley," about outsiders' perception of the Valley. *Harpers* online, April 23, 2015.

"The Ducks of Santa Nella." *Hobart* online, August 1, 2006.

"The Grapevine," about California wild grape, the Spanish naming and exploration of what became Grapevine Pass, and the deadly highway that runs through the old Cañada de las Uvas. *Threepenny Review* 132 (Winter 2013): 28–29.

"Highway Rest: Sex and Commerce in Rural California." *Columbia Journal* online, January 30, 2018.

"One of the All-Time Great One-Hit Wonder Novels: On Leonard Gardner's Novel *Fat City*," about this Stockton author's perfect novel and how it fits into the Central Valley literary canon. *Tin House* 54 (Winter 2012): 131–34; *LitHub* online, August 28, 2015.

"San Joaquin Fever: Journal of an Unlikely Obsession." *High Desert Journal* 8 (October 2008): 39–41.

"The San Luis Creek Rock 'n' Roll Rec Area." *The Rambler*, January–February 2008, 28–31.

"Seeing Clear to Pismo," about a homeless man who lives by his wits in the desert outside Lost Hills, making use of all the food we waste. *Dublin Review* 75 (Summer 2019): 5–21.

"Uncle Jeff's Cabin." *Southwest Review* 103, no. 2 (Fall 2019): 154–65.

"We Want to Be Unique: Kingsburg Swedish Village," about the small town of Kingsburg and marketing ethnicity. *Nowhere* online, December 27, 2019.

"The Worried Life," about the feral dogs that haunt a Motel 6 parking lot along the busy highway, living on the margins of society. *Southern Humanities Review* 4, no. 1 (Winter 2012): 11–13.

BIBLIOGRAPHY

So much of our success comes directly from the accomplishments and generosity of others, so I must loudly say how I would never have wrapped my mind around this area were it not for Robert Dawson's and Stephen Johnson's photos, and especially Gerald Haslam's detailed text, in their enormous *The Great Central Valley: California's Heartland.* Most of my historic re-creations, and many historic sections, were made possible because of William Brewer's careful journal entries, compiled in *Up and Down California,* and it would have been impossible to re-create little Valley towns like Las Juntas, Hill's Ferry, and Dos Palos were it not for Douglas E. Kyle's incredible book *Historic Spots in California.* Haslam's *The Other California* provided invaluable facts about Tulare Lake and details about the scale of habitat loss, and most importantly, it passed along the powerful dream that is California's vanished past, which is actually more of a snakebite whose venom I refused to suck out.

Of course, this story would not exist without Frank and Jeanette Latta. Details like the twenty-foot-tall brush at Tulare Lake's northern outlet, the island of skulls, and Terrapin Bay would not exist without their passion. And I doubt that future writers' imaginations could have dreamed a place as strange and magnificent as the facts of this place.

To narrate the journey of the *Alta II,* throughout this book, I relied on unauthored 1938 articles from the *Bakersfield Californian, Fresno Bee, Oakland Tribune Sun, Reno Gazette-Journal,* and the *San Bernardino County Sun* that tracked the crew's movements. It's a shame I can't thank their authors by name. In the introduction, numerous

1937 and 1938 articles let me set the scenes of hard rain and flooding that preceded the *Alta*'s journey, as did F. W. Panhorst's 1938 article in *Civil Engineering*; Robert W. Taylor and W. Leonard Taylor's informative "The Great California Flood of 1862" for the Fortnightly Club of Redlands, California; and the Department of Water Resources' Bulletin no. 159-65, *California Flood Control Program 1965*. These essential articles follow in chronological order:

"U.S. Engineers Study County's Flood Problem." *Bakersfield Californian*, October 16, 1937.

"Drive for Clovis-Fresno Flood Control Launched; Loss-Data Sought for U.S." *Fresno Bee*, March 8, 1938.

"Natural Storage Use Is Proposed to Halt Floods." *Fresno Bee*, March 8, 1938.

"Fresno, Merced Officials Confer on River Control." *Fresno Bee*, March 9, 1938.

"U.S. Speeds Study of Flood Control; May Build Project." *Fresno Bee*, March 9, 1938.

"Health Officer Gives Flooded Area Clean Bill." *Fresno Bee*, March 10, 1938.

"Rain Falling on High Sierra Snow Threatens Floods in Valley Areas." *Fresno Bee*, March 12, 1938.

"Cloudburst Flood Approaches Madera; Fresno Peril Wanes." *Fresno Bee*, March 13, 1938.

"Kern Levee Breaks, Workers Escape." *Bakersfield Californian*, June 10, 1938.

"Kern Boatmen on Way to S.F. via Water." *Bakersfield Californian*, June 18, 1938.

"Boat Marooned by Lake Storm." *Bakersfield Californian*, June 20, 1938.

"Crew in Small Boat Continues Journey North." *Bakersfield Californian*, June 20, 1938.

"Kern Boatmen Sail across Tulare Lake." *Bakersfield Californian*, June 21, 1938.

"Kern Boatsmen Reach Alpaugh during Evening." *Bakersfield Californian*, June 22, 1938.

"Boaters Start Trip to Coast on Flooded Inland Waterways." *San Bernardino County Sun*, June 23, 1938.

"Tranquility Is Next Objective for Tiny Craft." *Bakersfield Californian*, June 23, 1938.

"Kern Boat Crew Continues North." *Bakersfield Californian*, June 24, 1938.

"Latta Ship Races toward Bay Area." *Bakersfield Californian*, June 25, 1938.

"Inland Waterway Voyagers Near S.F. Bay Goal." *Oakland Tribune Sun*, June 26, 1938.

"Engine Troubles Halt Latta Ship." *Bakersfield Californian*, June 27, 1938.

"Latta Crew Near City of Stockton." *Bakersfield Californian*, June 28, 1938.

"Boat Crew Nears S.F. Bay District." *Bakersfield Californian*, June 29, 1938.

"Route of Alta II on Voyage from Bakersfield to Treasure Island, San Francisco," *Bakersfield Californian*, June 30, 1938.

"Alta II Ties Up at Fair." *Oakland Tribune Sun*, July 1, 1938.

"Bakersfield Trio Rides Skiff All the Way to S.F." *Reno Gazette-Journal*, July 1, 1938.

"Kern Boatmen Dock at S.F. Fair Island after 8 Days." *Bakersfield Californian*, July 1, 1938.

"Latta Reports on Famous Boat Trip." *Bakersfield Californian*, September 5, 1938.

"Boat Trip Experience Told at Club Meet." *Bakersfield Californian*, September 12, 1938.

Biographical details in *Peninsula Midweek, Pacific Historian, Los Tulares*, James B. Snyder's "Introduction to the Frank Latta Papers, 1922–1985," and Latta's own writing allowed me to profile him as a youth and developing historian in my introduction and elsewhere. It's a shame that some of these articles' authors weren't listed either, because their work helped me greatly:

"Frank Latta Fired by Supervisors." *Bakersfield Californian*, March 31, 1955.

"Latta 'Triumphant' on Tour of Museum." *Bakersfield Californian*, July 19, 1955.

"Historian-Teacher Latta Tells How He Came to Write." *Bakersfield Californian*, May 21, 1970.

"Museum Founder Latta Dies." *Bakersfield Californian*, May 10, 1983.

"Frank Latta Dies." *Los Tulares*, no. 134 (June 1983).

Curtis M. Hinsley's book *The Smithsonian and the American Indian: Making a Moral Anthropology in Victorian America* let me contextualize Latta's place among other important documentarians in my introduction. So did Christopher Cardozo's *Sacred Legacy: Edward S. Cutis and the North American Indian*, the Smithsonian's collection on Dr. John Peabody Harrington, and their online profile of Frances Densmore. Linda Yamane's quotes came from Patricia Jamie Lee and Milt Lee's indigenous interview series on their website Oyate. Various Valley agricultural and physical statistics and details about rivers, soils, and cities came from the EPA, NPR, Gerald Haslam,

William Preston, the American Rivers organization, reports from the California State Library, the U.S. Department of Agriculture, and Kenneth W. Umbach's excellent *A Statistical Tour of California's Great Central Valley*. Information about drought, crops, irrigation, aquifers, and wells came from *Slate*, *Mother Jones*, the *New Yorker*, the *Guardian*, *Sacramento Bee*, *Fresno Bee*, *National Geographic*, *Los Angeles Times*, AP, and Bonnie McInturf's "History of the San Joaquin County Resource Conservation District," prepared for the San Joaquin County Resource Conservation District.

Many sources, especially William Preston's book *Vanishing Landscapes* and brief email correspondence with Preston, allowed me to re-create the complex geology, hydrology, and ecology of this altered landscape in chapter 1 and elsewhere. Also indispensable were Hendrix and Warner's massive *California Riparian Systems*, Gerald Haslam's writings, Glen Martin's article "Bay Today, Gone Tomorrow: S.F. Region's Defining Feature Is Just a Transitory Puddle in Geologic Time," Charles W. Jennings and George J. Sauceda's "Simplified Fault Activity Map of California, 1999," the EPA's 2007 "Tulare Lake Basin Hydrology and Hydrography: Summary of the Movement of Water and Aquatic Species," the California Department of Fish and Wildlife, and the California Department of Water Resources.

Air pollution details came from William Brewer, the *Bakersfield Californian*, the *Guardian*, *Time*, and *Merced Sun-Star*. David Igler's *Industrial Cowboys* was priceless for helping me tell the story of Miller and Lux's domination and the story of the tule elk's disappearance and recovery; so were state and national park brochures about the elk, as well as J. D. Ballou and J. K. Fischer's "From Bottleneck to Metapopulation: Recovery of the Tule Elk in California." Buena Vista Lake and Slough history came from David Igler, John Parsons at the Buena Vista Aquatic Recreational Area, Mary Austin's work, and the unlisted author of "Buena Vista Reservoirs Named; They're Now Lake Webb, Lake Evans" from the *Bakersfield Californian*, November 27, 1974.

Tulare Lake is one of the most dizzying subjects I've ever tried to understand, and conjuring its ghost in chapter 2 required the labor and imaginations of many other curious people, especially Jihadda Govan, Frank Latta's interview subjects, and Mark Arax and Rick Wartzman in their indispensable book *The King of California*, whose research was vital to my own.

Understanding how groundwater works, salinization, selenium, soil toxicity, land retirement, and the environmental challenges facing the Tulare Lake basin required many books and articles, including material from the Land Retirement Technical Committee, the Tulare Basin Wildlife Partners, and the Trinity Lake Revitalization Alliance. Casual efforts by people outside magazines and books helped too, including various posts by Tyler (no surname listed) on the *Tales of a Nomad Biologist* blog, which let an outsider see what was happening at Atwell and Alpuagh. Now-dead links from the California Water Impact Network and from the Ryan Company helped me understand poisoned farmland and the Atwell Solar project, respectively.

You can't drop into a city for one day and expect to understand much, but the locals who spoke with me, and the many articles and books I read after my visit, deepened my understanding of Hanford, including *Central California Life Magazine*'s June 28, 2014, article "Hanford's Star Restaurant: Where History and Community Meet"; Mike Eiman's and Brandon Santiago's *Hanford Sentinel* articles; and some now-dead links by the California Cancer Registry about local history. Dairy industry details came partly from the *Guardian*, CNBC, the California Dairy Press Room and Resources, and Water INTER-face: An Interdisciplinary Graduate Education Program United by the Central Focus of "Water for Health."

Re-creating intimate moments between deceased people, especially historically important moments, is challenging, but Frank Latta's version of events in *Tailholt Tails* and Malcolm Margonlin's forward and Latta's introduction to *Indian Summer* allowed me to bring readers into the proverbial room with Latta and Uncle Jeff in chapter 4 and let me envision the rest.

The National Park Service's map of the Butterfield Overland Trail let me see how the route shaped the face of the Valley and the people

Latta spoke to, and Douglas E. Kyle's detailed *Historic Spots in California* let me bring the Butterfield stations and route to life. I found excellent details about the Mendota Canal, Pool, and Dam on the Revive the San Joaquin website and the Water Education Foundation website. Duane Hall's post "Where the Palm Meets the Pine: Madera County, California," on his blog *A Geographer's Scrapbook*, filled in many missing pieces about the story of the pine and the palm on Highway 99. Books like Gene Rose's *San Joaquin: A River Betrayed* and *Merced Sun-Star* articles helped me write about modern and historic Chowchilla, a subject still buried too deeply in the library stacks.

Chapter 6's epigraph came from page 421 of Arax and Wartzman's *The King of California*. Sometimes you search for specific information. Sometimes you stumble on the most illuminating passage while reading for something else. This chapter's John Muir history came from numerous common biographical sources, Muir's own writing, and Rose's vital *San Joaquin*. The Hill's Ferry info was pulled from various sources, including Brewer's *Up and Down California*, Kyle's *Historic Spots in California*, and Rose's *San Joaquin*. I also relied on Latta's "Pioneers of the San Joaquin" newspaper columns for his oral history work in this area, found in a bound compilation by that title in the Fresno library's San Joaquin Valley Heritage and Genealogy Center. It's one of his most interesting books and sadly one of the hardest to find.

Chapter 7's epigraph came from Sarah Vowell's book *The Partly Cloudy Patriot*. Many reliable, detailed sources, from *National Geographic* to Haslam to the USGS, provided information that went into this chapter's delta section, as did posts on the Association of California Water Agencies' website.

I gathered details about San Francisco buildings, businesses, and farmer's markets from the websites of the Ferry Building Market Place, the Heart of the City Farmer's Market, and the Bay Area Radio Museum and Hall of Fame, as well as John F. Schneider's collected articles and images from Voices Out of the Fog, at www.oldradio.com.

Bits from multiple unauthored 1938 newspaper articles allowed me to bring the *Alta*'s arrival in San Francisco to brief life, as did an untitled, unauthored typed page from July 1, 1938, about the Lattas' arrival in San Francisco, provided by staff at Bakersfield Reference Local History Room, Beale Memorial Library. Details about Latta's later years, retirement, and life outside the Valley came from June Morrall's writing at Half Moon Bay Memories and Jeanette Latta's obituary, submitted by Gale Stroud and Burta Herger to the California Tombstone Project. Titles of Latta's unpublished and planned book projects came from various published sources, some confirmed via email by Chris Brewer of Exeter, California.

Brewer also verified hazy details and provided new information about the Lattas—specifically, details about Frank's plan to turn their Santa Cruz ranch into a tourist attraction, the Lattas' children and inheritance, where Frank's papers ended up, and the family's collected artifacts. Although things didn't work out as I'd hoped in the end, I am grateful for Brewer's assistance, since his friendship with the Lattas and his knowledge as a historian and collector filled important gaps in my book.

Paul Rogers's, Joseph Serna's, and Amy Graff's articles from *Mercury News*, *Los Angeles Times*, and *San Francisco Chronicle* provided the hard facts in the story of California's recovery from its devastating drought. I apologize to anyone whose work I have failed to recognize. Omissions are not intentional, only proof of the limits of my abilities and the size of my piles of printouts and notes.

ARCHIVES

California State University, Fresno Library, Fresno, California.
    Latta, Frank F. "San Joaquin Valley Bandits." H. G. Schuut Collection.
Fresno Central Library, Fresno County, California.
    Latta, Frank F. *Pioneers of the San Joaquin*, 1935.
Huntington Library, Art Museum, and Botanical Gardens, San Marino, California.
    Frank F. Latta Collection: Skyfarming, 1802–1982. http://catalog.huntington.org/record=b1767823.
Huntington Library, Los Angeles, California.
    Latta, Frank F. "Sky Farmers and Mule Skinners."

Anderson, Gary Clayton, and Laura Lee Anderson, eds. *The Army Surveys of Gold Rush California: Reports of Topographical Engineers*. Norman OK: Arthur H. Clark, 2015.

Arax, Mark. "A Kingdom from Dust." *California Sunday Magazine*, February 2018.

———. *West of the West: Dreamers, Believers, Builders, and Killers in the Golden State*. New York: PublicAffairs, 2009.

Arax, Mark, and Rick Wartzman. *The King of California: J. G. Boswell and the Making of a Secret American Empire*. New York: PublicAffairs, 2003.

Associated Press. "Man Who Buried a Busload of School Children Alive in Quarry, Then Demanded Ransom, Released from Prison." News release, June 22, 2012.

Audubon, John Woodhouse. *Audubon's Western Journal: 1849–1850*. Tucson: University of Arizona Press, 1984.

Austin, Mary. *Isidro*. Boston: Houghton Mifflin, 1905.

———. *The Land of Little Rain*. Boston: Houghton Mifflin, 1904.

Bailey, Richard C. *Explorations in Kern*. Bakersfield CA: Kern County Historical Society, 1962.

Ballou, J. D., and J. K. Fischer. "From Bottleneck to Metapopulation: Recovery of the Tule Elk in California." In *Metapopulations and Wildlife Conservation*, edited by Dale Richard McCullough, 375–403. Covelo CA: Island Press, 1996.

Barich, Bill. *Big Dreams: Into the Heart of California*. New York: Vintage, 1994.

Berg, Nate. "Breathless in Bakersfield: Is the Worst Air Pollution in the US about to Get Worse?" *Guardian*, February 14, 2017.

———. "Why Does California's Central Valley Have Such Bad Air Pollution?" *CityLab*, September 28, 2011.

Bezzerides, A. I. *Thieves' Market*. New York: Bantam, 1950.

Boessenecker, John. *Bandido: The Life and Times of Tiburcio Vasquez*. Norman: University of Oklahoma Press, 2010.

Bogdanov, Vladimir, Michael Erlewine, Stephen Thomas Erlewine, and Chris Woodstra. *All Music Guide to Country: The Experts' Guide to the Best Country Recordings*. New York: Backbeat Books, 1997.

Brewer, Chris. *Historic Kern County: An Illustrated History of Bakersfield and Kern County*. San Antonio TX: HPN Books, 2001.

Brewer, William Henry. *Up and Down California in 1860–1864*. Berkeley: University of California Press, 1974.

Cardozo, Christopher. *Sacred Legacy: Edward S. Cutis and the North American Indian*. New York: Simon and Schuster, 2000.

Clark, William. "Flood Control Men Guard Kern Live: River Chief Fred L. Gribble Guides Reporter on Tour of Safety Levees." *Bakersfield Californian*, June 11, 1942.

Clarke, Thurston. *California Fault: Looking for the Spirit of a State along the San Andreas.* New York: Ballantine, 1996.

Coate, Bill. "Madera Almost Died in Infancy." *Madera Tribune,* May 2, 2017.

Darlington, David. *In Condor Country: A Portrait of a Landscape, Its Denizens, and Its Defenders.* New York: Houghton Mifflin, 1987.

Dawson, Robert, Gerald Haslam, and Stephen Johnson. *The Great Central Valley: California's Heartland.* Berkeley: University of California Press, 1993.

Dodge, Fred A., and Eugene L. Menefee. *History of Tulare and Kings Counties, California, with Biographical Sketches of the Leading Men and Women of the County Who Have Been Identified with Its Growth and Development from the Early Days to the Present.* Los Angeles CA: Historic Record Company, 1913. https://archive.org/details/historyoftularek00mene/page/n9.

Egan, Timothy. *Short Nights of the Shadow Catcher: The Epic Life and Immortal Photographs of Edward Curtis.* Boston: Houghton Mifflin Harcourt, 2012.

Eiman, Mike. "Debate over Posting of Founding Documents Continues." *Hanford Sentinel,* February 19, 2014.

———. "Vendome Building Rises from the Ashes." *Hanford Sentinel,* November 4, 2014.

———. "Vendome Hotel Demolition Begins." *Hanford Sentinel,* August 15, 2012.

Everson, William. *The Residual Years: Poems 1934–1948.* Santa Barbara CA: Black Sparrow Press, 1997.

Fagan, Brian M. *Ancient North America.* London: Thames and Hudson, 1995.

Farnham, Thomas Jefferson. *Travels in the Californias, and Scenes in the Pacific Ocean.* New York: Saxton & Miles, 1844. https://archive.org/details/travelsincalifor00farn.

Galloway, Devin L., Marti E. Ikehara, S. E. Ingebritsen, and David R. Jones. *Delta Subsidence in California: The Sinking Heart of the State.* U.S. Geological Survey FS-005-00. Washington DC: U.S. Department of the Interior, April 2000.

Gardner, Leonard. *Fat City.* New York: Farrar, Straus, and Giroux, 1969.

Garone, Philip. *The Fall and Rise of the Wetlands of California's Great Central Valley.* Berkeley: University of California Press, 2011.

Garvin, Cosmo. "Farmers Band Together to Stave Off Sprawl: In California's Central Valley, a Strategy for Steering Growth Takes Shape." *High Country News,* December 9, 2002.

Gia, Gilbert P. "Where Bakersfield Threw Its Garbage, 1872–1992." Author's website, 2016. https://hcommons.org/deposits/objects/hc:15014/datastreams/CONTENT/content.

Goodman, Marian. "History Project That Never Stops." *Peninsula Midweek*, supplement to the *Advance-Star*, November 13, 1968.

Haight, Robert G., Brian Cypher, Patrick A. Kelly, Scott Phillips, Hugh P. Possingham, Katherine Ralls, Anthony M. Starfield, P. J. White, and Daniel Williams. "Optimizing Habitat Protection Using Demographic Models of Population Viability." *Conservation Biology* 16, no. 5 (2002): 1386–97.

Haight, Robert G., Brian Cypher, Patrick A. Kelly, Scott Phillips, Katherine Ralls, Hugh P. Possingham. "Optimizing Reserve Expansion for Disjunct Populations of San Joaquin Kit Fox." *Biological Conservation* 117 (2004): 61–72.

Hallowell, Joell, and Coke Hallowell. *Take Me to the River: Fishing, Swimming, and Dreaming on the San Joaquin.* Berkeley CA: Heyday Books, 2010.

Hanson, Victor Davis. "The Scorching of California." *City Journal*, Winter 2015.

Haslam, Gerald. *Coming of Age in California: Personal Essays.* Walnut Creek CA: Devil Mountain Books, 1990.

———. "Historian Preferred Roughnecks' Tales to Bankers." *Bakersfield Californian*, April 21, 2013.

———. "A MELUS Interview: Arnold R. Rojas, the Last Vaquero." *MELUS* 13, no. 1/2 (Spring–Summer, 1986): 125–33.

———. *The Other California: The Great Central Valley in Life and Letters.* Reno: University of Nevada Press, 1994.

———. *Snapshots: Glimpses of the Other California.* Walnut Creek CA: Devil Mountain Books, 1985.

———. *Voices of a Place.* Walnut Creek CA: Devil Mountain Books, 1987.

———. *Workin' Man Blues: Country Music in California.* Berkeley: University of California Press, 1999.

Haslam, Gerald W., and James D. Houston. *California Heartland: Writing from the Great Central Valley.* Santa Barbara CA: Capra Books, 1978.

Heizer, Robert F., and M. A. Whipple. *The California Indians: A Source Book.* Berkeley: University of California Press, 1971.

Hendrix, Kathleen M., and Richard E. Warner, eds. *California Riparian Systems: Ecology, Conservation, and Productive Management.* Berkeley: University of California Press, 1984.

Hinsley, Curtis M. *The Smithsonian and the American Indian: Making a Moral Anthropology in Victorian America.* Washington DC: Smithsonian Institution Press, 1994.

Igler, David. *Industrial Cowboys: Miller and Lux and the Transformation of the Far West, 1850–1920.* Berkeley: University of California Press, 2005.

Jepson, Willis Linn. *Jepson Manual of Vascular Plants of California*. Berkeley: University of California Press, 2012.

Johnson, Susan Lee. *Roaring Camp: The Social World of the California Gold Rush*. New York: W. W. Norton, 2000.

Kay, Jane. "Delta Smelt, Icon of California Water Wars, Is Almost Extinct." *National Geographic*, April 3, 2015.

Kelley, Robert. *Battling the Inland Sea: Floods, Public Policy, and the Sacramento Valley*. Berkeley: University of California Press, 1998.

Kherdian, David. *Down at the Santa Fe Depot: 20 Fresno Poets*. Fresno CA: Giligia Press, 1970.

Kosloff, Laura H. "Tragedy at Kesterson Reservoir: Death of a Wildlife Refuge Illustrates Failings of Water Law." *Environmental Law Reporter* 15, no. 12 (1985).

Kroeber, Alfred L. *Handbook of the Indians of California*. Mineoloa NY: Dover Publications, 2012.

Kyle, Douglas E. *Historic Spots in California*. Stanford CA: Stanford University Press, 2001.

Laird, Carobeth. *Encounter with an Angry God: Recollections of My Life with John Peabody Harrington*. Albuquerque: University of New Mexico Press, 1993.

Lapham, Macy H. *Crisscross Trails: Narrative of a Soil Surveyor*. Berkeley CA: Willis E. Berg, 1949.

Latta, Frank F. *Black Gold in the Joaquin*. Caldwell ID: Caxton Printers, 1949.

——. *California Indian Folklore*. Exeter CA: Brewer's Historical Press, 1999.

——. *El Camino Viejo a Los Angeles: The Oldest Road of the San Joaquin Valley*. Exeter CA: Bear State Books, 2006.

——. *Handbook of the Yokuts*. Exeter CA: Brewer's Historical Publications, 1999.

——. "Historic Kern County Places: Grapevine." *Bakersfield Californian*, June 15, 1951.

——. *Little Journeys in the San Joaquin*. Livingston CA, 1937–38.

——. *Tailholt Tales*. Santa Cruz CA: Bear State Books, 1976.

Lochhead, Carolyn. "Blame the Drought: Wildlife Disappearing in Tulare Basin." *San Francisco Chronicle*, June 13, 2015.

——. "California Drought: Central Valley Farmland on Its Last Legs." *SF Gate*, March 24, 2014.

Lynch, George Gilbert. "The Late, Great, Buena Vista Lake." *Historic Kern Quarterly Bulletin*, 59, no 3 (Fall 2009).

Madison, Mike. *Walking the Flatlands: The Rural Landscape of the Lower Sacramento Valley*. Berkeley CA: Heyday Books, 2004.

Magruder, Genevieve Kratka. *The Upper San Joaquin Valley 1772–1870*. Bakersfield CA: Kern County Historical Society, 1950.

Marshal, Gail. "Chowchilla Bus Kidnapper James Schoenfeld's Own Words Add Insight to Crime." *Fresno Bee*, August 29, 2015.

Martin, Glen. "Bay Today, Gone Tomorrow: S.F. Region's Defining Feature Is Just a Transitory Puddle in Geologic Time." *San Francisco Chronicle*, December 20, 1999.

Masumoto, David Mas. *Harvest Son: Planting Roots in American Soil*. New York: W. W. Norton, 1998.

Mayfield, Thomas Jefferson. *Indian Summer: A True Account of Traditional Life among the Choinumne Indians of California's San Joaquin Valley*. Berkeley CA: Heyday Books, 1993.

McKinney, John. "Happy Trails at Former Ranch in Pacheco State Park." *Los Angeles Times*, June 6, 1999.

Mooallem, Jon. *Wild Ones: A Sometimes Dismaying, Weirdly Reassuring Story about Looking at People Looking at Animals in America*. New York: Penguin Press, 2013.

Morgan, Wallace M. *History of Kern County, California, with Biographical Sketches of the Leading Men and Women of the County Who Have Been Identified with Its Growth and Development from the Early Days to the Present*. Los Angeles CA: Historic Record Company, 1914. https://archive.org/stream/historyofkerncou00morg/historyofkerncou00morg_djvu.txt.

Morrall, June. "1957: Historical Museum at Pescadero." *Half Moon Bay Memories* (blog), August 8, 2007.

———. "1957: Historical Museum-Resort at Pescadero?" *Half Moon Bay Memories* (blog), August 8, 2007.

Muir, John. *The Eight Wilderness Discovery Books*. Seattle WA: Mountaineers, 1992.

———. *John of the Mountains: The Unpublished Journals of John Muir*. Madison: University of Wisconsin Press, 1979.

Norris, Frank. *The Octopus: A Story of California*. New York: Doubleday, 1901.

Panhorst, F. W. "Role of Highways in Recent California Floods: Road Network Takes On Added Value in Time of Emergency." *Civil Engineering* 8, no. 8 (August 1938). https://scvhistory.com/scvhistory/panhorst0838.htm.

Philpott, Tom. "California Goes Nuts." *Mother Jones*, November–December 2014.

Pitt, Leonard. *The Decline of the Californios: A Social History of the Spanish-Speaking Californias, 1846–1890*. Berkeley: University of California Press, 1966.

Preston, William L. *Vanishing Landscapes: Land and Life in the Tulare Lake Basin*. Berkeley: University of California Press, 1981.

Reisner, Marc. *Cadillac Desert: The American West and Its Disappearing Water*. New York: Penguin Books, 1993.

Rintoul, William. *Oildorado*. Santa Cruz CA: Valley Publishers, 1978.

Ritchie, Ryan. "No-Hurry History Beckons." *Los Angeles Times*, June 24, 2012.

Rose, Gene. *The San Joaquin: A River Betrayed*. Fresno: Linrose, 1992.

Santiago, Brandon. "The Story behind the Vendome." *Hanford Sentinel*, July 10, 2012.

Saroyan, William. *Fresno Stories*. New York: New Directions, 1994.

Schenker, Heath, ed. *Picturing California's Other Landscape: The Great Central Valley*. Berkeley CA: Heyday Books, 1999.

Schoenherr, Allan A. *A Natural History of California*. Berkeley: University of California Press, 1995.

Serna, Joseph. "California Snowpack Is One of the Biggest Ever Recorded, and Now Poses a Flooding Risk." *Los Angeles Times*, March 30, 2017.

———. "Shasta Dam Makes History as Water Flows from Top Gates for First Time in 20 Years." *Los Angeles Times*, February 23, 2017.

Smith, Wallace. *Garden of the Sun: A History of the San Joaquin Valley, 1772–1939*. Fresno CA: Craven Street Books, 2004.

Snyder, James B. "Inventory of the Ethnographic Papers of Frank Forrest Latta." Yosemite Research Library, National Park Service, 1990.

Soto, Gary. *The Effects of Knut Hamsun on a Fresno Boy*. New York: Persea Books, 2000.

———. *The Elements of San Joaquin*. Pittsburgh: University of Pittsburgh Press, 1977.

Steinbeck, John. *The Grapes of Wrath*. New York: Penguin Books, 2002.

Sutter, John D. "My 417-Mile Trip Down 'Apocalypse River.'" CNN, September 2014. https://www.cnn.com/interactive/2014/09/opinion/endangered-river-ctl/.

Taylor, Robert W., and W. Leonard Taylor. "The Great California Flood of 1862." The Fortnightly Club of Redlands, California, 2007. http://www.redlandsfortnightly.org/papers/Taylor06.htm.

Thomasson, Ron R., and Dennis W. Westcot. *Survey of Tributaries of Salt Slough Merced County, California*. Sacramento CA: California Regional Water Quality Control Board, August 1990.

Thomasson, Ron R., and F. Wayne Pierson. *Survey of Tributaries of Mud Slough (North) Merced County, California*. Sacramento CA: California Regional Water Quality Control Board, April 1989.

Trejo, Ernesto, and Jon Veinberg, eds. *Piecework: 19 Fresno Poets*. Albany CA: Silver Skates, 1987.

Tuggle, Troy S. "Historian of the Valley: Frank Forrest Latta." *Pacific Historian*, Summer 1970.

Umbach, Kenneth W. *San Joaquin Valley: Selected Statistics on Population, Economy, and Environment*. California State Library, California Research Bureau, May 2002.

——. *A Statistical Tour of California's Great Central Valley*. California State Library, California Research Bureau, August 2007.

Villa, Juan. "Restoration Project Atwell Island Shows Success in Reclaiming Tainted Farm Land." *Visalia Times Delta*, May 14, 2014.

Waldie, D. J. *Holy Land: A Suburban Memoir*. New York: W. W. Norton, 1996.

Walsh, Bryan. "See the Worst Place to Breathe in America." *Time*, September 21, 2014.

Watts, Jane. *Valley Light: Writers of the San Joaquin*. Poet and Printer Press, 1978.

Weber, Devra. *Dark Sweat, White Gold: California Farm Workers, Cotton, and the New Deal*. Berkeley: University of California Press, 1994.

Wells, Andrew Jackson. *The San Joaquin Valley of California*. Southern Pacific Railroad, 1905.

Woodard, Niki. "Why Should We Care about Native Lands?" *Visalia Times Delta*, July 30, 2015.

Yan, Holly. "California Mass Kidnapping: After Being Buried Alive, Victims Relive Nightmare." CNN, December 28, 2015, video by Alberto Moya and Nick Scott, 2:38, https://www.cnn.com/2015/11/19/us/rewind-chowchilla-school-bus-kidnapping/index.html.

Yogi, Stan. *Highway 99: A Literary Journey through California's Great Central Valley*. Berkeley CA: Heyday Books, 1996.